Contents

ɔl

Illustrations

FIGURES

TABLES

Introduction

Teaching – a learning relationship

Neil Kitson and Roger Merry

> Precisely what is to be learnt, what it is to be a learner, what it is to be a teacher, are not separately pre-specifiable, but emerge from the particular situations created by a set of reciprocal relationships. This is clearly at odds with those current approaches to curriculum planning which increasingly demand that all such things are carefully defined in advance. Clarity of purpose is thereby conflated with pre-set standards and goals, which run across and obscure the demands of real learning.
>
> (Bonnett 1994: 179)

Over the past few years, radical government reforms have meant that, for better or worse, primary education in Great Britain has come much more into line with that of most other countries in the world. Ironically, the establishment of the British National Curriculum came at a time when many countries, including some of our nearest neighbours, were looking critically at their educational systems and were seriously contemplating a shift away from such central government control (Merry 1991). Even if many British teachers were not necessarily opposed to the idea of a National Curriculum, most felt that they had not been properly consulted and that the whole thing had been thrust upon them, so that until quite recently they might have been forgiven for thinking that there was little point in reflecting about what went on in their classrooms.

Yet it is crucial that such reflection should take place not only in British schools but also in countries where different sorts of changes are being considered. If teachers anywhere feel so deprofessionalised and disempowered that they no longer reflect on their practice, they really will have become nothing more than deliverers of somebody else's curriculum. In Britain, hopefully such reflection was encouraged by the five-year moratorium on change and the post-Dearing attempt to restore at least some of the emphasis on teachers' own professional judgement in both teaching and assessment. In the so-called 'emerging' countries, reflection of a different sort is increasingly important, as they consider their changing educational needs, moving from subsistence societies to play their part in the technological revolution. Our starting point here must be to look at what actually goes on in classrooms. So, what sorts of things do we find if we look at the curriculum as it is set down for teachers and children?

Even at primary level, the British National Curriculum, like most others, is based on a rationale of 'teaching subjects to children'. This may seem to be reasonable enough, and indeed the only common-sense way to proceed, but the assumptions behind that simple and apparently innocuous phrase are important ones. The emphasis is on content and delivery – on traditional academic subjects and on what the teacher does, and on children only to the extent that they are rather passive recipients of it all. Yet the assumption that what is learned is necessarily identical to what is taught is a dangerous one, and most psychologists and many teachers now recognise that the successful learner is an active participant in a learning relationship with others, including teachers. This notion of learning relationships is, therefore, a central one for this book, which is divided for convenience into two sections. The first section emphasises the child's contribution, and the second the teacher's contribution, to their learning relationship.

As Sotto (1994) succinctly puts it, 'It makes no sense to decide how one is going to teach, before one has made some study of how people learn', and cognitive psychologists have long been interested in that which children bring to learning situations. However, they have tended to study it in isolation, often in rather artificial conditions which are deliberately closer to the science laboratory than to the home or school settings in which learning normally takes place. Such research has certainly advanced our understanding of what might be going on in children's heads, but it has rarely been used directly by teachers and has more recently come under criticism from psychologists themselves. The highly influential work of Piaget, for instance, has been attacked for portraying the child as a solitary little scientist rather than someone learning in the rich social context of home or school. In fact, such criticism may be unjust, in view of some recent work showing that Piaget was actually keenly aware of the importance of social factors in children's learning (Piaget 1995), but it is an emphasis which has been emerging only relatively recently, along with research in 'social cognition' (see, e.g., Rogoff 1990) and an interest in the work of writers like Vygotsky (1961).

Vygotsky's much-quoted phrase, 'the zone of proximal development' or ZPD (see, e.g., Newman et al. 1989), is one which strongly emphasises the role of teachers or other adults in the learning relationship, and a similar role is implied in Bruner's equally well-known notion of 'scaffolding' (see, e.g., Bruner and Haste 1987). Here, learning is seen very much in the public domain, and the teacher, far from standing helplessly by until the child is 'ready' to move on to the next stage, plays a crucial part in mediating between the culturally-defined demands of the task on the one hand and the individual child's understanding on the other. In such a view, successful learning depends therefore on the negotiated relationship between child and teacher, and it is definitely not an easy option for the latter! It is a 'child-centred' view, to the extent that what the child brings to the relationship is recognised as crucial, but there is more to it than that. It is also a view which not only fully recognises the social context in which individual children learn, but is also realistic about the public demands of the curriculum.

PART I: THE CHILD AND THE LEARNING RELATIONSHIP

Chapter 1 Just for fun?

The first chapter presents this central theme of the child as an active partner in the learning relationship. Babies and young children are natural learners, and we now know that they can demonstrate much higher levels of thinking than was previously thought. As teachers, we need to be careful that society's need for formal, 'disembedded' schooling does not result in children also learning to become sleeping partners in the relationship, passively giving up responsibility to the teacher and, in the process, losing the curiosity and enthusiasm that characterise the learning of most pre-schoolers. In this chapter **Janet Moyles** considers the process by which the child acquires concepts, skills, knowledge and attitudes towards learning and towards others, particularly through play. 'Play' happens in some mode or other even in those cultures where there are few apparent opportunities for it. Many modern learning theories are based upon the notion that children learn to make sense of the world by building up concepts through interaction with the environment. This chapter defines what is meant by concepts and by the related notion of schema, much in evidence in current writing in early years education, as well as exploring the range of learning strategies which children may adopt in different circumstances, such as the domain-specific and domain-general strategies.

Emphasis is placed on the need for adults to relate to children's ways of thinking, and to acknowledge that these ways are not somehow 'faulty' but represent the world as the child perceives and conceives it. The role of the teacher in understanding concept development and schema is emphasised.

Chapter 2 Cognitive development, 3–7

This chapter is the first of two to consider the child's contribution to the learning relationship, beginning at pre-school level and moving through the first formal learning settings to the end of Key Stage Two. Enormous changes take place, not only in individual cognitive terms, but also in the social settings and learning demands imposed on the child, and therefore in the whole nature of the learning relationships which evolve. Here **Linda and David Hargreaves** offer an introduction to current perspectives on children's development between the ages of 3 and 7 years. The two major foci of the discussion will be:

1 young children's socio-cognitive development, which is very briefly traced through the work of major theorists such as Piaget, Vygotsky and Bruner, and the research carried out by Donaldson, Rogoff and Lave;
2 young children's emotional development and current interest in the child's theory of mind.

Musical skills are briefly discussed and analysed as an example of how development occurs.

Chapter 3 Cognitive development, 7–11

This chapter continues the theme, outlining how cognitive, social and emotional development work together to enable children to take on increased responsibility for their own learning, so that their contribution to the learning relationship becomes not only more skilled but also shows an increased awareness of themselves as learners and an increased sensitivity to the thoughts and feelings of others. In this chapter, **Roger Merry** briefy considers the legacy of Piaget's work in the context of contemporary theorists, by examining the notion that he underestimated young children's potential and overemphasised 'disembedded' logical thought in older children. The chapter then goes on to explore more recent trends in the study of child development, social cognition and the idea that social factors are not merely a background for cognitive development but actually mediate experience and shape learning. It considers the importance of language and the role of the teacher in the Zone of Proximal Development, leading into the notion of domain-specific learning and the development of 'intelligences', and concluding with the importance of learning strategies and the development of metacognition in children at Key Stage Two.

Chapter 4 Children with special needs

It would clearly be misleading to present an idealised view of classrooms involving only successful and fulfilling learning. The central notion of the learning relationship means that totally 'within-child' explanations of learning difficulties are no longer adequate, and children with special needs are increasingly seen as the responsibility of all teachers. This chapter considers therefore not only the problems that can arise but also the sorts of learning relationships that teachers need to cultivate in order to try to meet the needs of all their children. Whereas those working in the field of child development are actively seeking elements that are universal and common across cultures, the notion of special needs is more culturally defined and specific. **Sylvia McNamara** looks at the concept of disability and handicap in this chapter. The notions of the continuum and the inherent difficulties with labeling rather than identifying are also considered. Within this consideration the importance of feelings and how children perceive themselves are explored alongside cognitive issues. The discussion also covers the notion of inclusion, its relation to integration, and the role of the whole school in creating an inclusive climate.

Chapter 5 Observing, assessing and recording children's development

This chapter acts as a bridge between the two sections of the book. The first four chapters, although they have set out some implications for teachers, have emphasised the child's contribution to the learning relationship. This chapter begins to shift the focus by looking at how teachers can observe, assess and record what their children do, as a first step towards making the learning relationship more effective. In this chapter **Sue Cavendish and Jean Underwood** present a discussion of the assessment of children's development and learning in primary schools. There is no one perfect way to assess children's development and learning. In planning and managing an assessment there will always be critical decisions, and these should be informed by considering (a) who or what will benefit; for example:

- school policy;
- the teacher's classroom practice;
- the children;
- outside agents;

and (b) the purpose or goal of assessment; for example:

- to improve a teaching programme;
- to determine the effectiveness of a teaching programme;
- to explain why something happens;
- to find a solution to a problem.

The authors conclude by discussing appropriate methods of collecting and recording evidence, the need to match method of assessment to goals and the differences between measurement and evaluation of development and learning.

PART II: THE TEACHER'S ROLE IN THE LEARNING RELATIONSHIP

The first section of this book looks at the underlying processes of learning and draws implications from these for the teaching of young children. Throughout, the thrust of the argument is that teaching is not something that is done *to* children *by* teachers; rather it is a relationship for learning. The second half continues this analysis by focusing on the role of the teacher as reflective practitioner within this complex relationship, exploring how teachers can be empowered to learn more about their role in the classroom and as a result become more effective practitioners.

Chapter 6 Primary culture and classroom teaching

Maurice Galton examines in this chapter the links between theories of learning and theories of teaching. He looks at typical practice in a number of countries, both developed and developing, in particular focusing on cultural assumptions which govern particular choices of classroom organisation such as the use of whole-class teaching or individualised approaches to learning. In addition he looks at the economic pressures which are leading many countries to modify existing practice in ways that would suggest a shift from the informal to the formal in developing countries and the opposite direction in the developed ones.

In the second half of the chapter the 'hidden curriculum' of these classrooms is explored. In many primary classrooms the apparent 'busyness' masks a variety of strategies designed to reach a 'steady state' between the teacher's requirements and what the pupils are prepared to do in return. In particular, consideration is given to the problem of over-dependency by pupils on teachers and ways of overcoming it.

Chapter 7 Look back and wonder: the reflective practitioner

It is not enough to look at how children function within the learning relationship. If the relationship is to grow then we must consider the teacher's role and explore strategies that will help them to be more effective in gaining insight into their own practice. We must understand the teacher's relationship to their work. In his chapter, **Neil Kitson** considers reflection as a key to teacher effectiveness. The ability to reflect upon present practice and make reasoned changes to improve the work of the individual within the classroom is what marks out the analytical and developing teacher. This is coupled with an increasing awareness that the professional growth of teachers no longer lies with paternalistic bodies such as the old local authorities but is now the responsibility of the individual practitioner within the school. There has been a considerable amount of research carried out which shows how, through the development of action planning, teachers are able to link their personal professional needs with the development of the school.

This chapter looks at the process of action planning, and couples this with the notion of competency-based learning for teachers. Consideration is also given to the effectiveness and limitations of this model.

Chapter 8 Teacher language and communication

Language is a central component of the classroom relationship. It is the basis for most forms of interaction, and yet it is simply seen as a functional device. By developing a greater understanding of the complex language structures that exist within the classroom, teachers can be helped to gain insight into the learning relationships they create and the effects that they have on the children's ability to learn. **Martin Cortazzi** looks at the process of teaching by considering the aspects of language which lead to effective communication. This chapter investigates the construction of meaning through socio-cultural models of interaction, linguistic register and through analysis of transcripts, exchange structure and its extensions. Following up on his research, both in this country and abroad, he considers a wide range of aspects of the communication between teacher and pupil, including:

- the function and effectiveness of teacher talk;
- cultural aspects;
- roles and context variation;
- discourse analysis;
- teacher stories.

Chapter 9 Management in primary education: a learning relationship

The broader issues relating to the school as a whole are taken up by **Paul Ryan** when he considers the the relationship between the individual and the learning organisation as a whole. He considers notions of responsibility to individuals and draws the conclusion that not only children and teachers, but also managers, should engage in learning relationships – in the case of managers with their colleagues. Management in the primary school, he argues, is most effective when it is collaborative and when the learning is through shared experience. Using a case study he illustrates this principle, showing how the development of the structure parallels the development of the individuals within it.

Chapter 10 Initial teacher training in the primary years: 'back to the future'

As professionals, none of us works in isolation. We teach and think as a direct result of the various influences upon us. Many of these influences are cultural, and this to some extent affects our interpretation of pedagogy. This can be seen most clearly in the relationship between the teaching process itself and the influences placed upon it by the teacher training institutions. In **Mark Lofthouse's** chapter the general discussion of initial teacher training is separated into three main sections as he considers:

1 A brief overview of teacher training up to the 1944 Act, placing the emphasis on British notions, how they were 'exported' to the Empire and how the original idea of 'training' teachers developed into 'educating' teachers with the involvement of higher education.
2 A survey of current routes to Qualified Teacher Status and how those routes are returning to the notion of training rather than continuing the emphasis on teacher education. The chapter looks at how and why this has happened.
3 An evaluation of this trend, with parallels between the current situation of payment by results and those of monitoring and 'sitting with Nellie'. Links are made to Neil Kitson's chapter on the Reflective Practitioner through a discussion of competencies for newly qualified teachers, arguing that this development is a retrograde step.

REFERENCES

Bonnett, M. (1994) *Children's Thinking – Promoting Understanding in the Primary School*, London: Cassell.
Bruner, J. and Haste, H. (1987) *Making Sense: The Child's Construction of the World*, London: Methuen.
Merry, R. (1991) 'Curriculum lessons from Europe?', *British Journal of Special Education*18, 2: 71–4.
Newman, D., Griffin, P. and Cole, M. (1989) *The Construction Zone: Working for Cognitive Change in School*, Cambridge: Cambridge University Press.
Piaget, J. (1995) *Sociological Studies*, trans. L. Smith *et al.*, London: Routledge.
Rogoff, B. (1990) *Apprenticeship in Thinking: Cognitive Development in Social Context*, Oxford: Oxford University Press.
Sotto, E. (1994) *When Teaching Becomes Learning: a Theory and Practice of Teaching*, London: Cassell.
Vygotsky, L. (1961) *Thought and Language*, Boston, MA: MIT Press.

Chapter 1

Just for fun?

The child as active learner and meaning maker

Janet Moyles

INTRODUCTION

For the past several decades in many parts of the world, play and active learning have been acknowledged as crucial to the cognitive and other developmental processes of children. That the child learns through making his or her own physical and mental connections with the world, through sensory explorations, personal effort, social experiences and the active seeking of meanings from experiences, has been established in the theories of psychologists and educationalists such as Froebel, Montessori, Isaacs, Steiner, Vygotsky and, later, Piaget and Bruner. Yet it is by no means easy for teachers and other adults in schools and kindergartens to achieve these ideals in practice, where so-called 'child-centred' education and individualised learning are either logistically, pragmatically or culturally considered inappropriate or unrealisable. Similarly, while many educators may see themselves as providing opportunities for children to be actively engaged in their learning, how far this is a reality will depend upon the interpretation and evaluation of these beliefs in practice.

In many countries, curricular debates have focused around the perceived imperative to balance the needs of society for a suitably educated workforce and the needs of children to learn at their own pace and in ways deemed appropriate to their current developmental phase. One view would suggest that we must allow young children to revel in their childhood and childhood experiences before we consider them to be future employees, with an entitlement to have the needs of their particular age group met before they, in turn, must meet the needs of an industrial society (Moyles, 1996). The whole concept of an industrially and economically dominated curriculum militates against a curriculum based upon individual learning needs which is deemed by many to be at the heart of effective primary school practices (Siraj-Blatchford and Siraj-Blatchford 1995).

This chapter sets out to identify the basis upon which these various beliefs about children's active learning as both part of their intellectual development and of their rights as children are justifiable. It also examines their substance in terms of the teaching and learning relationship and how such beliefs may be translated into curricular practices in different cultural settings. First, we explore the issue of how children perceive the world and are, in turn, perceived in the context of childhood by the dominant adults.

PRIMARY CHILDREN MAKING SENSE OF THE WORLD

> **The children in the kindergarten were told by the adult that it was nearly time to go outside for outdoor play. It was a beautiful, hot, sunny day though Anna, aged 4 years, moved towards the coat-racks and asked the adult to help her put on her coat. The adult laughed, saying, 'You don't need your coat. It's too nice out there. Go and feel how hot it is.' Anna stood on the steps outside the nursery door and was seen to stretch out her arms and then pinch her fingers and thumbs together in a 'feeling' action.**

As an example of 'intelligent' behaviour, the reader may wonder what on earth Anna was doing. But looked at from the child's perspective, Anna was doing exactly what she perceived the adult had told her to do: in Donaldson's (1978) words she was attempting to make 'human sense' of what had been said to her. The fact that she so literally interpreted the action behind the adult's words is not uncommon in young children for it takes some time for them to grasp the different interpretations implicit in the words and actions of others.

Children in the primary years learn directly about their immediate environment through exploration using their senses: by attending to the world around them through touching, listening, tasting, smelling and looking, they begin to make generalisations. By generalising from these experiences, children begin to form the basis of lasting understandings. Without the ability to generalise and put 'chunks' of learning into large wholes, we would all rapidly become overloaded and overwhelmed with information (McShane 1991). But this very need to generalise means that children will not always be 'right', for, as Edwards and Knight (1994: 21) emphasise, 'Young children have less information on which to build new understandings and their strategies for organising and holding information are less well developed.' It is interesting to note that this equally applies to adult learners in contexts which are new to them, such as learning a second language.

Sensory learning combined with existing experience leads children to perceive the world in certain ways which, at different stages in the child's development, leads to different levels of understanding being available to the child. As Merry (1995: 84) points out, 'Perception is not a passive taking-in of our surroundings but a highly active process in which the information supplied by our brains is at least as important as the information received by our senses'. Donaldson (1993: 19) also believes that

> Most of the knowledge that matters to us – the knowledge that consti-
> tutes our conception of the world, of other people and of ourselves – is
> not developed in a passive way. We come to know through processes
> of active interpretation and integration.

Reality from the child's perspective

Children's views of the world are very much human-centred: they per-ceive and conceive of events and things through the experiences they themselves encounter and in which adults offer support and models. But there are times when perception dominates children's thinking, and if they cannot perceive something they may well doubt its existence. Even when primary-age children do perceive something they frequently mis-interpret what the reality is by attending only to those aspects which are immediately recognisable, adopting what Piaget and Inhelder (1969) called 'unscientific causations'.

From much research (see, e.g., Langford 1987, Willig 1990, Bonnett 1994) it is clear that children bring a different kind of 'logic' to situations from which it is possible for the practitioners[1] to learn a great deal with which to inform primary practice. Consider the following: after a short discussion about how they learned to read with a group of 11-year-olds clustered around a computer, the writer was presented with the follow-ing text and asked to 'read' it:

Ωηψ χαν τ ψου ρεαδ τηισ? Ιτ ισ περφεχτλψ σιμπλε – προωιδεδ ψου υνδερστανδ τηε λανγυαγε ανδ τηε σψμβολσ ιν τηε φιρστ πλαχε!

The children explained that this was how many of them had perceived reading as young children, a series of squiggles on paper which meant very little to them but which they knew that somehow they were intend-ed to read. (The text, in Symbol font, actually says 'Why can't you read this? It is perfectly simple – provided you understand the language and the symbols in the first place!')

Other instances spring to mind. Consider the child who answered '11' to the seemingly simple sequence of numbers 2, 4, 6, 8, _. Although we would immediately perceive the answer from a numerical base as 10, this child's interpretation was equally valid because she was actual-ly perceiving the numbers to relate to a social and personal (egocentric) context: she is one of five children whose ages are 2, 4, 6, 8 and *11* years. The misinterpretation of the context of learning needed to be understood by the adult in order for the child's 'error' to be understood.

Language proves to be no less confusing. Consider the child who has just had a large dish of their favourite food and is asked if they would like to have some 'more'. What will they inevitably get? Well, certainly *less* than they had the first time! Or the child who, when asked which out of two ribbons is the longer, the red or the yellow, confidently responds 'The yellow one – because I like that colour'. As Hughes (1983) points out, whereas adults would recognise that they have insufficient information, children do not always know the appropriate questions to ask and assume that a response is possible because the question has been asked by an older person.

Abstraction and symbolism

As adults, we are in danger of forgetting just how abstract – and symbolic – much of what we present to children really is. What must be recognised is that children's thinking is not inferior to adults, but rather that it is different in form and experience. Their thinking is embedded in a context which has some meaning to them, whereas much school activity, such as filling in the blanks in a workbook, is what Donaldson (1993: 19) describes as 'disembedded' tasks: tasks divorced from a context in which children can see purpose and meaning and which, therefore, make the processes of learning much more difficult. Sotto (1994: 44) suggests that meaning emerges slowly from the learner's active involvement in thinking through and understanding the 'patterns' which underlie understanding, and emphasises that learning is not the same as remembering. Wood (1988: 35) stresses that 'Learning involves the search for pattern, regularity and predictability', and urges us to view children as 'limited information processors'. These findings propose a very different model of the child as learner from the one which suggests that they are passive recipients of handed-down information and ideas. As Bruce *et al.* (1995: 59–60) suggest,

> Adults seize on the child's developing ability to make and use symbols and often cannot wait to begin to teach directly the symbols of their particular society. In some cultures this begins at a very young age. . . . What is it that activates these important symbolic developments in children and . . . what turns them into ever deeper levels of symbolic learning? The key issue in answering this revolves around what kind of symbols children are most at ease with in their early years. This will dictate what symbols they can most readily engage with.

Bruce and her colleagues go on to propose that the development of the use of symbols in children is most likely to take place through 'real experiences' and 'a consideration of the links among play, experience, relationships and creativity', rather than pressure from adults to conform to learning which is outside the children's current potential to understand.

It is acknowledged that, towards the end of primary schooling, children are more able to cope with disembedded tasks as their thinking becomes more abstract. However, as primary practitioners, we need to consider (and observe for) embedded thinking when we set out to teach different kinds of knowledge and understanding, for, whatever the content demands of a curriculum subject, the children need to have tasks presented to them which offer a meaningful context in which they can bring their previous experiences and understandings to bear and which fit in with the new experiences and patterns of understanding they are already acquiring. As Donaldson (1993: 20) suggests, ' . . . it is even more important to recognise that the *processes* of coming to know transform us. This is particularly so when these entail sustained, self-directed effort.'

Teaching must acknowledge the learner's role in the essential links between teaching and learning effectiveness. This means particularly recognising that the ability to think abstractly about things has a starting point in *action*, a feature of the work of Piaget, Bruner and Vygotsky which often manifests itself in the process we call 'play'. It is to the links between play and active learning that we now turn.

ACTIVE LEARNING AND CHILDREN'S PLAY

The primary classroom is carefully arranged with all materials necessary for the morning's session. The teacher has planned an active lesson for the children aimed at helping them to understand the concept of electricity. Each group of tables is equipped with a collection of bulbs, wires, batteries and switches, a new experience this term for this class of 9-year-olds. The active learning session has arisen because the teacher has recognised that, despite telling the children in a class session yesterday about electricity, they still do not appear to understand how a circuit is made.

When the children enter the room from the playground, many of them rush to the tables and, in the teacher's words, start 'messing about' with the materials and arguing over them. It takes some time to bring the class back to order and to gather in the electricity resources. The teacher gives out a worksheet in which the children complete a series of sentences regarding issues to do with electricity.

Children appear to need to play regardless of whether society approves or not. Clearly this teacher did not 'approve' of these children's play, yet indeed that is what it was: play as exploration, in this case, of resources in an effort to understand them. While feeling an empathy with this teacher that his carefully conceived plans were not fulfilled, it is also vital to think of the activity from the learners' point of view. This was the first time in many weeks that the children had been given the opportunity to play with resources which brought electricity to their immediate level of engagement – which gave a direct embedded context for their learning – and they were keen to explore the wires, batteries, bulbs and switches and understand their patterns and purposes. In so doing they were engaging in a form of play – exploratory play – through which they are able to learn about the properties and functions of materials as a preliminary to being able to manipulate them for a given purpose (Hutt *et al.* 1989, Moyles 1994).

In Brunerian terms, in this activity children were still at the *enactive* stage in their learning; they needed to learn by actively doing, whereas the teacher was expecting them to operate at an *iconic* (image or pictorial) or even *symbolic* (abstract) stage by filling in the sentences on a worksheet. What distinguishes 'active learning' from 'play' is to do with the processes in which the children engage and with concepts such as 'ownership' and 'locus of control' which, in play, rest with the player but in active learning situations can be under the direction of another person, e.g. the teacher (see Bruce 1991 and Moyles 1991).

Holt (1991: 160) raises issues to do with active learning in the following terms:

> What do we do when we make learning? Well, we observe, we look, we listen. We touch, taste, smell, manipulate and sometimes measure or calculate. And then we wonder. . . . This process creates learning and we all do it. . . . And this is exactly what children do. They are hard at work at this process all their waking hours. . . . They are observing, thinking, speculating, theorising, testing and experimenting . . . and they're much better at it than we are!

Like Holt, Vygotsky (1978) suggests that play and play processes *lead* children's development (rather than development leading play). He suggests that play acts as a catalyst for children's learning and ensures that they are able to perform ahead of their current developmental level. Children acquire concepts, skills, knowledge and attitudes towards learning and towards others in their play and, for this reason, play should occupy a central part in children's lives. Play happens in some mode or another even in cultures where there are few apparent play opportunities (Curtis 1994), and many studies have indicated how effective play is in ensuring motivation in learning and providing the context for lasting understanding. For example, much primary-level learning focuses around developing schema which are the amalgamation of smaller pieces of information which have entered consciousness through children's active engagement in seeking meaning. As an example, children build up a 'cat' schema by gradually accommodating all those facets which make up a cat (body, head, tail, eyes, legs, then sizes, shapes, breeds), until one has a full concept of 'cat' – the more sophisticated the schema, the deeper one's knowledge. Schema, in turn, enable the formation of *concepts* – big ideas, which are capable of being generalised and which enable us to use the knowledge gained in one situation in a new context. Research by Athey (1990), Gura (1991) and Nutbrown (1994) with children under six has shown clear evidence of schema development in children's play and in their representations of the world, particularly in pictures and model-making. There is no evidence to suggest that this does not apply equally to older primary children.

One tangible element of play is that it is an *observable behaviour* and, therefore, one could argue that at least one value of play is being able to observe and assess the outcomes of the learning process through what one sees. Schwartzman (1983) supports this view in suggesting that children play what they know and, therefore, through play we can find out about their deeper understandings.

Indeed, there is now a plethora of research showing that play and active learning allow children to understand the meanings behind the symbols they create, whether it is in art, music or pretend play (Matthews 1994). Socio-dramatic play, in particular, has been shown to be at a level between the concrete and the symbolic where one meets the other in the child's world (Kitson 1994). Not only is this an important link for primary children's developing skills in the area of number, reading, writing and representation, but it is also believed by some writers (see Smilansky and Shefataya 1990) to contribute to greater cognitive gains in such areas as verbalisation, richer vocabulary, higher language comprehension, better problem-solving strategies, higher intellectual competence, better performance on conservation tasks and greater concentration.

Play and learning theory

Play provides children with an active learning mode in which to

1 explore;
2 use their developing skills;
3 solve problems;
4 practise skills;
5 rehearse.

These five aspects link closely with established theories of learning, such as that developed by Bennett and his colleagues (1984) from an earlier model by Norman (1978) which suggests that learners need to show evidence of their ability to

1   acquire new knowledge and skills;
2   use existing knowledge and skills in different contexts;
3   recognise and solve problems;
4   practise what they know;
5   revise and replay what they know in order to retain it in memory.

As well as offering a sound theory, this model also offers a clear relationship to classroom practice, in terms of both children's play and active learning opportunities. It has been found by many writers (see Sylva *et al.* 1980, Smith and Cowie 1992, Moyles 1994) that children's first need in learning about an object or situation is to have opportunities to *explore* the properties, textures, shapes, colours, forms and so on in order to gain basic factual knowledge and handling skills. Having done so, this then enables the child to begin to *use* this knowledge and skill in ways which should eventually result in the *recognition* and *solution* of problems. In returning to a related activity or situation at a later time, the child will be required to *practise* and *revise* as the basis for future learning activities.

It now becomes clear that the children in the electricity cameo were attempting to acquire new knowledge about, and skills in handling, the various materials which, in turn, would have given them a sound basis on which to use that knowledge to develop a circuit. In completing the circuit, they will have needed both to recognise and attempt to solve particular problems in ensuring that a light appeared. A later return to a similar electricity experiment would afford the children opportunity to practise and revise what they have previously learned and commit it to memory. Memorising of 'facts' alone would be difficult without the developing concept of electricity which has, in turn, been refined through further additions to developing schema.

Trial-and-error learning

One of the things which seems to be important in relation to play and active learning situations is that, because having real, first-hand experiences is in itself motivating to children, the processes of play provide a valuable means of allowing children to learn through their own efforts and their own mistakes. Play also increases children's powers of concentration which, in itself, has been found to be a good indicator of children's potential (Keough 1982). As well as knowledge, skills and opportunities to practise, children need to believe that they *can* achieve in school: they need confidence and a good image of themselves as 'learners'. This is much more capable of being achieved in situations where success is not judged only in terms of recognisable outcomes, but where making mistakes is itself valued as part of a successful learning process.

In the process of 'coming to know' something it is likely that most of us will not achieve success every time (Holt 1991). Unfortunately, many learning situations in school accept only 'right' answers: mistakes are not something to be learned from but seen as a sign of 'failure'. Yet, as we have seen, many psychological theories over the past few decades have suggested strongly that children's learning occurs more effectively in the context of trial-and-error opportunities where fear of failure is replaced with open-ended challenges which are under the control and direction of the child and, furthermore, do not undermine children's self-esteem. Yet practitioners insist on emphasising right answers, particularly in countries with a heavily dominated paper-and-pencil-based curriculum where children either can or cannot do the tasks presented to them and are, therefore, either right or, if they do not peform correctly, wrong. The question must be raised as to whether children should be penalised for not understanding or whether practitioners need to rethink their practice in terms of allowing children opportunities to learn through exploring their own understandings without fear of failure. This leads us to examine the role of adults in children's play and learning, to which we now turn.

THE PRACTITIONER'S ROLE IN ACTIVE LEARNING APPROACHES

The teacher sits down beside a group of four 10-year-old children who are attempting to design and make a pulley system from a range of different materials. The children have been having some difficulty in making their pulleys work and concentration has begun to wane. The teacher, without speaking, manipulates the various pieces of wood, pulley wheels and string under the watchful eye of the children. One child approaches and asks her what she is doing. The teacher replies that she has a problem in trying to make her pulley work and wonders if the child can think of a way of doing so. The rest of the children gather round and make various suggestions, all of which the teacher tries until one achieves the desired result and the pulley is made to work. The children analyse with the teacher how success has been achieved and evaluate the outcome, then they quickly return to their own efforts and consult with each other on producing the desired outcome. The teacher leaves the technology table, returning around ten minutes later to find a series of different pulleys being eagerly discussed and experimented with by the children.

In the 1960s there was a view which still prevails today among some people in Western societies, that children's active learning and play should not be 'interfered' with by adults: that it is somehow sacrosanct to the child and that adults cannot have a role in it other than as providers. This is now seriously in question, since studies (like those of Bruner 1980, Smilansky 1968, Hutt *et al.* 1989, and Smilansky and Shefataya 1990) have shown clearly that children's play and active learning can be significantly enhanced educationally and academically by adult involvement (see also Clark 1988).

Can the teacher in the cameo be said to be 'teaching'? The answer to this lies, of course, in what perception one applies to the teaching role. In the previous section, the case for children's active engagement in their own play and learning has been argued in relation to children creating meaning and making sense of the world.

Through the actions of the teacher in the cameo, the children were enabled to be successful in their learning outcomes *and* to retain the ownership and control of their own play and active learning. This is surely at the heart of good teaching when applied to the model of learning which has been previously outlined. For children to achieve learning goals set by others and to add to their existing schema, they need adults who can 'scaffold' their attempts (Bruner 1973) and allow them to use first-hand experiences within what Vygotsky terms 'the zone of proximal development': i.e. the gap between what the child can currently do alone and what he or she could do with support.

The teacher could have approached the children with a range of questions about what they were doing or, indeed, have given directions as to what they should do to achieve the desired outcome. This would, however, have meant that the teacher needed to understand exactly what level each child was capable of achieving with her support – no mean feat! This approach could also have left the children with the feeling that only someone outside of themselves could provide the answer to their problem, rather than the answer coming from within the children's own intellect and experiences.

Children's independence and adult models

With the adult operating both as model and as facilitator of the children's own thinking and questioning, the children were challenged to provide their own solutions rather than generating a dependency upon the teacher. The latter has been shown by researchers to create impossible situations in classes of thirty and more children, who are then all potentially dependent upon the teacher for their learning actions (see Barrett 1986, King 1978, Bennett and Kell 1989). This in itself creates environments in which, according to Galton (1995: 18), there are often queues of children waiting for the teacher, which decreases the time that children are able to devote to their learning tasks. Darling (1994: 4/5), in discussing learner-centred education, proffers the Dewey view that

Once children see education as something that other people do to them . . . they lose the ability to take any initiative or responsibility for their own learning. . . . In particular the kinds of enquiry that children naturally pursue are not reflected in the way traditional schooling categorises knowledge into different 'subjects'. It is this lack of correspondence which accounts for children's low motivation . . . child-centred educational theory suggests that we could and should have classrooms where learning is largely self-motivated and the atmosphere is fairly relaxed.

A model that perceives children as having a central role in their own learning also has to acknowledge teachers as *learners* themselves, rather than as general purveyors of existing knowledge (see Pollard and Tann 1992). This means a fundamental shift in some teachers' thinking and in the strategies they apply to children's learning. Dweck and Legett's (1988) research has indicated that, through the kind of learning support they receive, children either develop 'learning goals' or 'achievement goals'. The latter are characterised by children attempting to gain favourable judgements from others, developing very little sense of control and attributing success to ability rather than to effort. Children tend to avoid struggle and trial-and-error situations. The former – learning goals – involve the children in a concern for personal competence and ways of increasing mastery. Children are actively engaged, need to struggle and solve problems, leading to personal standards of success. The writers emphasise, like Bruner and Vygotsky, children's need for support as they struggle to understand and make sense. One might also add the children's need to be *trusted* to negotiate, discuss and understand their own learning needs and be responsible for some of the outcomes. This requires practitioners who have a clear view of their own role.

Based upon the kind of learning model explored earlier, teachers should consider several factors shown in Table 1.1, which will lead to the active learner retaining some control over the learning activities and having opportunities to reflect on their own cognitive processes. The order can be adjusted according to the task.

This model is readily applied to a range of teaching and learning situations and links with the kind of teacher action shown in the cameo at the start of this section. The teacher's entering strategy was to model the kind of actions undertaken by the children in order to enable them to understand not only the processes of their own learning but the content of the technological activity. The children could see from the teacher's actions what they were intended to learn and had opportunities to reflect on her outcomes and evaluate them in terms of their own potential achievement. The adult valued and trusted the children, giving them the responsibility and ownership of their task by leaving them to complete it,

Table 1.1 Teaching strategies for active learning

1. *Entering strategy*
   What will be your starting point(s)? Introduction?

2. *Exploration mode*
   What exploration will the children undertake? What materials/resources need to be available? How/by whom would they be set up?

3. *Contents*
   What do you intend the children should learn? Subject and/or processes and/or skills?

4. *Ownership and responsibility*
   How/at what point will it be possible for the practitioner to withdraw and allow the children ownership? How will the children know what they are supposed to learn through their active involvement?

5. *Adult value strategies*
   What will the practitioner role be? How will you interact/intervene in the learning and sustain/extend it? What level of support will the children require?

6. *Evaluation and analysis*
   How/when will you observe to see what children were learning in relation to concepts covered?

7. *Reflection*
   What opportunities will you provide for children to reflect on their learning and be part of the evaluation/analysis of processes and outcomes?

8. *Justification*
   What kind of outcomes will you expect? How will the value of these be communicated to others?

having scaffolded their attempts. She valued and evaluated the active processes of their learning equally with the outcomes. This is what could be termed 'the learning relationship'.

Ownership, control and the sensitive teacher

The concept of *ownership* is one worth exploring a little further. Even in exploratory play children do not necessarily have a sense of ownership: it is when they take things on board intrinsically that ownership is established. Teachers can support this by the way they present tasks to children within the curriculum. It can be the teacher's idea or learning objective, but then the children need to be persuaded to make it part of their learning. Much of the research already discussed has shown the long-term value of programmes which are characterised by the latter type of learning involvement and of children taking ownership and responsibility: e.g., the outcomes of the longitudinal High/Scope study in the United States (see Royal Society of Arts 1994, Sylva 1994).

It is worth noting from the research that what children choose to do (even if by adults' perceptions it is work) is still deemed 'play' by children and is often characterised by greater motivation, persistence and concentration (Karrby 1989, Moyles 1989, Robson 1993). Edwards and Knight (1994: 21) note that 'Teaching is above all led by sensitivity to the state of the learner. A learner's state will include motivations, confidence and existing understandings.'

Teachers do have several dilemmas when engaging in making this kind of learning provision for children; large class sizes, the dictates of imposed curricula, pressures from others (including parents) to provide paper evidence of children's learning, to mention but a few. Practitioners should consider, however, the outcomes of *not* providing appropriate experiential learning: the result is often demotivated children, who can 'perform' and conform to adult requirements but who often have little understanding of learning intentions and little responsibility for themselves as learners (Bennett and Kell 1989). An example would be the young child who can readily count to ten and beyond but has no concept of the 'fiveness' of five, or what constitutes 5 + 1. Hughes (1986) has shown clearly that, when adults allow children to manipulate the numbers in concrete terms through having the objects to handle and move, they are capable of much greater levels of understanding, not only of numbers but of their own metacognitive processes.

The practitioner's sensitivity to/empathy with the way children make sense of learning opportunities is vital, for, as Willig (1990: 184) shows,

> Teaching is about negotiation of meanings between teachers and pupils . . . skilled teachers encourage pupils' contributions and look for links between the knowledge children bring to the situation and the new experiences to which they are being introduced. The act of learning then becomes an exchange of viewpoints where the learner works hard on the new material, grafts it on to existing learning and comes out of the experience with fresh insights.

– a true learning relationship.

The final topic in this chapter concerns the provision of an appropriate curriculum for this type of learning

Figure 1.1 Environmental geography

PROVIDING FOR AN ACTIVE, PLAY-BASED CURRICULUM

A teacher, new to the Infants School, was presented with a series of headings under which each term's curriculum was to be presented to the children in different year groups. The first-year children were to undertake some of their work based on the subject of 'Environmental Geography'. The teacher had some concerns as to how she could develop this into an appropriate scheme of activities for these 5-year-olds. She decided to ask the children at discussion time what they understood of 'environmental geography' and, despite great keenness on the children's part to explore all kinds of things to do with their homes, toys, families and so on, her own concerns were confirmed when children appeared unable to offer any explanation of the subject. However, some time later, Leigh came to her with a drawing which the child explained showed 'environmental geography'. When asked to describe what she had drawn, Leigh said 'This is the whole wide world, with some people in the grass, some flowers and some trees.' (see Figure 1.1)

As teachers, we are often set seemingly impossible tasks in trying to teach children about issues which are not directly within their experience but which 'society' in its broadest sense, through a designated curriculum, feels it appropriate for children to learn. It is vital that those directly responsible for the curriculum in action in classrooms are sensitive not only to what they must teach but to the children's starting points in setting out to learn about different aspects (Blenkin and Kelly 1994). As Doyle affirms, 'tasks communicate what the curriculum is to students' and 'meaning is seldom at the heart of the academic tasks they work on' (Doyle 1986: 366, 374).

In discussing with the children the concepts behind 'environmental geography', this practitioner was able to draw from at least one child what her perception of the subject involved, and was, therefore, able to evolve activities within the curriculum which would operate from the basis of the children's existing knowledge and understanding.

In fact, learning experiences were planned which involved considering the earth beneath the children's feet and the things which grew upon it and lived underneath. The activities were within the children's understanding, with scaffolding from the teacher. While the child's interpretation of environmental geography may, by adult standards, be very incomplete and rather naive, as we have seen earlier in this chapter practitioners need to relate to children's ways of thinking and to acknowledge that these are not somehow 'faulty' but represent the world as the child perceives and conceives it. This must be the starting point for any active learning curriculum, for how can any child actively engage with something about which they have no schema, or, as Sotto (1994) suggests, no 'model inside the head'? Sotto goes on to state:

[I]f I do not have such a working model, I find I may understand the individual words said to me, but I do not really understand their full *meaning*. The result is that I begin to lose track of what is being said to me . . . until I am actively engaged [in developing this model] I do not really learn.

(Sotto 1994: 33)

In observing and evaluating children's approaches to activities, practitioners gain a clear understanding of how to match curriculum intentions to children's learning. For, as Bruce (1991: 87) suggests,

It is not in children's best interests to give them successes with low-level activities, because these leave them without the ownership and the self-esteem to believe in themselves as creators. They deny them control, and discourage them from the effort of struggling . . . play is an example of the way that children apply, use and integrate the inputs of first-hand experiences.

So the curriculum, as it is imposed upon the children from outside, needs also to be considered in terms of what is developed through the kinds of learning experiences which match with children's capacity to understand and make sense of the world at any given time. Broadly it could be said that the curriculum is everything the child experiences in the context of schooling which is intended to foster learning. The curriculum must acknowledge the central role of the learner and have a relationship to the child's life, otherwise the learning will be sterile and will not create opportunities for the child to make sense. Curriculum activities should ensure that children are motivated and want to try and to succeed. Above all, what children can do alone and with support, evidenced in their attempts to make sense of the world and gain meaning from their experiences, must be the starting point, rather than what they cannot yet do alone. The curriculum has its own processes which can be seen to link effectively with learning processes if one conceives of it in this way. The curriculum is the medium through which children should be enabled to think, feel, do, acquire knowledge and skills, solve problems, investigate, apply knowledge, practise, revise, cooperate and communicate.

What practitioners will be attempting to do is to ensure that all of these processes are engaged in by children during most of the school day. The interaction between the teacher, the child – the learning relationship – and the curriculum is crucial. McAuley (1990: 89) rightly emphasises that

[I]t is the teacher–child interaction that is at the heart of the educational process and it must always be *about* something. That 'something' is the task which, if it is routinely conceived as an exercise for skills and competences rather than a problem, will devalue the teacher–child interaction. The latter will become demonstrational, instructional, transmissional rather than the exploration of making sense and figuring out.

SUMMARY

The Piagetian emphasis on learning through doing which instigated 'activity'-based learning methods in the UK and other countries has formed the focus of this chapter. Through looking at children's active engagement in abstracting meaning from their environment and their interaction with others, it is possible to evolve a series of models which support practitioners in understanding how children's learning develops, how children construct their own meanings and how teaching and curriculum links can be made. These ideas perhaps involve a concept of childhood which is new to many practitioners, one in which children are not necessarily thought of merely as 'adults in waiting' (Dowling 1988) but as young people with a contribution to make to our understanding of different perceptions and conceptions of the world. Only if we offer children the opportunities to create their own meaning and understand their own learning through play and active engagement at a developmentally appropriate time in their lives are we likely to ensure our future citizens have the necessary adaptability, flexibility and clarity of understanding to be the source of technological innovation so necessary for economic survival.

NOTE

1 I have used the term 'practitioners' throughout in the belief that not all those who work with primary children, particularly younger primaries, will be qualified teachers.

REFERENCES

Athey, C. (1990) *Extending thought in young children*, London: Paul Chapman.
Barrett, G. (1986) *Starting School: An Evaluation of the Experience*, Final Report to AMMA. CARE. Norwich: University of East Anglia.
Bennett, N. and Kell, J. (1989) *A Good Start? Four Year Olds in Infant Schools*, Oxford: Blackwell.
Bennett, N., Desforges, C., Cockburn, A. and Wilkinson, B. (1984) *The Quality of Pupils' Learning Experiences*, London: Lawrence Erlbaum.
Blenkin, G. and Kelly, A. (1994) *The National Curriculum and Early Learning: An Evaluation*, London: Paul Chapman.
Bonnett, M. (1994) *Children's Thinking: Promoting Understanding in the Primary School*, London: Cassell.
Bruce, T. (1991) *Time to Play in Early Childhood*, London: Hodder and Stoughton.
Bruce, T., Findlay, A., Read, J. and Scarborough, M. (1995) *Recurring Themes in Education*, London: Paul Chapman.

Bruner, J. (1973) *Beyond the Information Given*, London: Allen and Unwin.
—— (1980) *Under Five in Britain*, London: Grant McIntyre.
Clark, M. M. (1988) *Children Under Five: Educational Research and Evidence*, London: Gordon and Breach.
Cullingford, C. (1990) *The Nature of Learning: Children, Teachers and the Curriculum*, London: Cassell.
Curtis, A. (1994) 'Play in Different Cultures and Different Childhoods', in J. R. Moyles (ed.), *The Excellence of Play*, Buckingham: Open University Press.
Darling, J. (1994) *Child-Centred Education and its Critics*, London: Paul Chapman.
Donaldson, M. (1978) *Children's Minds*, Glasgow: Fontana.
—— (1993) *Human Minds: An Exploration*, London: Penguin.
Dowling, M. (1988) *Education 3–5*, London: Paul Chapman.
Doyle, W. (1986) 'Classroom Organisation and Management', in M. Wittrock (ed.), *Handbook of Research on Teaching* (3rd edn), New York: Macmillan.
Dweck, C. and Leggett, E. (1988) 'A social-cognitive approach to motivation and personality', *Psychological Review*, 95(2), April, pp. 956–73.
Edwards, A. and Knight, P. (1994) *Effective Early Years Education: Teaching Young Children*, Buckingham: Open University Press.
Fisher, R. (1990) *Teaching Children to Think*, Oxford: Blackwell.
Galton, M. (1995) 'Do you really want to cope with thirty lively children and become an effective primary teacher?', in J. R. Moyles (ed.), *Beginning Teaching: Beginning Learning*, Buckingham: Open University Press.
Gura, P. (1991) *Exploring Learning: Young children and blockplay*, London: Paul Chapman.
Holt, J. (1989) *Learning All the Time*, Ticknell: Education Now.
—— (1991) *Never Too Late*, Ticknell: Education Now.
Hughes, M. (1983) 'On asking children bizarre questions', in M. Donaldson, R. Grieve and C. Pratt (eds), *Early Childhood Development and Education: Readings in Psychology*, Oxford: Basil Blackwell.
—— (1986) *Children and Number*, Oxford: Basil Blackwell.
Hutt, S. J., Tyler, S., Hutt, C. and Christopherson, H. (1989) *Play, Exploration and Learning: A Natural History of the Pre-School*, London: Routledge.
Karrby, G. (1989) 'Children's perceptions of their own play', *International Journal of Early Childhood*, 21(2), pp. 49–54.
Keough, B. K. (1982) 'Children's temperament and teachers' decisions', in R. Porter and G. Collins (eds), *Temperamental Differences in Infants and Young Children*, London: Pitman.
King, R. (1978) *All Things Bright and Beautiful?*, London: John Wiley.
Kitson, N. (1994) 'Please Miss Alexander: will you be the robber? Fantasy Play: a case for adult intervention', in J. R. Moyles (ed.), *The Excellence of Play*, Buckingham: Open University Press.
Langford, P. (1987) *Concept Development in the Primary School*, London: Croom Helm.
McAuley, H. (1990) 'Learning structures for the young child: A review of the literature', *Early Child Development and Care*, 59, pp. 87–124.
McShane, J. (1991) *Cognitive Development: An information-processing approach*, Oxford: Basil Blackwell.
Matthews, J. (1994) *Helping Children to Draw and Paint in Early Childhood: Children and Visual Representation*, London: Hodder and Stoughton.
Merry, R. (1995) 'Take some notice of me! Primary children and their learning potential', in J. R. Moyles (ed.), *Beginning Teaching: Beginning Learning*, Buckingham: Open University Press.

Moyles, J. R. (1989) *Just Playing? The role and status of play in early education*, Milton Keynes: Open University Press.

—— (1991) *Play as a Learning Process in your Classroom*, London: Collins.

—— (ed.) (1994) *The Excellence of Play*, Buckingham: Open University Press.

—— (ed.) (1995) *Beginning Teaching: Beginning Learning in the Primary School*, Buckingham: Open University Press.

—— (1996) 'Nationally Prescribed curricula and early childhood education: The English Experience and Australian comparisons–identifying the rhetoric and the reality.' *Australian Journal of Early Childhood*, 21 (1), pp. 27–31.

Norman, D. A. (1978) 'Notes Towards a Complex Theory of Learning', in A. M. Lesgold (ed.), *Cognitive Psychology and Instruction*, New York: Plenum.

Nutbrown, C. (1994) *Threads of Thinking*, London: Paul Chapman.

Piaget, J. and Inhelder, B. (1969) *The Psychology of the Child*, London: Routledge and Kegan Paul.

Pollard, A. and Tann, S. (1992) *Reflective Teaching in the Primary School: A Handbook for the Classroom* (2nd edn), London: Cassell.

Robson, S. (1993) 'Best of all I like Choosing Time. Talking with children about play and work', *Early Child Development and Care*, 92, pp. 37–51.

Royal Society of Arts (1994) *Start Right* (The Ball Report), London: RSA.

Schwartzman, H. (1983) 'Play as a mode', *Behavioural and Brain Sciences*, 5, pp. 168–9.

Siraj-Blatchford, J. and Siraj-Blatchford, I. (eds) (1995) *Educating the Whole Child*, Buckingham: Open University Press.

Smilansky, S. (1968) *The effects of Socio-Dramatic Play on Disadvantaged Preschool Children*, London: Academic Press.

Smilansky, S. and Shefataya, S. (1990) *Facilitating Play: A Medium for Promoting Cognitive, Socio-Emotional and Academic Development in Young Children*, Gaithersberg: Psychosocial and Educational Publications.

Smith, P. and Cowie, H. (1992) *Understanding Children's Development* (2nd edn), Oxford: Basil Blackwell.

Sotto, E. (1994) *When Teaching Becomes Learning*, London: Cassell.

Sylva, K. (1977) 'Play, Exploration and Learning', in K. Sylva and D. Harvey (eds), *The Biology of Play*, London: Spastics International.

—— (1994) 'The Impact of Early Learning on Children's Later Development', in Royal Society of Arts, *Start Right* (The Ball Report), London: RSA, pp. 84–96.

Sylva, K., Roy, C. and Painter, M. (1980) *Childwatching at Playgroup and Nursery*, London: Grant McIntyre.

Tizard, B. and Hughes, M. (1984) *Young Children Learning: Talking and Thinking at Home and at School*, London: Fontana.

Trevarthen, C. (1991) Commentary to the BBC TV *Horizon* programme *Play for Tomorrow*.

Vygotsky, L. (1978) 'Mind in society: the development of higher psychological processes', in M. Cole, V. John-Steiner, S. Scribner and G. Souberman (eds), *Mind in Society*, Cambridge, MA: Harvard University Press.

Willig, C. J. (1990) *Children's Concepts and the Primary Curriculum*, London: Paul Chapman.

Wood, D. (1988) *How Children Think and Learn*, Oxford: Blackwell.

Chapter 2

Children's development 3–7
The learning relationship in the early years

Linda M Hargreaves and David J Hargreaves

INTRODUCTION

Children aged between three and seven are passing through a rich and fascinating period of development in which they experience a great variety of learning relationships. For most children this period includes the major transition from the typically small network of relationships with family, family friends and neighbours to the wider world of pre-school groups and school, in which they meet adults and other children who are not known to their parents. In other words, the child's sphere of potential learning relationships undergoes a radical change during this period. Psychologists have been particularly interested in the cognitive development of children in this age group, but recently this interest has broadened to take in:

- the role of the social world in shaping and supporting children's learning;
- children's understanding of how the people around them think and feel;
- the importance of real-life contexts;
- the concept of development throughout the life span.

This chapter will look, therefore, at studies of young children in their homes and with their families, at their friendships, and at the more formal relationships set up in classrooms. It begins with brief sketches of three major cognitive theories of child development, namely those of Piaget, Vygotsky and Bruner, followed by Bandura's social learning theory. We shall consider children's language acquisition, sibling relationships and the development of gender role identity. Children's acquisition of singing will be described to exemplify development in a very specific domain, and to demonstrate parallels with the development of drawing. We shall move on then to look at children's informal learning relationships with family and friends as compared with the formal learning contexts typical of schools. The chapter ends with the possibility of a better understanding of the importance of social learning relationships for children's achievement in and adjustment to school. Several of these themes will be taken up again in the following chapter.

THEORIES OF CHILD DEVELOPMENT

In the next few paragraphs we look very briefly at the main ideas of three important developmental psychologists, Piaget, Vygotsky and Bruner, whose work is described at length in widely available books on developmental psychology (see, e.g., Smith and Cowie 1991, Berryman *et al.* 1991, Butterworth and Harris 1994, Lee and Das Gupta 1995; see also Wood 1988, who looks specifically at their contributions to children's thinking and learning).

Jean Piaget (1896–1980)

Jean Piaget is probably the best known and most influential of developmental psychologists, who, after making detailed and careful observations of his own children's development, proposed the existence of four developmental stages in children's cognitive growth:

1 sensori-motor (roughly from birth to two);

2 pre-operational (from about two to seven);

3 concrete operational (from about seven to eleven);

4 formal operational (from about eleven onwards).

For Piaget, children's thinking develops through the dynamic interaction of two processes – *assimilation*, in which new information is taken into their existing concepts, and *accommodation*, in which these concepts change to fit new information. Among other things, he claimed that young children are *egocentric* in their thinking – that they cannot see things from another person's point of view – and that they lack *conservation*. This refers, for example, to the ability to recognise that things do not change in number when re-arranged, or that a liquid does not change its volume when poured into a differently shaped container. Children begin to appreciate these constancies as they approach age seven.

These two features of Piaget's theory have influenced a good deal of thinking in contemporary developmental psychology, in particular his conceptions of developmental *stages* and the critical role of *interaction* between child and environment in development. Piaget's work has been criticised, however, on the grounds that the rather artificial and socially awkward situations in which he observed children led him to underestimate children's thinking. Donaldson (1978), for example, showed that young children's sensitivity to such social contexts as those found in Piaget's studies has a strong influence on their ability to succeed in conservation tasks. Very recently, however, newly translated work provides strong evidence of Piaget's recognition of the role of social encounters on development (Smith 1995).

Lev Vygotsky (1896–1934)

Lev Vygotsky was a Russian psychologist whose work was not available in the West until the 1960s, when Jerome Bruner (see below) was asked to review Vygotsky's book, 'Thought and Language' (Vygotsky 1961). Vygotsky proposed that children develop through *social interactions*, particularly those involving language, which they then *internalise* to form their own concepts. Teachers and other adults, therefore, play a major role in collaborating with children in learning relationships. One of Vygotsky's best-known developmental concepts is what he called the 'zone of proximal development' (ZPD), which refers to the difference between what children can do alone and what they can do with help from an adult or an older child (see Wood 1988 for more information about Vygotsky). We shall return to this concept later in the chapter.

Jerome Bruner

The ideas of the American psychologist Jerome Bruner are similar to those of Piaget and Vygotsky in many ways, though Bruner was particularly keen to develop a theory of *instruction* as well as a theory of development. He described three increasingly powerful ways of *representing* the world (Bruner 1966):

- *enactive representation*, in which thought is based only on actions;
- *iconic representation*, in which the child can form and use images of objects without the actual objects themselves having to be present;
- *symbolic representation*, in which the child can use and think in terms of symbols such as words, which do not necessarily have anything in common with what they represent.

The idea of the learning relationship is also important for Bruner because adults can provide valuable temporary behavioural 'scaffolding' which consists of words and actions to support children's learning through the ZPD (see Wood 1988).

The learning theory approach to child development

The theories of Piaget, Vygotsky and Bruner are referred to as cognitive or socio-cognitive theories of development. Another way of explaining development has been through behaviourism. The most prominent behaviourist theorist is Burrhus F. Skinner, who assumed that intellectual growth involves the formation of associations between stimuli and responses as a result of reinforcement. Thus the behaviourist view is that children learn language, social behaviour and their understanding of the physical world through the rapid, continuous and often unconscious accumulation of associations, which are strengthened or weakened throughout the child's waking hours. Simple behaviourist theory, however, cannot explain common but complex behaviours such as imitation and demonstrations of empathy, both of which involve internal representation, and which occur without apparent reinforcement. Social learning theory, however, overcomes the problems of simple Skinnerian behaviourism by incorporating cognitive constructs, notably identification and imitation, which enable it to deal with more complex developmental phenomena such as sex typing.

Social learning theory was put forward by Bandura and Walters (1963) and their colleagues. In a well-known series of experiments, children watched an actor, or a filmed cartoon character, behave aggressively towards a large, inflatable, self-righting 'Bobo' doll. After an intervening session in which the children were frustrated by not being allowed to play with some desirable toys, Bandura then observed the children while they waited in a room which contained a similar Bobo doll. The children imitated, very precisely, the aggressive behaviour they had seen, even though there was no reinforcement provided for that type of behaviour. Bandura found that the aggressive behaviour was learned, and could be strengthened when, for example, the aggressive model was a cartoon character, or the child was rewarded for aggression. Thus Bandura revealed a very powerful mechanism of social learning.

Now we shall go on to see how these established theories try to explain development, first in the context of the home and family, and then as the child's world expands in school and beyond. We begin with language, because this is a medium which can link the people encountered in a familiar place with those in a new and unfamiliar one, and which can be used to transfer stories about events which occurred in one place to another. It enables children to bring their widening world into the security of home.

DEVELOPMENT IN THE CONTEXT OF HOME AND FAMILY

Language development, 3 – 7

[I]n fact by the age of five children from all cultures understand and use most of the grammar rules of their language, communicate effectively with peers and adults and demonstrate inventive ways of expressing themselves in words.

(Smith and Cowie 1991: 281)

Smith and Cowie's comment on the remarkable, universal and rapid rate at which children acquire language might explain why psychologists and linguists have a special interest in understanding the origins of language development, and the relationship between language, thought and social development.

The process of language acquisition goes through a similar series of phases regardless of the actual culture or language learnt, and these are summarised in Table 2.1.

Table 2.1 Summary of process of language development

Age	Form of communication	Example
Birth	Cries and grunts	Cries of hunger, anger and pain can be identified by parents
	Cooing	'ooo' sounds, in 'conversations' with parent
		Pitch and stress variations
	'Vocal play'	More vowel sounds and some consonants
6 – 9 months	Babbling	Repeated sounds: 'mumumumum'
	Echolalia	Social turn-taking (Snow 1977)
12 months	First 'words'	With intonation and stress – sounds like language
18 months	20 words	First words generalised to classes of objects e.g. 'gam' = foods: jam,
21 months	200 words	ketchup, porridge; 'jus' = drinks
18 months – 2yrs	Telegraphic speech	First two-word sentences, e.g. 'allgone jus'
2 3 yrs	3 – 4 word sentences Grammatical rules applied	Negatives: 'not daddy work' Questions starting with 'wh-' Word order becoming conventional
3 – 5 yrs	1000 words; more complex sentences but cannot yet understand passive Show sensitivity to listeners' age	4-year-olds used simpler sentences for 2-year-olds than for adults (Gelman and Schatz 1977)
5 – 9 yrs	Adult language forms Complex semantics understood	Not until 9 years old can children answer reliably whether a blind-folded doll is 'easy to see' or 'hard to see' (Chomsky 1969)

Theories of language acquisition

There are three main ways of explaining how children acquire language. These are based on: (a) behavioural psychology; (b) biological programming; and (iii) social interaction.

The behavioural explanation, developed by Skinner in the 1950s, suggested that parents reinforce and shape their baby's early vocalisations by rewarding those that sound like words and ignoring those that do not. Gradually, as words are learned, certain combinations are rewarded if they fall into patterns resembling sentences. Language develops further as children imitate their parents' talk and are rewarded for doing so in the appropriate situations.

Although this theory is intuitively plausible, it cannot explain why children produce sentences that they have never heard before, nor why they make 'virtuous errors'. For example, if a child says, ' I eated my biscuit', she is applying a rule which states that adding '-ed' to a verb produces the past tense. If she was imitating her parents, however, she would be more likely to say, ' I ate my biscuit', since 'eat' is an irregular verb. The prevalence of virtuous errors in young children's speech suggests that they are able to apply rules and generate new language forms which they have not heard before.

Noam Chomsky, also writing in the 1950s, rejected Skinner's theory of language acquisition. He argued that children would not have heard enough language to be able to produce the complex grammatical rules which they are able to apply and understand simply on the basis of imitation. Chomsky suggested that human beings are biologically preprogrammed to generate language and to communicate through it. He postulated the existence of a biological structure, which he called the 'Language Acquisition Device' (LAD), to explain young children's ability to use complex rules.

Chomsky's theory takes little account of social interaction, however, and yet the purpose of a language within the species must be for communication. The role of social interaction in language acquisition is the basis of the third type of language acquisition theory, which sees language development as an aspect of cognitive and/or social development, and is concerned with the relationships between language and thought. Piaget, as the first proponent of this view, argued that thinking precedes language, or that cognitive development precedes linguistic performance. Vygotsky, on the other hand, emphasised interaction between language and thought as complementary processes in the child's cognitive development. He suggested that talking about events plays a crucial role in the development of thinking. Jerome Bruner, however, has been most influential in developing a *social* interactionist theory of language development which takes account of babies' *pre-verbal* social skills, such as:

- turn-taking in 'conversations' with a parent (Snow 1977);
- 'joint attention' as a baby follows its mother's gaze to see what she is looking at;
- pointing and reaching behaviour which tell a parent that the child wants a particular object.

Bruner suggested that parents and infants structure language development together through social exchanges, which he refers to as the 'Language Acquisition Support System' (LASS) (Bruner 1983). Gradually the LASS gives way to language which is a more effective form of communication. However, while Bruner saw these pre-verbal exchanges as essential precursors to language development, infants in some cultures, such as South American Mayan children, experience no LASS-type social interaction, but still acquire language (Pye, writing in 1986 and cited by Bancroft (1995)). It may be, therefore, that Bruner's language precursors assist language development without being essential to it.

Before we move on to consider studies of children's language experiences at home and in school, we shall take a brief look at an area which is sometimes called a universal language – namely, music. Hargreaves (1986) provides a detailed examination of children's musical development, an important part of which is the development of singing, which spontaneously emerges in young children. In many cultures, singing is also an important learning medium, used, for example, to help children learn a basic vocabulary such as numbers, days of the week and parts of the body, through rhymes and action songs, or to pass on historical or moral tales to younger generations.

The development of song in children

Singing, like language, appears to go through several stages in its acquisition. It has some revealing parallels, also, with developmental stages in other artistic domains, such as drawing and writing (Hargreaves and Galton, 1992). The work of Dowling (1984) and Davidson *et al.* (1981), for example, is based on the idea that cognitive schemes exist which determine the nature of songs at different ages within the pre-school period. These studies have been typically conducted by obtaining rich and detailed information over long periods of time from a small number of individual children. The 'babbling' singing of the young infant, in which pitch and phrasing are as yet unstable, is analogous to the scribbles which children make with pens on paper and which gradually become more organised and predictable. At the age of two or so, babbles give rise to what have become known as 'pot-pourri' songs, or coalescences between the child's spontaneous babbles or improvisations and songs in the culture. Elements of nursery rhymes and pop songs from the media are incorporated into the child's own song creations, and numerous examples of these have been collected. These songs might be considered to be characterised by global schemes, in that the overall shapes of the songs can be identified but the precise tonal details within them are as yet not established. In the later part of the pre-school period, interval relationships, phrasing and melodic construction become more regular and schematic, so that the child's songs become more recognisable. The songs of the five-year-old might be thought of as 'first draft' songs which only become fully operational with respect to musical conventions later in childhood. Full-scale development of intervals and scales in singing, along with analytic recognition of keys and the development of sensitivity to musical styles and conventions, gradually becomes established between the ages of eight and fifteen or so, although there are considerable individual variations according to training and experience.

In comparison with oracy, literacy and drawing, children's musical development has been comparatively ignored, but the above outline does show some interesting parallels. However, we now return to an emphasis on language development, with a focus on the role of social behaviour. This leads us to look at children's linguistic experience as they become more proficient linguistically around the age of four. In particular, we shall look at Dunn's studies of young children in their homes, and later, at Tizard and Hughes' (1984) comparisons of the language of four-year-olds at home and at nursery school.

Young children at home

Judy Dunn and her colleagues have explored children's developing social understanding and have also examined the relationship between children's actual social behaviour at home and their performance on tests and measures of social and emotional understanding (Denham 1986, Dunn et al. 1987).

Dunn has carried out detailed observations of pre-school children in their homes with their families. She and her colleagues observed and analysed the conversations of children aged three and four with their mothers, siblings and friends, and then analysed episodes which were especially likely to reveal children's social understanding, such as arguments, jokes and pretend play. The analyses showed that children with advanced understanding of other people's minds were more likely to have:

- engaged in pretend play more when they were two years old;
- more 'connected' interactions with friends at age three;
- taken part in conversations about why people behave as they do;
- witnessed an intense relationship between two other family members.

One interesting finding was that the *same* children used *different* arguments about the *same* issues with *different* people (e.g. mother and friend). This is particularly surprising if we recall Piaget and Inhelder's (1956) finding that the young children who did the well-known 'three mountains' task seemed unable to take the perspective of another person. Piaget and Inhelder found that they could describe their own view of a model of three mountains but, when asked to say what a doll sitting on the opposite side of the model would be able to see, the children once again described their own view, and could thus be described as 'egocentric'. However, Dunn's observations suggest that, far from being egocentric, young children could not only respond to, but also anticipate or even pre-empt, what the other person might say or do. An important difference between Piaget's and Dunn's studies is that Dunn's were purposeful interactions which took place in a natural context. Piaget's task, while its subject matter would be familiar and relevant to Swiss children, did not provide them with real reasons to adopt different perspectives. Dunn and her colleagues have shown that children's emotional understanding shown in social relationships at age three is related consistently to their understanding as measured by tests at age seven. (This developing awareness of other people's thinking is taken up again in the next chapter.) Dunn suggests that

> [I]f we are to make progress in understanding children's development we should surely include a focus on the relationships within which that development takes place. Naturalistic studies have a special value for such research in childhood.
>
> (Dunn 1995: 346)

This developing awareness of other people's thinking is taken up again in the next chapter.

The role of play in social and cognitive development

A widely-held view in nursery schools and pre-school play groups is that 'children learn through play' (Moyles 1989, and Chapter 1 of this book). This is supported by several well-established theories, of which the most prominent is that of Piaget (1951). Since Piaget first formulated his theory, a good deal of experimental research has been carried out which has looked in more detail at the precise function of play in promoting problem solving, creative thinking and social development. Generally speaking, different studies have shown that there are positive gains in all of these dimensions, although some studies have methodological limitations and the typical timescales of experience claimed to promote particular cognitive effects could be as little as ten minutes (Smith 1984). It would seem safer to conclude, therefore, that 'play is one way to learn';

that different kinds of play promote different kinds of learning; and that we must be careful in attributing too many cognitive and social advances to free play *per se*. In other words, we need to be more precise about what kinds of play promote what kinds of learning.

The development of gender role identity

One characteristic of play behaviour in children aged three to seven is the existence of gender differences. In North American and European homes, boys typically engage in larger-scale physical activity, whereas girls are more likely to be engaged in quieter activities, perhaps playing with dolls or doing domestic activities. This is a clear manifestation of the phenomenon of *gender role development* in the pre-school period. Slaby and Frey identified three stages in the development of gender roles (see Smith 1986). The first stage is *gender identity* and labeling, which occurs when a child can reliably label his or her own gender and the gender of other people. Children can usually do this by the ages of two to three years. The second stage is that of *gender stability*, which refers to a child's knowing that they were, are, and will be a girl or a boy. Gender stability is usually reached by about four to five years. Finally, when children are aged seven to nine, they achieve *gender constancy*, that is, the understanding that boys stay as boys and girls stay as girls regardless of changes of clothes, contexts and situations.

Gender identity and gender constancy involve the way children see themselves, and there are different explanations as to how gender role identity develops. The focus on self-concept with respect to gender is a central part of a cognitive developmental explanation (Kohlberg 1966). In this explanation, the child is thought to have a generalised concept of gender role, and the specific attachments with fathers for boys and mothers for girls follow the development of the generalised concept. In contrast, in the social learning theory explanation of gender role development, generalised gender role identity follows on from the individual attachments which are initially formed with parents and other significant figures as a result of the reinforcing power of these models. As we saw earlier, social learning theory builds on basic principles of reinforcement in incorporating cognitive concepts such as imitation and identification, and gender role identity is one clear and basic example of this. The idea has been developed further in Sandra Bem's *gender schema theory* which adapts contemporary ideas about social cognition to the issue of gender role development (Bem 1981).

It is also very clear, for the four to seven age range, that girls tend to be more advanced than boys in many intellectual activities, such as reading. There are various possible reasons for this. One is simply that girls mature physically more quickly than boys up to the age of six or seven, although this physical difference then diminishes. Another is that pre-schools and nursery schools tend to be dominated by female staff, and the feminine atmosphere which this creates could serve to exaggerate further the advantage that girls possess. Another suggestion is that boys' play is more *object-oriented*, involving impersonal, mechanical and scientific interests, whereas girls' play is more *person-oriented*, involving empathetic relationships with their peers. There is a good deal of empirical support for this idea, but it is not quite so clear that sex-typed play styles in children necessarily lead on to sex-differentiated patterns of attitudes and personality in adult life. However, the notion that masculine and feminine styles of behaviour may have their origins in styles of early play is an interesting one which is developed further by Archer (1984) in his proposal that 'development pathways' exist. This proposal involves seeing gender roles in a lifespan perspective in which pre-school play may form an important early part, and which may lead on to differences in school achievement in different subject areas and in adolescent interests and career choices.

Widening the sphere of learning relationships: from home to school

The evidence presented so far suggests that children about to enter school are 'logical but of limited experience . . . are actively trying to make sense of their world, and use encounters with significant other people as a means of doing so' (Hughes 1991: 147). In contrast to this view of young children as skilful and active learners, Hughes reported that reception teachers, when interviewed, consistently described new children coming to school as

> egocentric, immature, lacking in confidence, over-dependent, and lacking in basic skills and knowledge . . . unable to socialise . . . with little evidence of any social training in the home . . . and frequently bad-mannered, disruptive and disobedient. . . . spoken language was commonly singled out for criticism and [was] often seen as being the cause of other problems, such as aggression. . . . they were unable to give explanations . . . and there was a reluctance to ask questions, discuss stories or relate experiences.
>
> (Hughes 1991: 148)

This gap between psychologists' and teachers' perceptions of young children suggests that children's learning relationships in school may be very different from those that they experience at home or out of school. In the next section, we shall look more closely at how these different views might arise.

LEARNING RELATIONSHIPS IN AND OUT OF SCHOOL

In this final section of the chapter we review the child's development in the specific context of the school. The transition from home to school, pre-school playgroup, nursery or kindergarten is marked (a) by a substantial increase in the number of children and adults, (b) by making new acquaintances often unknown to the child's parents, and (c) by an increase in extended periods of time spent away from the home. It requires young children to enter into *formal* learning relationships not only with adults called teachers, but also sometimes with other children. In order to develop these relationships, the children may have to compete for the teacher's attention, within the formal setting. They will have to learn also to distinguish between informal and formal learning relationships: (a) with peers, in play situations; (b) with peers in work situations; (c) with teachers and other adults in school; and (d) with the same adults who might be family friends out of school.

Are schools the only effective places to learn? Are teachers the only people who can teach?

One way to investigate the effects of formal schooling on development is to study learning and teaching situations in a variety of different cultures (Wagner and Stevenson 1982). Stevenson (1982), for example, investigated the performance of Peruvian children on a series of cognitive tasks involving memory skills, spatial representation and concept learning. The sample included children of the same age, some of whom attended school and some who did not. Stevenson concluded that schooling made a significant independent contribution to children's performance on cognitive tasks even after the effects of sex, location, parental education, home quality and home teaching example had been removed (see also Chapter 9 in this book for a discussion of school effectiveness). Other studies of this type which have tested children's performance on standardised tests of cognitive ability, and report similar results (Wagner and Stevenson 1982), have usually found that schooling is associated with enhanced test performance, but this type of study does not consider how the learning or teaching takes place. Furthermore, many of the tests used are designed to be insensitive to cultural differences, and may be limited indicators of learning outside the school context. We shall look next, therefore, at two studies which have focused on children's development in non-school settings.

Learning and teaching out of school

Greenfield and Lave (1982) compared children's learning in three different contexts which represented increasingly formal instructional contexts. They were:

1 young Mexican weavers learning to weave in their homes;
2 children as apprentice tailors in Liberia;
3 children learning in school.

Analysis of the learning relationships in each case showed that carefully scaffolded learning, cooperative learning and graded task setting did take place within the more informal settings, thus contradicting the idea that it is only in school that children are exposed to a variety of teaching and learning strategies. The more naturalistic situations also provided rich learning relationships. Rogoff (1989) provides a review and discussion of research on scaffolded learning, or 'guided participation', of different types, e.g. with verbal versus non-verbal emphasis, in relation to several cultures.

Making 'human sense'

One aspect of learning outside school is that what is being learned is usually of some intrinsic value in the child's life. Donaldson (1978) used the term 'human sense' to discriminate between tasks which have a purpose and make sense in everyday life, and those which are 'disembedded' from real or human contexts, such as school tasks. For Donaldson, the issue of whether a task makes 'human sense' explains the discrepancy between Piaget's findings and those of Sinha and Walkerdine, who in 1977, reported an investigation in which they made Piaget's standard conservation of volume task *active*. In the standard task, children are asked to say whether the amount of water in a tall, thin glass is the same, or more, or less than it was when it was in a short, wide glass. Piaget found that children under the age of seven typically reply that the amount of water has changed. Sinha and Walkerdine changed the standard task slightly. They asked the child to shout 'Stop' when both the child and the adult had 'exactly the same amount to drink', as the adult poured orange juice from a jug into two differently shaped glasses. Seventy per cent of the five-year-olds who failed Piaget's task succeeded in shouting 'Stop' at the appropriate point. Similarly, children could conserve number at younger ages than Piaget's theory suggested, when a 'naughty teddy' altered the array of counters (McGarrigle and Donaldson 1974), or when the task did not involve asking the child the same question twice (Rose and Blank 1974).

All of these tasks have been modified so as to make more 'human sense', such that the child is either actively involved in the task or can identify reasons for what happens. In contrast, many school learning tasks appear to be 'disembedded' from any real context. For the child, the difference between embedded and disembedded tasks signifies the difference between informal and formal learning relationships, which must be recognised. This difference has been explored by Tizard and Hughes (1984) in their study of four-year-olds in conversations at home and at school.

Conversations at home and at school

Tizard and Hughes recorded 30 four-year-old girls' conversations with their mothers at home, and with their nursery teachers at school, and analysed the language and learning in these two highly influential learning relationships. The results contradicted the common assumption that 'what teachers do in a classroom is *ipso facto* educational while what a mother does is only "upbringing or child-rearing". Parents themselves often accept this view . . . ' (Tizard and Hughes 1984: 17). They found not only that the girls asked a significantly larger number of questions at home, but also that the adults' answers were much more frequently 'adequate and full' at home than at school. The girls asked three main types of question. About a quarter of the children's questions were *business questions*, concerned with carrying out activities, e.g. 'Where are the scissors?'. *Curiosity questions*, such as 'What's that?', 'How do you do that?', 'Why is it . . . ?', made up two-thirds of the girls' questions to their mothers. *Challenge questions*, such as 'Why?', 'Why should I?', which challenged the relationship between mother and daughter, accounted for only about 10 per cent of the children's questions, but these seemed to have particular educational importance in eliciting informational content in the mothers' answers. In addition, Tizard and Hughes identified what they called 'passages of intellectual search', that is, conversations in which the child asks a sequence of questions which take account of the adults' answers, often finding them unsatisfactory and so actively pursuing understanding. Formal school or nursery settings, however, specifically discourage children from asking challenging questions, or from persisting in their questioning, and, in a serious challenge to the effectiveness of teachers, Tizard and Hughes concluded that 'children's intellectual and language needs are much more likely to be fulfilled at home than at school'. In school, 'the puzzling mind of the four-year-old has no outlet in a setting where the child's basic role is to answer and not ask questions' (Tizard and Hughes 1984: 255–6).

Children learning together: friendships and groupwork

Before they start school, children are likely to have some regular play-mates or companions with whom they may have made a variety of dis-coveries about physical, social, emotional and environmental matters. Once in school, children are often expected to work with other children on common tasks, such as making a model or making up a story, for, as we saw earlier, Piaget, Vygotsky and Bruner all suggested that learning relationships between peers can be particularly powerful. In the final part of this section, we shall consider peer learning in informal relation-ships, such as children's friendships, and then in formal learning rela-tionships, such as cooperative groups.

Children's friendships

Hartup's (1992) review of the literature on children's friendships con-cludes that 'we can better argue that friendships are developmental advantages than argue that these relationships are developmental neces-sities' (p. 201). Friendships provide children with relationships which might be called egalitarian, symmetrical or horizontal, in contrast to the assymmetrical, vertically structured relationships which they have with adults. Hartup summarises five stages in the development of relation-ships, including friendships. These are:

- acquaintance;
- build-up;
- continuation;
- deterioration;
- endings.

Among young children, the first stages depend on physical proximity, successful social overtures, the occurrence of complementarities, and smiling, laughing or other indications of positive affect (Howes 1983). The middle stage is characterised by stability in interactions and aware-ness of commitment, although children younger than ten or eleven do not necessarily mention commitment and their friendships do not always develop this far: many younger children's friendships end as they simply drift apart or cease to interact. Hartup points out, however (Hartup 1992), that research on younger childrens' friendships, and on the end-ings of friendships in childhood, is lacking.

Hartup' s review shows that friendships have several functions, some of which depend on childrens' developmental stage. Friends typically interact more with each other than non-friends and, among pre-school children, social behaviour with stable friends was more competent, led to more successful group entry, more complementary and reciprocal social play, and more engagement in pretend play. Thus, those children who have the social skills to obtain and maintain stable friendships also have more opportunity to extend and practise their social skills of communication, cooperation and conflict management. Quarrels, too, are an important part of friendship. 'They illuminate the "fit" between individuals, i.e. by demonstrating when the skills, interests and goals of two children are not concordant as well as by marking relationship boundaries' (Hartup 1992: 190). Conflicts and disagreements also vary with age and context. Friends had fewer disagreements in open contexts such as playgrounds, but disagreed more often and more intensely than non-friends in closed situations where they could not change partners or activities. The implication for teachers is that, as the gap in social skills widens between friend-makers and others, teachers may need to teach children strategies for how to make friends (see, e.g., McNamara and Moreton 1995, and related discussion in Chapter 4 of this book).

Friendships enable children to learn about themselves, others and the world. According to Hartup, children not only teach one another in many situations but also use methods 'remarkably similar to those employed by adults in teaching children' (Hartup 1992: 186). When set problems to solve, for example, Newcomb and Brady (1982) found that boys who were friends explored the situation more, conversed with more vigour and connectedness, and could remember more about the problem afterwards. Research needs to be done on the effects of friendship groupings on the effectiveness of collaborative and cooperative learning in school, a topic to which we now turn.

Cooperative learning in school

In cooperative learning, children work together on some common task. In English schools, the Plowden Report (1967) had advocated groupwork as a cost-effective use of teacher time when compared with the use of individualised programmes. Teachers who use it argue that it not only contributes to higher achievement levels but also promotes social development and raises children's levels of self-esteem. What is the theoretical basis for this classroom organisation strategy, however?

Piaget's theory suggests that cognitive development is more likely to occur when children work with peers than when they interact, either with older children or adults, or work by themselves. This is because development, or adaptation, is brought about by conflict between what the child already knows and what, Piaget suggested, he or she perceives in a situation. Whereas children are likely to give way if an adult or older child's interpretation of an event differs from their own, they would expect friends of their own age to agree with them, and therefore would be more likely to argue with friends or peers. The existence of disagreement will force the children to attend to aspects of the event which they would have missed if working alone. Thus, the conflict will create disequilibrium in the children's minds and so motivate reconstruction of their understanding of the event, thus moving them towards a new developmental stage. Vygotsky and Bruner, on the other hand, stressed that development occurs through social cooperation rather than through conflict. Development will take place when a more experienced child, parent or teacher guides the child's participation in a task, or, in other words, scaffolds the child's progress through the ZPD. By learning from more experienced members of their social group, children absorb cultural expectations, approaches, and methods as a natural part of the learning process (Tharp and Gallimore 1991, Rogoff 1990). In schools, however, structured peer groupwork has been associated with higher achievements (Johnson *et al.* 1981).

'Cooperative groupwork' has many meanings and purposes, including working together in small groups as well as the more circumscribed technique of 'peer tutoring', in which a more able or experienced child works with a less able or experienced child. There are also different cultural interpretations. Topping (1992), for example, has contrasted the 'extremely rigid, rule-bound and prescriptive' North American approaches to cooperative groupwork with the British 'warm, fuzzy and comfortable' ones (see also Galton and Williamson's (1992) review of research on groupwork in the primary classroom, and Chapter 6 of this book for a discussion of general cultural differences). While structured groupwork appears to be more effective for cognitive gains (Slavin 1990), it can also lead to social and affective developments, and be used specifically to promote teamwork and cooperative attitudes. Peer tutoring, used particularly as a strategy in the teaching of reading, has shown gains in attitudes and achievement across gender, race and social class divisions, especially for the 'tutors' (Topping 1992). Studies of the effects of cooperation on self-concept, self-esteem and self-image have tended to have only slight or neutral effects, however, despite positive anecdotal claims about their benefits (Osguthorpe and Scruggs 1990). Finally, positive social benefits have been found in studies of cooperative grouping in multi-ethnic classes. These included improved social relationships, liking for others, more cross-race and cross-gender preference choices and reduced negative stereotyping (see, e.g., Sharan 1990).

The social world of children's learning

One of the aims of this chapter, in keeping with the central theme of learning relationships, has been to emphasise young children's social development, a field which has become increasingly prominent in developmental psychology. Pollard (1996), in a unique and original longitudinal study of five children's first years in school, has attempted to bring together evidence about their social lives with friends, family and teachers, their learning experiences and their formal school achievements. Using case study data, he has derived frameworks to facilitate analysis and synthesis of the social influences on the children's self-identity and approaches to learning. He has concluded that the children who learned most effectively could manage their classroom identities so as to derive support from both teacher and peers. The children could be effective learners when 'their self-confidence is high, the classroom social context poses manageable risks and they receive sufficient appropriate instruction and support. The need for suitable social conditions in classrooms complements the necessity for appropriate levels of cognitive challenge' (Pollard 1996: 311). Pollard's analysis provides some explanation of, and a way forward from, the yawning gap portrayed by Hughes (1991) between young children's capabilities and teachers' perceptions of them.

CONCLUSION

This chapter has considered several aspects of children's development between the ages of three and seven. While cognitive development has a central place in most research on child development, we have emphasised the complementary role of social development, focusing on the child's widening circle of social relationships. Each of these is potentially a new learning relationship for children's understanding of themselves and of their social and physical worlds. The recent attention to the social world in the psychological literature in recent years is one that educationists are now beginning to assimilate.

REFERENCES

Allen, V. L. (ed.) (1976) *Children as teachers: theory and research on tutoring*, New York: Academic Press.
Archer, J. (1984) 'Gender roles as developmental pathways', *British Journal of Social Psychology*, 23, 245–56.
Bancroft, D. (1995) 'Language Development', in V. Lee and P. Das Gupta (eds), *Children's cognitive and language development*, Oxford: Blackwell (in association with The Open University).
Bandura, A. and Walters, R. (1963) *Social learning and personality development*, New York: Holt, Rinehart and Winston.
Bem, S. L. (1981) 'Gender schema theory: a cognitive account of sex-typing', *Psychological Review*, 88, 354–64 .
Berryman, J., Hargreaves, D., Herbert, M. and Taylor, A. (1991) *Development psychology and you*, London: The British Psychological Society in association with Routledge.
Brown, R. Cazden, C. and Bellugi, U. (1969) 'The child's grammar from I to III', in

J. P. Hill (ed.) *Minnesota Symposium on Child Psychology* Vol 2, Minneapolis: University of Minnesota Press.

Bruner, J. (1966) *Toward a theory of instruction*, New York: W. W. Norton.

—— (1983) *Child's talk; learning to use language*, Oxford: Oxford University Press.

Butterworth, G. and Harris, M. (1994) *Principles of Developmental Psychology*, Hove: Lawrence Erlbaum.

Chomsky, C. (1969) *The acquisition of syntax in children from 5–10*, Cambridge, MA: MIT Press.

Cowie, H. and Rudduck, J. (1988, 1990, 1991) *Learning together; Working together* (Vols 1–5), available from BP Educational Service, PO Box 30, Blacknest Road, Blacknest, Alton, Hampshire, GU34 4PX.

Davidson, L., McKernon, P. and Gardner, H. (1981) 'The acquisition of song: a developmental approach', in J. A. Mason *et al.* (eds) *Documentary Report of the Ann Arbor Symposium on the applications of psychology to the teaching and learning of music*, Reston, VA: MENC.

Denham, S. A. (1986) 'Social cognition, prosocial behaviour and emotion in preschoolers; contextual validation', *Child Development*, 57, 194–201.

Donaldson, M. (1978) *Children's Minds*, London: Fontana.

Dowling, W. (1984) 'Development of musical schemata in children's spontaneous singing', in W. Crozier and A. Chapman (eds) *Cognitive processes in the perception of art*, Amsterdam: Elsevier.

Dunn, J. (1995) 'Studying relationships and social understanding', in P. Barnes (ed.) *Personal, social and emotional development of children*, Milton Keynes: Open University Press (in conjunction with Blackwell).

Dunn, J., Brown, J. R. and Beardsall, L. (1987) 'Why are children of the same family so different from one another?', *The behavioural and brain sciences*, 10, 1–16.

Dunne, A. and Bennett, N. (1990) *Talking and learning in groups*, London: Macmillan Education.

Galton, M. and Williamson, J. (1992) *Groupwork in the primary classroom*, London: Routledge.

Gelman, R. and Schatz, M. (1977) 'Appropriate speech adjustments: the operation of conversational constraints on talk to two-year-olds', in M. Lewis and L. Rosenblum (eds) *Interaction, conversation and the development of language*, New York: Wiley.

Goodlad, S. and Hirst, B. (eds) (1990) *Explorations in peer tutoring*, Oxford: Blackwell.

Greenfield, P. and Lave, J. (1982) 'Cognitive aspects of informal education', in D. Wagner and H. Stevenson (eds) *Cultural perspectives on child development*, San Francisco: W. H. Freeman.

Hargreaves, D. (1986) *The developmental psychology of music*, Cambridge: Cambridge University Press.

Hargreaves, D. and Galton, M. (1992) 'Aesthetic learning, psychological theory and educational practice', in B. Reimer and R. Smith (eds) *The arts, education and aesthetic knowing*, 91st Yearbook of the National Society for the Study of Education, Chicago, IL: University of Chicago Press.

Hartup, W. (1992) 'Friendships and their developmental significance', in H. McGurk (ed.) *Childhood social development*, Hove: Lawrence Erlbaum.

Howes, C. (1983) 'Patterns of friendship', *Child development*, 54, 1041–53.

—— (1989) 'Peer interaction of young children', *Monographs of the Society for Research in Child Development*, 53 (Serial no. 217).

Hughes, M. (1991) 'The child as a learner: the contrasting views of developmental psychology and early education', in C. Desforges (ed.) *Early childhood education*, British Journal of Educational Psychology, Monograph Series No. 4, Edinburgh: Scottish Academic Press.

Johnson, D., Maruyama, G., Johnson, R., Nelson, D. and Skon, L. (1981) 'Effects of cooperative, competitive and individualistic goal structures on achievement: a meta analysis', *Psychological Bulletin*, 89, 47–62.

Kohlberg, L. A. (1966) 'A cognitive developmental analysis of children's sex-role concepts and attitudes', in E. Maccoby (ed.) *The development of sex differences* Stanford, CA: Stanford University Press.

Lee, V. and Das Gupta, P. (eds) (1995) *Children's cognitive and language development*, Oxford: Blackwell (in association with The Open University).

Light, P., Sheldon, S. and Woodhead, M. (eds) (1991) *Learning to think*, London: Routledge (in association with The Open University).

McGarrigle, J. and Donaldson, M. (1974) 'Conservation accidents', *Cognition*, 3, 341–50.

McNamara, S. and Moreton, G. (1995) *Changing Behaviour*, London: David Fulton.

Moyles, J. (1989) *Just playing? The role and status of play in early childhood education*, Milton Keynes: Open University Press.

Newcomb, A. F. and Brady, J. E. (1982) 'Mutuality in boys' friendship selections', *Child Development*, 53, 392–5.

Osguthorpe, R. and Scruggs, T. (1990) 'Special education students as tutors: A review and analysis', in S. Goodlad and B. Hirst (eds) *Explorations in peer tutoring*, Oxford: Blackwell.

Piaget, J. and Inhelder, B. (1956) *The child's conception of space*, London: Routledge and Kegan Paul.

Plowden Report, The (1967) *Children and their primary schools*, Report of the Central Advisory Council for Education in England, London: HMSO.

Pollard, A. (1996) *The social world of children's learning*, London: Routledge.

Rogoff, B. (1989) 'The joint socialisation of development,' in M. Lewis and S. Feinman (eds) *Social influences and behaviour*, New York: Plenum. Reprinted in Light *et al.* (1991).

—— (1990) *Apprenticeship in thinking: cognitive development in social context*, New York: Oxford University Press.

Rose, S. and Blank, M. (1974) 'The potency of context in children's cognition: an illustration through conservation', *Child Development*, 45, 499–502.

Sharan, S. (1990) 'Cooperative learning and helping behaviour in the multi-ethnic classroom', in H. C. Foot, M. J. Morgan and R. J. Shute (eds) *Children helping children*, Chichester: Wiley.

Sinha, C. and Walkerdine, V. (1977) 'Conservation: a problem in language, culture and thought', in N. Waterson and C. Snow (eds) *The development of communication: social and pragmatic factors in language acquisition*, London: Wiley.

Slavin, R. E. (1990) *Cooperative learning: theory, research and practice*, Englewood Cliffs, NJ: Prentice Hall.

Smith, L. (1995) *Sociological Studies*, trans. L. Smith and others, London: Routledge.

Smith, P. (1986) 'Exploration, play and social development in boys and girls', in D. Hargreaves and A. Colley (eds) *The psychology of sex-roles*, London: Harper and Rowe.

—— (ed.) (1984) *Play in animals and humans*, Oxford: Blackwell.

Smith, P. and Cowie, H. (1991) *Understanding children's development* (2nd edn), Oxford: Blackwell.

Snow, C. (1977) 'The development of conversation between mothers and babies', *Journal of Child Language*, 4, 1–22.

Stevenson, H. (1982) 'Influences of schooling on cognitive development', in D. Wagner and H. Stevenson (eds) *Cultural perspectives on child development*, San Francisco: Freeman.

Tharp, R. and Gallimore, R. (1991) 'A theory of teaching as assisted performance', in P. Light, S. Sheldon and M. Woodhead (eds) (1991) *Learning to think*, London: Routledge (in association with The Open University).

Tizard, B. and Hughes, M. (1984) *Young children learning: talking and thinking at home and school*, London: Fontana.

Topping, K. (1992) 'Cooperative learning and peer tutoring; an overview', *The Psychologist*, 5, 151–62.

Vygotsky, L. (1961) *Thought and language*, Boston, MA: MIT Press.

Wagner, D. and Stevenson, H. (eds) (1982) *Cultural perspectives on child development*, San Francisco: Freeman.

Wood, D. (1988) *How children think and learn*, Oxford: Blackwell.

Chapter 3

Cognitive development 7–11
The learning relationship in the junior years

Roger Merry

INTRODUCTION

For whatever reasons, there has been rather less written about the cognitive development of children from around the age of seven onwards than from birth to six. Part of the explanation could lie in the nature of development itself. The changes that take place in the first few years of life are enormous, crucial and fascinating, especially since advances in electronics and the ingenuity of psychologists over the last twenty years have allowed us to make inferences about the thinking of even very young babies. It could also be that we as adults are simply programmed to be more interested in young and dependent children – we certainly see them as more cute than their older siblings, as the declining number of family photographs of a growing child at different ages shows.

The changes taking place in children's thinking between the ages between around seven and eleven may be less dramatic, but they are certainly there, and it is just as important for teachers to have thought about them. This chapter, therefore, will consider some of these changes and their implications for teachers.

A GENERAL SHIFT IN THINKING

One important legacy from Piaget, mentioned briefly in the previous chapter, was the notion that during this period most children begin to make a transition from being able to think only in concrete terms to being capable of more abstract thought – what Piaget called the transition from concrete to formal operations. Although it is now clear that there are times when many seven-year-olds can think in an abstract way, and times when many eleven-year-olds (and even adults) do not, Piaget's general idea still seems to be valuable, and Bruner for instance proposed a similar development from 'iconic representation', with a need to use mental images in order to think, to the ability to use purely 'symbolic representation'. (See Chapter 2; for a detailed discussion of these theories, see Wood 1988.)

More recently, Donaldson (1992) characterised children's thought as moving from 'point mode' to 'line mode', 'construct mode', and finally to 'transcendent mode'. In 'point mode' the infant is restricted to thinking in the here and now, whereas with 'line mode' the child's thoughts can move backwards and forwards in time. With 'construct mode' there is generalisation taking place, though still in concrete terms, until finally with 'transcendent mode' the limitations of space and time are overcome. Perhaps an example will make this abstract idea clear, by putting it in more concrete terms.

POINT MODE: 'I want to watch my favourite TV programme right now but my brother is watching something else and he won't let me.'

LINE MODE: 'The same thing happened yesterday, but I'll make sure I'm there first tomorrow.'

CONSTRUCT MODE: 'My brother always decides what we watch because he is bigger than me.'

TRANSCENDENT MODE: 'Brute force and size usually win – life isn't fair!'

Piaget's interest in the universal development of thought is also at odds with more recent views suggesting that children's learning develops at different rates in different areas or 'domains'. A domain might be, for example, chess or mathematical learning, so that a child could reach a much higher Piagetian level in one domain than in another, rather than development occurring in a smooth and universal way (Moran 1991).

This is particularly important for the learning of older children, because cognitive development must always interact with learning demands. As children grow older, these demands in school become based much more on different subjects. In most countries by the time they are eleven, children are expected to be able to think in a mathematical way or in a musical way according to the lesson. On the other hand, during these years, schools also require increasingly 'disembedded' thinking which is not tied to any particular set of circumstances. Children are therefore expected, for example, not only to be able to multiply given numbers, but also to recognise a multiplication problem embedded in any context.

The different domains of thinking are, of course, not restricted to school subjects. Other psychologists have come up with the idea of 'scripts' or 'scenarios' which children have to learn about and which shape their thinking across a whole range of situations, such as going to the cinema or going to a restaurant (Hudson 1993). They learn what sort of behaviour is expected of them and can predict what others are likely to do. Behaviour in school is obviously one such general area, but the increasing importance of different subjects towards the end of primary education means that children may have to learn to carry out a series of steps predetermined by the teacher to get the right answer in one lesson, then be willing to discuss publicly their innermost anxieties with that same teacher a few minutes later! Under these circumstances, the notion of the learning relationship at the heart of this book changes not only when the child goes to school, as outlined in the previous chapter, but becomes increasingly complex and differentiated as the child moves through the later primary years.

One of the most popular and influential discussions of different ways of thinking, one which has once more come to enjoy popularity, was proposed by Gardner in 1983. Gardner suggested that there might be seven such intelligences: linguistic, musical, spacial, logical-mathematical, bodily-kinaesthetic, inter-personal and intra-personal. However, he was careful to point out that 'these intelligences are fictions and most useful fictions – for discussing processes and abilities that (like all of life) are continuous with one another' (Gardner 1983: 70).

The general shift in thinking, therefore, does not happen smoothly, but is much affected by the context of each particular situation and the sorts of thinking involved. Bearing this in mind, we can now look more closely at some more specific cognitive changes which tend to occur in the 7–11 age range.

STRATEGIES

Confronted with an apparently simple problem like the need to remember a short list of words, it is clear that many seven-year-olds simply don't know what to do. Close studies of eye movements using electronic equipment show that younger children tend to behave in the same way whether they are asked to remember the words or simply to look at them. Similarly, if they forget some of the words and are asked to try again, they will probably look equally at all the words and not pay any special attention to those they forgot. (For a review of this area of research, see Simmons 1994.) As adults, we may find this quite surprising, since we would tend to use a variety of strategies without even thinking about them. (You might like to pause for a moment to think what you yourself would do, given a list of a dozen words and half a minute to remember them, in any order.) For instance, we would almost certainly say the words over to ourselves several times, and repeating out loud is a common technique used in classrooms all over the world to learn things by heart. We might well do other things too, of course. Without even realising it, we would probably try to picture the items in our mind's eye, and bearing in mind the general shift in thinking mentioned above, it is significant that abstract words such as 'hope' or 'revolution' are harder to remember than words which we can image easily, like 'door' or 'feather'.

But that isn't all. We might also note any links between the words, so that if, say, some were names of fruits, we would tend to remember them together rather than in the order in which they had been presented. And if we had been asked to recall the words in order, we would almost certainly use different strategies, perhaps linking the items together in some sort of story.

The years roughly between 7 and 11 mark the start of a transition towards this more adult use of strategies. Repetition (sometimes called 'rehearsal' or 'rote' learning) tends to be the first strategy to appear, and by the time they are 10, about 85 per cent of children are able to use it, though they may not always do so without being reminded (Kail 1990). This basic strategy helps because, if we don't use it, things disappear after a few seconds from our short-term memory. Repetition literally 're-presents' the material before it can disappear, and enables it eventually to become part of our long-term memory, but on its own it isn't a very efficient strategy, and other, more powerful techniques are also beginning to emerge during this period.

Unlike straightforward repetition, these other strategies don't simply prolong the information for a few seconds, but transform or elaborate on it, enriching it and linking it to things we know already. Thus, forming visual images for words might seem to be making the task more difficult by increasing the amount to remember, but it brings into play the very powerful visual memory system and makes it much more likely that the items will be retrieved. If the order of words isn't important, re-grouping into categories forges links between the items, so that recalling one makes it likely that it will remind us of the others in that category. If on the other hand the word order was important, linking the words in a different way in order to preserve the sequence, for example in a story, similarly makes it much more likely that each item will be remembered in turn. Imposing structure or meaning seems to be the key.

Without such strategies, we would be able to remember very little – indeed, McShane (1991) says that 'much of development can be seen as the construction of efficient representations and procedures to overcome the resource limitations of the information processing system' (p. 342). In fact, there is still some disagreement about whether the child's actual thinking capacity increases with age or whether it is simply that better use is made of the same capacity (Halford 1993, Meadows 1993), though most psychologists probably incline towards the latter view, and there is certainly considerable interest now in how these strategies develop in older children.

METACOGNITION

But simply having strategies available isn't enough to guarantee improvements in learning, and there are at least two other sorts of cognitive skills that children need to develop. Both of these require an ability to reflect on your own thinking, and therefore come under the general heading of what psychologists call 'metacognition'.

First, they need to be able to recognise *when* a strategy is appropriate and must generally be able to *control* their use of different strategies to choose the best ones. To do this, of course, they need to be able to compare new problems with familiar ones and to transfer or generalise from previous experience. Thus, for example, a successful learner with the metacognitive skills to recognise that they have forgotten some items or are finding others difficult will concentrate more on those items than on the rest. Such self-checking begins to emerge as a very important general strategy, applicable across a wide range of problems.

In this respect, apparently 'negative' information can be just as useful as 'positive', though younger children may not always appreciate this in their desire to get 'the right answer'. For instance, some children are very reluctant to practise the valuable skill of estimating the answer first in case their estimate is wrong, not realising that the error can provide useful feedback. Similarly, Holt (1984) describes how he used to think of a number between, say, one and 100 and his children would try to guess it. They eventually developed the strategy of asking questions like 'Is it more than 50?', but they tended to be disappointed if the answer was negative, apparently not realising that this gave just as much information as a positive answer! So children need not only to have a range of strategies available, but also to develop skills in deciding which strategies are appropriate, and in making use of feedback to monitor their success.

It is obviously difficult to obtain information directly about children's metacognitive skills, and the best we can hope for is to design studies which allow us to make inferences about their thinking or ask them to 'introspect' – to talk to us about what goes on inside their heads. McShane (1991) is rightly cautious here. He notes that children may have such skills without necessarily being able to describe them to someone else, and points out that a correlation between improved learning and reported use of metacognitive skills could mean that either one could be the cause of the other. In spite of potential problems with methodology, however, a great deal of research has been generated, and it is clear that the growth of metacognition is a major factor in children's development which affects not only their success in school but also enables them to feel increasingly involved in and responsible for their own learning (see, e.g., Galloway and Edwards 1991).

ATTITUDES AND EMOTIONS

Even this isn't really enough, however, because it suggests that children are rather passive learners, simply waiting for problems to come along and presumably doing nothing in the meantime. In contrast, successful learners are good at recognising problems in the first place, and actively seeking them out for themselves. As Karmiloff-Smith (1992: 88) says:

> Children are not just problem-solvers. They rapidly become problem generators and move from successful data-driven actions to theory-mediated actions that are often not influenced by environmental feedback.

Cognitive development should not be considered in isolation, however, and this active 'search after meaning' also implies certain attitudes towards problem-solving, such as a willingness to admit that you don't yet know the answer or that there may be a better solution than the one you've just thought of. Successful learners are not afraid of failing, and do not feel threatened by it – on the contrary, they may relish finding apparently pointless problems to solve, or insist that they do not want to be told the answer even when it is readily available. If this sounds rather odd, you have probably never done a crossword puzzle or read a mystery novel! Moreover, such positive attitudes towards potential problems go hand-in-hand with positive attitudes about yourself as a learner, and there has been considerable research into the importance of self-esteem in successful learners (See Chapter 4 of this book).

THE SOCIAL CONTEXT

Another general criticism of Piaget was that he tended to see the child as a rather solitary thinker, developing in isolation, and therefore did not pay enough attention to the social contexts in which learning takes place, though the previous chapter has suggested that such a view of Piaget may now be inaccurate. Vygotsky and Bruner, whose work was also very briefly outlined in Chapter 2, are recognised as being much more interested in these social factors and in the role of the adult in facilitating children's cognitive development. A whole new area of research, 'social cognition', has now emerged, linking the work of social and cognitive psychologists and emphasising not only the immediate social situations in which learning takes place, but also the wider cultural context which shapes all thinking (see, e.g., Rogoff *et al.* 1989).

Most developmental psychologists would now accept that the child is not a solitary thinker, though many would still be wary of suggesting that an emphasis on social factors implies a passive view of learning. As Halford (1993: 470) says:

The child is not simply a repository of socially and culturally provided information, like a file cabinet. The child actively selects, observes, codes, stores, interprets, and, where it is inconsistent with experience, rejects, information about the world.

The years between about 7 and 11 are therefore particularly interesting, because these social and cultural factors are beginning to interact with the child's metacognitive skills referred to earlier. In Gardner's (1983) terms, two sorts of intelligences are therefore involved – 'intra-personal' and 'inter-personal'. The former refers to the emerging sense of self and the detachment from the here and now which are needed in order to reflect on your own thinking, and the latter to the growing awareness of and sensitivity to other people needed to develop as a successful and valued social being.

COGNITIVE, SOCIAL AND EMOTIONAL DEVELOPMENT COMBINED IN 'THEORY OF MIND'

Although the first part of this chapter has considered cognitive, social and emotional factors separately, they are clearly all linked together in the way children actually develop. A particularly interesting area of recent research which illustrates this interdependence nicely concerns children's development of a 'theory of mind' or understanding of other people's behaviour, thoughts and feelings (see, e.g., Perner 1991).

Some ingenious experiments have shown that quite young children can have a surprisingly sophisticated understanding of the views of others, in contrast to Piaget's emphasis on egocentric thought at this age. Thus, studies which use a 'false belief' paradigm put children in a situation where they know something that someone else doesn't know, and ask them to predict what the other person will think or do. In a typical experiment, the child watches while Person A puts something in a box and then leaves the room. Person B then removes the object and hides it somewhere else. Person A returns, and the child is asked not where the object is, but where Person A thinks it is, even though that belief is false and not shared by the child. By the age of five, most children respond correctly, though those diagnosed as autistic are a notable and revealing exception. Even this is not the end of the story, however, and children continue to develop an increasingly sophisticated theory of mind as they grow older, including 'second order' mental states which involve an understanding of other people's understanding of other people! The fact that you may have to re-read the previous sentence to grasp it properly shows how complicated it can get.

Because of the inseparable nature of thoughts and feelings, a developing theory of mind involves not only an understanding of what other people may or may not know, but also an awareness of their emotions. Terwogt and Harris (1993), for example, asked children aged six, eleven and fifteen if it was possible to hide your feelings from others. (Before you read what happened, you might like to exercise your own theory of mind by predicting what the children in each age group said.) In fact, about two-thirds of the six-year-olds said it was possible, while the rest didn't know, and all the eleven-year-olds were confident that they could hide their feelings. But some of the fifteen-year-olds had their doubts, apparently because they realised that someone who knew them well might not be fooled.

THE DEVELOPMENT OF LEARNING IN THE WIDER CULTURAL CONTEXT

The dynamic interplay between self-awareness and social awareness has long been apparent in contrasting philosophical views about the whole nature of learning. Bonnett (1994), for example, compares the traditional Rationalist emphasis on publicly agreed knowledge and rules with the Existentialist notion that the only true or 'authentic' understanding is that of the individual. She concludes that the two are not incompatible but can be combined into what she calls 'poetic' teaching, which both 'respects the integrity of the self of the learner and the nature of the things to be learnt'.

Such potentially contrasting views are manifested in different ways in different cultures. In most Western societies, for example, the individual's sense of self is seen as particularly important because successful members of society are expected to act with a high degree of autonomy. This can be apparent in many ways, including the educational aim of encouraging children to take responsibility for their own learning, and the promotion of self-advocacy for those with special needs who would otherwise depend largely on others. In contrast, some other countries place more value on the needs of society in general, and see it as more important to be a good citizen than a successfully competitive individual. In turn, these differences will be reflected and promoted by differing educational systems using different methods of teaching and learning, sometimes to the bafflement of other societies. British teachers tend to be disbelieving when they hear that their Chinese counterparts successfully teach classes of 50 children, and to be dismissive of methods involving rote learning, while Chinese teachers may find it hard to understand a system which, for many years, seemed to them to leave children to their own devices and to the mercy of the personal whims of their teachers. We can certainly learn from each other, but our learning needs to recognise underlying differences in aims and ideology.

These differences are equally crucial when we consider not just different systems, but also how children may develop in the social context of the school. Several writers have contrasted children's learning at home and in school, often to the detriment of the latter. While agreeing that the comparison is not entirely justified, Wood (1991) describes classrooms as contrived learning situations in which the child's learning depends on the teacher, while, in contrast, parents teach their children spontaneously and naturally, depending on the child's needs. To be fair, most parents would probably prefer not to be faced with thirty children who are replaced every year (or every forty minutes in secondary schools), nor to have the pressures of a compulsory curriculum, regular assessments, league tables comparing them with other parents, visits from teams of inspectors, or the need to produce policy statements and to state their prior objectives every time they played with their child.

The contrast, of course, lies not in differences between teachers and parents but between the child's home and the need for developed societies to set up formal systems of education, and it is a contrast which has only occasionally been examined directly by psychologists interested in children's learning. Carraher *et al.* (1990) carried out a particularly interesting study of Brazilian child street vendors who were very adept at calculating costs and giving change when selling snacks and sweets, but could not do exactly the same calculations written down in a classroom context. To use Donaldson's (1978) term, the latter tasks were 'disembedded' rather than set in a real and meaningful context, so the children demonstrated a much lower level of competence.

In contrast with the open, informal and largely successful experience which was seen in the previous chapter as being apparently characteristic of young children's learning before they go to school, formal attempts to teach in a school setting seem, to some writers, to be doomed to fail. Thus, Holt (1991) claims that real learning is not the result of teaching but the product of working things out for yourself.

The first few sections of this chapter looked at some cognitive, emotional and social factors in the development of children between the ages of about seven and eleven, while recognising that they cannot really be separated in practice. This section has emphasised the wider cultural context in which children's learning develops, seeing it not just as a background, but as being inextricably bound up with the complex development of each individual. Classrooms have not emerged as being necessarily ideal places to learn, but the situation is hopefully not as gloomy nor the solution as radical as the de-schoolers suggest, and the final section of the chapter will take up the main themes discussed so far and consider some of their implications for teachers.

REVIEW

The general shift in conceptualisation, moving away from a need for concrete experience towards an ability to deal with more abstract ideas. This shift has been discussed by various writers, and although they are not directly comparable, some of the key terms mentioned in this chapter are:

- Concrete operations
  Formal operations

- Enactive and iconic representation
  Symbolic representation

- Point and line modes
  Construct and transcendent modes

- Embedded, contextualised
  Disembedded, decontextualised.

Whichever way the changes are expressed, they clearly represent such major conceptual shifts that the teacher's role is going to be a complex and long-term one. What are some of the things that teachers can do to encourage such development?

One of the most straightforward things that teachers can do is simply to give children more *time* to reflect and respond. Teachers understandably feel uncomfortable and even pressurised by a lack of immediate response, and Rowe (1986) found that the average 'wait time' for teachers was very short. Some children, therefore, learn to avoid having to think by simply keeping quiet, knowing that the teacher's nerve will almost certainly break first and that they will either ask an easier question or move on to plague someone else. Rowe found that simply waiting for a few seconds improved not only the number of responses, but also the quality of what the children said. Other writers have made similar suggestions. Sotto (1994), for example, suggests that teachers should ask a question and, having got an answer, *not* immediately evaluate the response or ask another question (which would seem the obvious thing to do), but instead simply smile and wait, looking round for further responses and shifting the responsibility and centre of attraction away from themselves on to the class ('teacher talk' is discussed in detail in Chapter 8 of this book).

Changes like this imply a conceptual shift for teachers, and certainly suggest different sorts of roles which are more in line with the views of children's learning and development proposed by writers like Bruner, Vygotsky and Feuerstein. Bruner's notion of 'scaffolding' (see, e.g., Bruner and Haste 1987) requires teachers who make suggestions, corrections and amplifications, and use questions to offer reasonable challenges rather than to check on the acquisition of facts. Vygotsky's much-quoted 'zone of proximal development' (see, e.g., Wood 1988, Rogoff 1990, and Chapter 2 of this book) has the teacher in a very similar role, enabling the child to cope with problems which they could not manage alone. Similarly, Feuerstein sees the teacher as a crucial figure, providing 'mediated' learning experiences, particularly for children who find it hard to make sense of the world for themselves (Sharron 1987).

What all these approaches have in common is that they portray the teacher as a facilitator of children's learning, rather than as the source of the knowledge to be passed on. In turn, this of course means that the teacher must also be willing to reflect on their own practice, as outlined in Chapter 7 of this book. What is certainly not implied is a parody of 'child-centred' education, in which children are left to their own devices to learn what they like as best they can. In fact, the teacher's role becomes a complex one involving what Rogoff (1990) calls 'guided participation', combining support and challenge to construct the learning relationship which is at the heart of this book.

The development of strategies represents another sort of shift, from having little idea of what to do when confronted with a problem, through the emergence of rehearsal, to the development of elaborative strategies which enrich and transform the stimulus and enable the learner to relate it to previous knowledge.

Overall, attempts to teach children directly to use more effective strategies have met with mixed success. (For a debate about the value of teaching children strategies, see Howe 1991 and the peer reviews which followed his article.) In the short term, it has certainly proved possible to improve children's learning by showing them how to use various sorts of mnemonic strategies, but the long-term results are often disappointing, with children failing to apply the same strategies spontaneously when confronted with similar problems later on (Levin 1993). This is why earlier discussion in this chapter emphasised the need, not only to have strategies available, but also to be able to select them appropriately and monitor their use.

Ashman and Conway (1993) suggest five levels at which the teacher may intervene to help children towards independent and successful use of strategies, in a sequence which is very much in line with Vygotsky's view of thought as internalised language:

1 teacher models the strategy;
2 teacher gives instructions as child carries out the task;
3 child instructs him/herself aloud;
4 child whispers the instructions;
5 child uses internalised (possibly private) language for self-instruction.

Another factor which is likely to help children to take strategies on board for themselves is the use of feedback to demonstrate that the strategies really are effective. Thus, McShane (1991) compares experiments which succeeded in teaching children to rehearse for themselves with experiments that failed, and concludes that such feedback is the crucial variable.

A rather more controversial area of related research concerns the question of whether 'knowledge-free' materials develop skills more effectively than materials involving actual curriculum materials. Feuerstein, for example, deliberately advocates the use of 'content-free' puzzles to develop specific cognitive skills in children who may associate familiar-looking materials with failure (Sharron 1987). On the other hand, as we saw earlier, growing research evidence suggests that much learning is domain- or content-specific, supporting claims that the most effective materials will be very closely related to actual curriculum demands (Howe 1991). The SPELT programme, described by Andrews *et al.* (1989) is one example, while the Somerset Thinking Skills course (Blagg *et al.* 1988) is an attempt to apply some of the ideas of Feuerstein more directly to the curriculum.

Metacognition, or the ability to reflect on your own mental processes, is clearly linked to strategy development, and among other things allows the child to select the best strategies and to monitor their success, as discussed earlier. In general, the teacher's task will be not so much to *instruct* as to *intervene* in the child's cognitive processes (Adey and Shayer 1994), to try to bring these processes out into the open, and ultimately to enable the child to take on responsibility for their own learning. Language will obviously be crucial here, but unfortunately there could be a potential conflict for teachers:

> What appears to be the dominant teaching register, involving frequent teacher-directed questions, may be effective in achieving certain managerial and instructional ends, but it seems unlikely to provide good conditions for developing children's powers as narrators, informants and, perhaps, self-regulating learners.

> (Wood 1988: 145)

Clearly, a different sort of learning relationship, with a different sort of language, is called for, taking us back to one of the oldest teaching techniques – Socratic dialogue. Meadows and Cashdan (1988) discuss the effectiveness of this approach, where the teacher talks the pupil through the problem with the ultimate aim of enabling the child to become 'self-running'. Similarly, 'conferencing' uses one-to-one discussion, partly to help children become more self-aware and partly as an informal assessment device for teachers. The Primary Language Record (CLPE 1988) is one of the best-known British examples.

For experienced teachers, a problem immediately springs to mind, of course. Where is one supposed to get the time to have one-to-one dialogues with thirty children? One possible solution is to use the children themselves as 'talk partners', while another is to carry on the dialogue in written form, allowing the teacher to communicate with each child when the teacher chooses. A particularly lively example of this technique is described in 'The Thinking Books' (Swan and White 1994). Each child simply wrote down something they had learned that day, plus any questions they wanted to ask, and the teacher wrote a brief response. Significantly, the children found it far from simple at first, and their comments and questions provided the teacher with some valuable insights about what they really had (or had not) learned. Moreover, encouraging the children to reflect on their own learning seemed to have long-term benefits which were still apparent eight years later.

Attitudes and feelings have been seen as inextricably bound up with cognitive development because successful problem-solving requires not only appropriate strategies, but also positive attitudes both towards the problem and towards yourself as a problem solver. So exactly what sorts of positive attitudes should teachers try to encourage, and what sorts of negative attitudes should they be aware of as potentially damaging? At risk of parody, the attitudes of good and poor learners after a few years' experience of school success or failure can be briefly summarised:

- Successful learners don't mind if they don't yet know the answer – indeed they will often relish not knowing and feel confident that they will find out eventually, to the extent that they may prefer not to be told the answer even if it is readily available. They will also run the risk that a line of thought may prove wrong, and be willing to try other solutions when they already have one. They have an 'internal locus of control' which attributes success largely to their own efforts, and prefer tasks which are moderately difficult, in line with the previous idea of 'comfortable challenge'. They see themselves as good learners and have high self-esteem.
- Unsuccessful learners may latch on impulsively to the first answer that seems reasonable and to persist with it in the face of contrary evidence. They attribute success to external factors, including pure luck, and see their learning as the teacher's responsibility, often acting in helpless or passive ways. They may develop strategies for avoiding tasks on the grounds that, if you don't try, you can't fail, and they prefer tasks which are either very easy (thus presenting no challenge) or impossibly difficult (so that no-one can blame them for failing). They see themselves as poor learners and have low self-esteem.

Developing a classroom climate and learning relationships where positive attitudes can flourish is clearly a long-term task and, again, the teacher's willingness to act as a model can provide a starting point, demonstrating not only appropriate learning strategies but also showing the child that not knowing something is acceptable. Allowing children to experience success is one apparently obvious way, though we do need to recognise that success can actually be a threat to children who see themselves as failures. Equally, however, we should perhaps not try to avoid failure at all costs, since it is only through experiencing failure that children can learn how to cope with it, and deciding not to get involved in a new learning situation may sometimes be the right decision (Claxton 1996). The ideal is therefore to present children with an appropriate challenge, but in a secure context. Chapter 4 of this book describes a range of classroom techniques which encourage self-esteem and develop social skills, often using the support of the peer group, which becomes increasingly important as children reach puberty (see McNamara and Moreton 1993 for more detail.) Conversely, preparing something for younger children may help those in the junior years by emphasising what they do know and enabling them to help others for a change.

The social context of learning has also been seen not just as a background, but as inextricably involved in individual cognitive development, in both the general context of the child's culture and in the immediate social situations of family or classroom which reflect that culture. Indeed, many of the ideas already mentioned imply a learning relationship which shifts both adult and child away from the traditional teacher and pupil roles. Such a shift will not be easy, particularly in cultures which themselves seem to require the teacher to maintain an authoritarian role, and, even in apparently 'progressive' classrooms, the teacher must retain social control in order to manage the class. Nor would it be sensible to emphasise individual cognitive processes and strategies at the expense of culturally-defined knowledge, since clearly both are involved in learning if that learning is to be both meaningful and useful. Ideally, as teachers, we would like children to learn for themselves what we just happen to have planned for them.

Bearing this in mind, it is still possible for teachers to encourage the sorts of cognitive development discussed in this chapter, within the social constraints of the classroom. As suggested earlier, teachers can model good practices themselves, for instance by admitting (or even pretending) that they don't know something and demonstrating how they find out, in line with the notion of 'apprenticeship'. Reading in class is another example, and ideas like USSR (uninterrupted sustained silent reading) or ERIC (everyone reads in class) propose that the teacher should sometimes read silently at the same time as the children, showing that adults read too and that reading is not just something that children have to do out loud for the teacher. Similarly, Waterland (1985) proposes a whole approach to reading based on the notion of the child as apprentice.

The role of the teacher as mediator between child and culture has already been mentioned, and is emphasised by writers like Rogoff (1990) who are interested in the whole process of social cognition. (Significantly, Rogoff called her book *Apprenticeship in Thinking*.) Successful teachers use what she calls 'guided participation' to involve the child at 'a comfortable but slightly challenging level' . Writing as a philosopher rather than a psychologist, Bonnett (1994) uses the term 'empathetic challenging' in a very similar way to denote a teacher role which is both accepting and demanding. The comfortable, accepting side of the role acknowledges the existing understanding of the child, while the challenging, demanding side recognises culturally-defined needs for certain knowledge and skills.

Such shifts in role can be subtle and even temporary, rather than radical and permanent, though it is important for teachers to signal when they wish to change from being unapproachable autocrats to sympathetic mediators! Simply changing the seating arrangements can help, and devices like 'circle time' encourage other sorts of learning relationships. Nor is it purely a matter of teachers teaching differently, since getting children to help each other is very much in line with the other suggestions in this section. (Chapter 4 discusses the value of genuine cooperative groupwork, as opposed to children sitting in groups but ignoring each other.) Rogoff (1990: 22) sees peer interaction as 'especially important in its encouragement of children's exploration without immediate goals (as in play or curious fooling around), its motivating nature that channels children's choice of activities, and its availability.' Similarly, Boden (1994) regards peer cooperation and discussion as crucial in developing cognitive as well as social skills.

CONCLUSION

This chapter has briefly discussed some of the major developments which take place in children's learning between the ages of about seven and eleven. The beginning of a general shift towards more adult ways of thinking obviously involves cognitive changes, like the ability to select, use and monitor a wider range of strategies, but appropriate attitudes and social awareness are equally vital during these years, as formalised schooling plays an increasingly important part in what children learn. In turn, this means that psychologists, if they are to have anything directly useful to say to teachers, must also continue to further our understanding of the wider cultural context in which schools function and in which children's learning develops.

REFERENCES

Adey, P. and Shayer, M. (1994) *Really Raising Standards: Cognitive Intervention and Academic Achievement*, London: Routledge.

Andrews, J., Peat, D., Mulcahy, R. and Marfo, K. (1989) 'Developing social competence within regular classrooms through a cognitive strategies approach', in C. Violato and A. Marini (eds) *Child Development: Readings for Teachers*, Calgary: Detselig Enterprises.

Ashman, A. and Conway, R. (1993) *Using Cognitive Methods in the Classroom*, London: Routledge.

Blagg, N., Ballinger, M. and Gardner, R. (1988) *Somerset Thinking Skills Course Handbook*, Oxford: Basil Blackwell.

Boden, M. (1994) *Piaget* (2nd edn), London: Fontana.

Bonnett, M. (1994) *Children's Thinking: Promoting Understanding in the Primary School*, London: Cassell.

Bruner, J. and Haste, H. (1987) *Making Sense: The Child's Construction of the World*, London: Methuen.

Carraher, T. N., Carraher, D. W. and Schliemann, A. D. (1990) 'Mathematics in the streets and in schools', in V. Lee (ed.) *Children's Learning in School*, Milton Keynes: Open University.

Claxton, G. (1996) 'Integrated learning theory and the learning teacher', in G. Claxton, T. Anderson, M. Osborn and M. Wallace (eds) *Liberating the Learner: Lessons for Professional Development in Education*, London: Routledge.

CLPE (Centre for Language in Primary Education) (1988) *The Primary Language Record: A Handbook for Teachers*, London: CLPE.

Donaldson, M. (1978) *Children's Minds*, Glasgow: Fontana/Collins.

—— (1992) *Human Minds: An Exploration*, London: Penguin.

Galloway, D. and Edwards, A. (1991) *Primary School Teaching and Educational Psychology*, London: Longman

Gardner, H. (1983) *Frames of Mind: The Theory of Multiple Intelligences*, London: Heinemann.

Halford, G. S. (1993) *Children's Understanding: The Development of Mental Models*, Hillsdale, NJ: Lawrence Erlbaum.

Holt, J. (1984) *How Children Fail*, Harmondsworth: Penguin

—— (1991) *Learning all the Time*, Ticknall: Education Now.

Howe, M. J. A. (1991) 'A fine idea but does it work?', *British Psychological Society Education Section Review*, 15(2), 43–6.

Hudson, J. A. (1993) 'Script knowledge', in M. Bennett *The Child as Psychologist: an Introduction to the Development of Social Cognition*, New York: Harvester Wheatsheaf.

Kail, R. V. (1990) *The Development of Memory in Children*, New York: W. H. Freeman.

Karmiloff-Smith, A. (1992) *Beyond Modularity*, Cambridge, MA: MIT Press.

Levin, J. R. (1993) 'Mnemonic strategies and classroom learning: a twenty-year report card', *Elementary School Journal*, 94(2), 235–44.

McNamara, S. and Moreton, G. (1993) *Teaching Special Needs*, London: David Fulton.

McShane, J. (1991) *Cognitive Development: An Information-Processing Approach*, Oxford: Blackwell.

Meadows, S. (1993) *The Child as Thinker: The Development and Acquisition of Cognition in Childhood*, London: Routledge.

Meadows, S. and Cashdan, A. (1988) *Helping Children Learn: Contributions to a Cognitive Curriculum*, London: David Fulton.

Moran, A. (1991) 'What can learning styles research learn from cognitive psychology?', *Educational Psychology*, 11(3/4), 239–45.

Perner, J. (1991) *Understanding the Representational Mind*, Cambridge, MA: MIT Press.

Rogoff, B. (1990) *Apprenticeship in Thinking: Cognitive Development in Social Context*, New York: Oxford University Press.

Rogoff, B., Gauvain, M. and Ellis, S. (1989) 'Development viewed in its cultural context', in P. Light, M. Sheldon and M. Woodhead (eds) *Child Development in Social Context: 2 – Learning to Think*, London: Routledge.

Rowe, M. B. (1986) 'Wait time: slowing down may be a way of speeding up!', *Journal of Teacher Education*, 37, 43–50.

Sharron, H. (1987) *Changing Children's Minds: Feuerstein's Revolution in the Teaching of Intelligence*, London: Souvenir Press.

Simmons, P. R-J. (1994) 'Metacognition', in T. Husen and T. N. Postlethwaite *International Encyclopedia of Education* (2nd edn), Oxford: Pergamon.

Sotto, E. (1994) *When Teaching Becomes Learning: A Theory and Practice of Teaching*, London: Cassell.

Swan, S. and White, R. (1994) *The Thinking Books*, London: Falmer.

Terwogt, M. M. and Harris, P. L. (1993) 'Understanding of emotion', in M. Bennett (ed.) *The Child as Psychologist: An Introduction to the Development of Social Cognition*, New York: Harvester Wheatsheaf.

Waterland, L. (1985) *Read with me: An Apprenticeship Approach to Reading*, Stroud: Thimble Press.

Wood, D. (1988) *How Children Think and Learn*, Oxford: Blackwell.

—— (1991) 'Aspects of teaching and learning', in P. Light, M. Sheldon and M. Woodhead (eds) *Child Development in Social Context: 2 – Learning to Think*, London: Routledge.

Chapter 4

Children with special educational needs
Supporting the learning relationship

Sylvia McNamara

INTRODUCTION: THE INTEGRATION–SEGREGATION DEBATE

Although most Western countries have put a great deal of effort into the development of separate special educational systems (Pijl and Meijer 1991), the whole notion of segregation has increasingly come under attack. A major effect of segregated systems was the development of expertise in teachers, resources and special instructional methods in the special schools, but one unfortunate consequence of this separation was the belief by some teachers in mainstream schools that they were unable to teach pupils with special needs because they lacked the skills to do so. Some were not motivated to acquire such skills and saw children with special needs as being outside their remit. Integration challenged both the idea that segregation was best for students with special needs and the idea that mainstream teachers lacked the expertise to deal with such students.

This integration movement came about for several different reasons. Some parents and administrators supported the pressure for change, leaving other groups of parents and administrators defending the *status quo*, that is to say the segregated, specialist settings. Those who were against integration wanted separate specialist resources and provision for children with special needs, while those who were for integration did not want children stigmatised, labeled and separated from their peers in the immediate community. There were also strong moral and human rights arguments voiced for social cohesion, social equality and social equity (Welton and Evans 1986). In addition,

> analysis of the outcomes of students of special educational provision, together with first-hand accounts of the experience of special educational treatment, provide a dissenting view of the benefits of the traditional assumptions and practices of special education.
>
> (Slee 1995: 33–4).

In summary, the rationale for integration is that segregation is damaging for people because they have at some stage in their lives to live in an integrated setting, and neither group of people, special or mainstream, will have had much practice in dealing with each other. It is also damaging because of the stigma of separation. It is an argument which states that any gains which can be had from the centralisation of specialist resources are actually outweighed by the social losses (Dessent 1987).

With the 1988 Education Act, the introduction of competition, market forces and value for money, integration has come to mean more in the UK than the right of access and entitlement for the child with special needs. As Fish and Evans (1995) point out, parental choice means that parents expect to be able to choose between two sets of provision, special and mainstream. This duplication of provision has serious financial implications, as has been outlined by the Audit Commission (1992), but for some teachers and administrators, it has led to a situation where the challenge is now to produce such an attractive combination of peer support, local schooling and progression in academic work in the mainstream setting that the special provision will dry up due to lack of clients.

INCLUSIVE EDUCATION

The most recent development in the special needs debate has been the notion of inclusive education. While this word may have different meanings in different countries, and while the classroom practice of one inclusive setting may be very different to that of another, even within one country, let alone between countries, it is still helpful to examine the US explanation, as there are parallels with classroom practices in other settings.

> Inclusive education is an umbrella term used in the United States to describe the restructuring of special education to permit all or most students to be integrated in mainstream classrooms through reorganisation and instructional innovations (e.g. co-operative learning, collaborative and instructional innovations and team teaching).
>
> (Ware 1995: 127)

The Warnock Report (DES 1978) in the UK drew a useful distinction between locational, social and functional integration, and inclusive education could be said to be an illustration of the last of these.

Locational integration is where, for example, a special unit exists on the same site as the mainstream school and the children share facilities but rarely meet or play with one another. Social integration is where children will eat or play together but attend the majority of their lessons separately. Functional integration is where children with special needs are able to access the curriculum fully and maintain good social relation-ships with their peers.

Some would argue that locational integration exists when children with special needs are in the mainstream classroom but are given differ-ent work, have the almost constant help of a welfare assistant or a spe-cialist special needs teacher, but may be excluded, shunned or dismissed by their peers. In such situations, it is felt that inclusive education rather than integration should be the goal.

> Rather than thinking about how to bring pupils with SEN *into* the ordinary school system why have an education system which pre-sumes exclusion? This point was firmly stated in the Declaration of the 1994 UNESCO World Conference on special needs (UNESCO 1994).
>
> (Wedell 1995: 100)

The similarities, both in terms of policy legislation and changes in sys-tems in the UK and the USA, are identified by Croll and Moses (1994). They highlight four major themes: inclusion; extension of the concept of special educational need; integration; and individualisation; although they point out that the legislation in both countries concentrates more on systems of identification and assessment than on methodology.

However, as Chapter 6 of this book implies, the concept of integration, like other important educational issues, is based on cultural values which are in turn interpreted by social institutions. Thus, in much of the Western world, there is an emphasis on the rights and entitlement of the individual, while elsewhere the emphasis is more on the contribution which the individual can make to the community. It may also be the case that, in some countries, the priority of education has, for economic rea-sons alone, focused on education for 'normal' children, specialist schools for those who are 'mentally handicapped and have sensory impairment', with little or no provision for those with learning difficulties:

> Despite substantial progress in reaching and teaching children with learning difficulties less than one per cent of those with significant learning disabilities attend any form of school in most developing countries (UNESCO 1995). The rest remain at home, often leading lonely and isolated lives.
>
> (Mittler 1995: 105)

This is the case in China, for example, where the categories used to assess special needs are hearing and speaking disabilities, visual disabili-ty, mental disorder and multiple disabilities. There has been a dramatic increase in provision for these categories in recent years. For instance, for children categorised as mentally retarded, the provision had increased from 131 special schools and 599 special classes in 1987 to 856 special schools and 2,651 special classes by 1990 (Potts 1995). Despite the enormous drain on resources of such an expansion, there has also been a clear attempt to integrate those in the mental retardation category. Potts cites a project of peer tutoring to support children with IQs of 60 on her visit in 1992, for example.

Ashman also indicates that developments in special education in China may follow similar lines to those in the UK:

> Where the expertise of Chinese Special Education has been long and where there has been constant contact with overseas education and research (as in hearing and visual impairment) programmes and techniques are much the same as in other countries. In the area of intellectual disabilities and speech and language disabilities however the process of programme and curriculum development may have to pass through a similar evolutionary process to that which has occurred in the West.
>
> (Ashman 1995: 56).

In order to understand this evolutionary process, the next section will look at how it originates in a 'traditional' view of special needs education.

THE TRADITIONAL VIEW OF SPECIAL NEEDS

The traditional, or 'within-child', view is based on the 'psycho-medical paradigm' (Clarke *et al.* 1995: 76). That is to say it is a view of special needs that locates the problem with the child and their difference. Thus, a child is seen as having a problem because she is blind. She is not normal, and we must either do as much as we can to make her as normal as possible, or we must lower our expectations of her because she is blind. But this concept of normality and the attendant educational strategies that accompany it have been challenged by some of those who are disabled and have been on the receiving end of such an approach.

Hearing impairment presents an interesting illustration of some of the issues. In the Western world there is a furious debate that continues among both the hearing and the hearing-impaired communities. Those in the 'deaf world' insist that they should be allowed to sign, because signing helps those who are deaf to communicate. Many parents and teachers think that children should not be taught to sign but made to speak, because signing makes them different. So there are 'non-signing' Local Education Authorities which have a hearing-impaired support service of experts who are banned from signing.

In the traditional paradigm, the identification of children with special needs and the placement of them in an appropriate educational setting depends on testing, and particularly on IQ testing. For many Western and Pacific rim countries, there is a clear relation between IQ and special provision. Thus, moderate and mild learning difficulties will usually be defined by IQs of 50–75, severe learning difficulties will be 20–49 and profound and multiple will be below 20 (Ware 1990). In contrast, in the UK a statement of need based on a multi-professional assessment is used. This will probably contain an IQ score, but will also contain a profile of strengths and weaknesses.

For some workers in the field of special education, progress towards integration and inclusion was accompanied by a more positive view of special needs. There was a move away from explaining poor academic achievement in terms of low intelligence, towards a more optimistic view emphasising a pupil's capacity for learning. This was accompanied by a questioning of the usefulness of the IQ test as an assessment tool, summarised by Thomas and Feiler:

> Intelligence was supposed to be inherited, uninfluenced by teaching, could be measured accurately, and was unchanging over time. . . . It is now widely accepted that intelligence quotients do not remain constant over time and that performance on such tests is influenced by cultural and educational factors (Clarke and Clarke 1976).
>
> (Thomas and Feiler 1992: 35)

From the traditional view of IQs developed programmes of work:

> These were based on the idea that academic skills such as reading and writing depend on the existence of a core set of sub-skills. It was proposed that if one could measure a child's ability in these underpinning areas it should then be possible to identify deficits, present the children with suitable programmes to compensate for these weaknesses and therefore improve the academic outcome.
>
> (Thomas and Feiler 1992: 16)

Unfortunately, research evidence has shown that, while children do get better at the sub-skills such as visual sequencing, there is no carry-over into academic skills (Newcomer and Hammill: 1975).

THE BEHAVIOURAL APPROACH

A related but slightly different instructional methodology that is a hallmark of the traditional view is the behavioural approach. This has spawned a number of different teaching strategies, including teaching to objectives, small steps, task analysis and individual programmes. There are obviously some advantages to such techniques, summarised by Burman *et al.* (1983):

1 They help teachers to know where to begin with new children and facilitate smooth progression between classes within the school.
2 They are useful for assessing progress.
3 Structured curriculum means that teachers no longer need to worry about *what* to teach and can spend time deciding *how* to teach.
4 They promote parent–teacher cooperation.
5 They imply a positive, optimistic approach.

The testing of children to work out where they are and where they should begin on a programme is a key element here, and screening and diagnostic tests of reading or maths difficulties become vitally important. The person who regularly administers such tests becomes familiar and expert in them and rapidly assumes the mantle of special needs expert. Thus, many assume a connection between knowledge of tests and special needs expertise about programmes that can be devised once the results of such tests are revealed. There is not necessarily such a connection, and there are several problematic assumptions underlying objectives approaches.

One such assumption is that the tests tend to see cognitive development in the skills of reading and maths and science as sequential and hierarchical. This may not be accurate and it may not be the best way for all children to learn. Gardner's work on multiple intelligences has led to the creation of some interesting projects in the USA in which children are being taught a particular subject, such as maths, in a way that fits their particular intelligence strength, like music for instance (Gardner 1993). Certainly there is a renewed interest in both the US and the UK on teaching styles that match the learning styles of children (Goleman 1996).

Another assumption is that people with severe or multiple learning difficulties can be taught social and cognitive basic routines through repetition, reward and 'chunking', in other words breaking a piece of curriculum down into small enough pieces for the person to master the skill before moving on.

> Early research findings indicated that people with severe learning difficulties did not learn things *incidentally* in the way that non-handicapped children did, but that they *could* acquire skills previously thought to be beyond them if the task was broken down into small steps and carefully and specifically taught (e.g. Clarke and Herman-Fleiss 1955, Gold 1973, Horner and Keilitz 1975).
>
> (Ware 1990: 159)

INDIVIDUAL EDUCATION PROGRAMMES

The result of this rationale has been an emphasis on individualised learning programmes to the point where special education is almost synonymous with individual programmes in the UK and Europe. Indeed, the guidance accompanying the Code of Practice, the latest legislation on special needs in the UK, specifies the production of Individual Education Programmes (IEPs) for all children who are identified as having Special Educational Needs. These programmes are designed for an individual, based on the diagnosis of where that person is on a given set of skills.

They can, however, lead to another assumption: that is that, since the expertise resides in special schools which cater for the 'most severe', then mainstream teachers who wish to integrate children with special needs will need to adapt and use the approaches and instructional methods from special schools. This means using individual educational programmes for some in classes of thirty or more, which most classroom teachers regard as exhausting and therefore unfair on both themselves and the other children in the class.

There is also an assumption about age-related development norms. In the UK, this assumption is combined with a pedagogy which is child-centred and purports to use a combination of individual exploration and collaborative groupwork approaches to teaching. British teachers try to cope in various ways:

1   They try to protect the child from the bad feelings of failure associated with doing the work the 'rest' are set, so instead they give the children different work to do. A problem with such 'differentiation by task' is the danger of low expectations. It is interesting to note that, in the first few years of the SATs tests in the UK, children with special needs at all key stages usually did better on the national SATs than on teacher assessment. OFSTED and HMI have highlighted low expectations, especially for children with literacy difficulties, for the past fifteen years.

2   Teachers ask for another adult to work with the child in the classroom, either a support teacher or a classroom assistant, a welfare assistant or an ancillary. The problem with this solution is to do with learned helplessness and attribution theory and low self-esteem, which are discussed later in the chapter.

3   Teachers try to be all things to all children, suffer stress and get burnt out. Many teachers in the UK are currently leaving the profession after only three or four years, or taking early retirement at fifty.

4   To protect themselves from burn-out, the teachers send the child to a special unit or school and pass on the responsibility to others whom they regard as more 'expert'.

5   The child is effectively punished for having special needs and is permanently excluded from school if the associated behaviour problems become severe.

However, if the instructional technique uses rote routines and learning in hierarchies in the mainstream classroom, there will be less of a problem in terms of adapting and individualising work for individual children. In this case the work is already delivered in an objectives, sub-skills approach to the whole class, though it does require extra effort from the teacher. In some countries this emphasis on the individual with problems comes down to offering more teacher attention and more reinforcement in order to get the child to produce work of a similar nature to the others in the class.

Reynolds (1995) notes that countries like Taiwan, Korea and Hong Kong are very successful in reducing the standard deviation or range of their pupils' achievements. They do this by getting all their children through the hurdles of basic skills acquisition by age eight or nine.

> In our schools within Hong Kong and Taiwan, this success is brought about at the cost of formidable investment of teacher effort in the education of children with special educational needs.
>
> (Reynolds 1995: 123)

He goes on to describe teachers walking up and down the rows, giving almost all of their attention to such children, the children attending extra catch-up classes, having more homework than other children, and ending up not differing from their peers as much as those with special needs in the integrated system in the UK.

However, there would probably be arguments against adopting the Taiwan and Hong Kong approach in the UK. For example:

1 The teacher would be spending time almost exclusively with the children with special needs and virtually ignoring the rest. In a child-centred culture, this would be viewed as helping children with special needs at the expense of the rest, and would be unacceptable. Alternatively, another adult must be brought in to focus on one of the two groups, each of which is actually getting different treatment.
2 The children with special needs are getting extra – and therefore different – tuition during the day.
3 The children with special needs are getting extra – and therefore different – homework.

In the UK, this would add up to something close to a segregated provision under the guise of locational integration.

SELF-ESTEEM AND ACADEMIC ACHIEVEMENT

As has already been suggested, there are clear advantages for teachers in using objectives approaches and related techniques. They facilitate planning and record keeping, and there is evidence of success in terms of the specific goals, even if generalisation to academic success is rare. On the other hand, these advantages emphasise the views of the parent and the teacher more than those of the child. The more that one is interested in child involvement, the more that teaching to objectives needs to incorporate an element of discussion, negotiation and child-identified target setting.

The disadvantages centre mainly on the issue of motivation. Many children with learning difficulties also have associated behavioural difficulties, which result in them refusing to do tasks which have been identified as being within their grasp. The reasons for these behavioural difficulties seem to be linked to some of the psychological motivation theories, such as self-esteem, attribution theory and learned helplessness, and it is to these that we now turn, beginning with self-esteem.

There have been a number of studies relating self-esteem and academic achievement, showing a strong, persistent link between the two (Purkey 1970). These research results have since been replicated with numerous studies covering countries throughout the world and all phases of education (Piskin 1996). Skaalvik and Hagvet (1990) provide a recent example. Burns (1982) also noted the powerful correlation between low academic achievement and low self-esteem:

> Where tests of general self concept were used most studies found a consistent relationship of about 90% of the variance common to the two measures. When a measure of academic self was used about 30% of the variance was common to both measures; correlations of between 0.5 and 0.6.
>
> (Burns 1982: 209)

If the sense of self-worth is so powerfully linked with academic achievement, and there is no clear causal relationship, then it is possible that a focus on raising self-esteem instead of a focus on sub-skills and hierarchies could provide an increase in academic achievement. Moreover, approaches using objectives, small steps, individual programmes and differentiation by task may actually reduce self-esteem by accentuating differences. For example, Wade and Moore (1993) interviewed a number of students from all phases of education in both the UK and New Zealand – one of the few studies which actually consulted the customer. They asked students with special needs their views on the following issues: teachers, lessons, parents and school, changing schools, feeling different, friends and enemies, fun and games, getting into trouble, being assessed and tested. Their sample expressed more negative views about testing than about any other category. Given that testing is the backbone of the objectives approach, this does not bode well for a strong sense of self-worth, and 'responses to the questionnaire and sentence completions suggest that the self concept of our students was unacceptably low' (Wade and Moore 1993: 161).

They also found that the students generally expressed positive views about their teachers – 'they liked helpful, understanding teachers who were fair, had a sense of humour and made lessons interesting' (Wade and Moore 1993: 40).

Like other groups, the students with special needs were more negative about lessons, finding some enjoyable, but worrying about difficulties with work. 'Very few students had strategies of self-reliance when faced with problems, and few sought the collaboration of classmates. Students in difficulty either stewed in inactivity or worry or relied on their teachers for help' (Wade and Moore 1993: 56).

They were anxious about their parents, although these anxieties varied from not enough help with homework to wanting more love and care, while their views about changing schools revealed a 'split between those who were positive about making a change and the majority who focussed on worrying about losing and making friends' (Wade and Moore 1993: 85).

In relation to feeling different, many appeared to view themselves negatively and 'a summary of responses indicated that students do not feel different so much as not so good academically' (Wade and Moore 1993: 101). As for friends and enemies, 'students who were fully integrated have stronger friendships although they argue more', and 'many students perceived that others disliked them because of differences emanating from their disabilities or special educational needs' (Wade and Moore 1993: 116).

The students in the sample had positive attitudes to fun and games, but the majority were not happy at playtime, being bored, lonely, uncomfortable or unhappy (Wade and Moore 1993: 130).

ATTRIBUTION THEORY

Attribution theory shows that those with high self-esteem have realistic and accurate explanations of success and failure: 'I got a low mark in that test because I did not revise,' or 'I do well in French because I enjoy the subject and I spend time learning the vocabulary.'

Those with low self-esteem, however, are more likely to attribute success to luck or chance, and failure to their own lack of ability. 'I got high marks in my science test because I was lucky with the questions that came up,' or 'I got low marks in maths because I am no good at maths.'

This may start to account for the reason why some children with special needs aggressively refuse to carry out tasks that the special needs teacher has carefully planned by identifying sub-skills and breaking these into smaller steps. Some children become verbally aggressive to other children, and are the ones most disliked by their peers (Wade and Moore 1993). Other children destroy the work set, or simply refuse to do it. Still others seem to show or experience no sense of pride when they receive help from other adults to carry out the work. This then means that the welfare assistant, who is often the 'extra resource' provided for the child with special needs, cannot perform a helpful function.

Other children seem totally unable to get started on a task without an enormous amount of adult help and support. This is known as Learned Helplessness.

LEARNED HELPLESSNESS

Learned Helplessness is the term used when people stop trying things for themselves because they believe they cannot do them. It is the belief that stops them, not their actual ability (Abrahmson *et al.* 1978, Craske 1988). This was articulated by the chess player Kasparov when he played against a computer (1994). The computer won, but, when interviewed, Kasparov said that he did not think the reason he lost was because the computer was actually so fast, and therefore better than him. He thought he had lost because he was *afraid* that the computer would win.

Craske (1988) noticed that children with poor academic self-concept appear to be particularly susceptible to learned helplessness. Abrahmson *et al.* (1978) found that a state of learned helplessness is reached when an individual perceives that he lacks control in obtaining his desired outcome. The type of explanation (attribution) that an individual makes for his lack of control determines the features of his helplessness.

Craske separated out a population of primary school children who were failing at maths into two groups: those whose deteriorated performance after failure is a consequence of Learned Helplessness, and those whose performance is motivated by Self-Worth considerations. She carried out an attribution retraining programme with all of the children and found that, while the Learned Helplessness group did respond to retraining, the Self-Worth group did not. This supported the findings of Dweck (1975). There are, however, different programmes which can be carried out to increase self-esteem (Lawrence 1973, 1988; Borba and Borba 1978; Gurney 1988; Mosley 1993, 1994; McNamara and Moreton 1993, 1995, in press).

These two theories seem to shed light on the reactions encountered when working with a child as a support teacher or when 'withdrawing' youngsters, for example for extra help with handwriting or spelling. It sometimes seems as if the problem is not so much that a pupil cannot do the work, but more that they do not *want* to do it. It is as if they refuse to acknowledge that other adults know that they have difficulties and that the task is one that has been set especially for them and is within their capabilities. Their tactics of either total withdrawal, aggressive refusal or clowning about, seem to be avoidance tactics because they *believe* that they cannot do the work. It seems that it is better for them to pretend that they do not care about the work because *the risk of* failure is too painful. In addition, some pupils seem to behave badly in order to deflect the cause of failure from lack of skill, so that both the teacher and the child can attribute the poor academic progress to the bad behaviour.

Approaches to special needs which pay attention to these theories of motivation will probably encompass the following:

It is most important that

(a) children with special educational needs feel they have something to contribute to develop their self-esteem;

(b) their motivation is increased by being treated as partners in their own learning;

(c) we obtain sufficient feedback (including feelings and attitudes) to help us properly direct our contributions, interventions, and provisions;

(d) we maximise the potential of every child by consultation, partnership and interaction;

(e) we avoid creating handicap, and treat pupils with special educational needs as normal (and according to the 1981 Education Act's concept of a continuum).

(Wade and Moore 1993: 11)

Wade and Moore, in common with the authors of several chapters in this book, emphasise the social context of learning, and it is obviously equally important to recognise this context when examining children's learning difficulties. The next section, therefore, turns to the ecological model, which is perhaps particularly relevant to special needs education.

THE ECOLOGICAL MODEL

This is the model which says that the child's needs are special in relation to their environment. It is a relative view, challenging the idea of normality. It suggests that the first step in the identification of a child's needs should not be to administer an IQ test or some assessment to see where they fit into a given programme, but instead to observe the context in which a child's learning difficulties take place. The second step is a review by the teacher to see if any of that context can be changed.

> The ecological model is a synthesis of the individual-centred and the context based understanding of situations. It takes as its starting point the fact that a child's behaviour cannot be separated from the context in which it occurs. Given such a simple starting point, it is not discordant with models which have traditionally been separated by wide differences both on methodology and content.
>
> (Thomas and Feiler 1992: 27)

Sheila Wolfendale (1987) also outlines an ecological model for primary schools.

In summary, then, this approach states that if a child acts up in the classroom and the parents say that this is not happening elsewhere, maybe the problem is not with the child but with the context of the classroom, which does not suit the child's needs. Given that it is teachers who are in charge of the classroom and actually create the context, then maybe it is us!

In this case, the imperative to examine teaching and learning styles is powerful. How *can* we make schools more effective?

THE EFFECTIVE SCHOOLS VIEW

The effective schools argument takes the ecological model one step further than the arrangements in the classroom, arguing for changing whole school ethos and management systems. It notes that, although integration has been espoused in the Western world, the incidence of children with special needs actually learning alongside their peers and interacting as equals is small (Ainscow 1994).

The argument then focuses on changing the school *system*, the teaching arrangements, the pedagogy, the teachers' ability to work in teams, the leadership and vision in the school, with different authors emphasising different aspects. Thus Clarke, Dyson, Millward and Skidmore (1995) argue that it is virtually impossible that teachers will never reach a point where there is a common ethos, but Ainscow (1994) focuses particularly on in-service training and has developed a pack of materials to try to bring about this change, while Hopkins (1995) argues that effective teachers are ones who use a range of teaching styles appropriately.

This author has developed a strategy for increasing the range of a teacher's styles so that the teaching methodology takes into account the motivational issues outlined above, and the ecological considerations, and also incorporates a skills approach. The approach differs from previous training programmes, however, because the skills training focuses not on the child with special needs, but on 'the rest' – the child's peers in the classroom. It is based on the principle that the difficulty is not the child and the child's difference, but the others in the group. This programme is called 'Inclusion Skills Training'

CLASSROOM ORGANISATION – SKILLS TRAINING FOR INCLUSION

Inclusion skills involve a method of teaching the curriculum to ensure that every member of the group has a healthy self-esteem; it is a specialist pedagogy (McNamara and Moreton 1993). The skills training approach builds on the premise that what is needed in the classroom is not necessarily an extra adult as a support for the pupil with special needs, but more urgently a change in teaching and learning styles (Slavin 1983; Johnson and Johnson 1975; Ainscow 1991, 1994; McNamara and Moreton 1993, in press; McNamara *et al.* 1996).

This change means giving more power and control to the students, teaching them to manage themselves and others. It also means a classroom that has much more pupil talk and much less reliance on reading and writing, or on worksheets – differentiated or not (Vygotsky 1962; DES 1975; Tough 1977; Wells 1985, 1986; DES 1989).

The starting point then is oracy – that is to say, 'talk'. For many children and adults with special needs, talk is a way of learning that takes away one of the major impediments, i.e. reading. This is not to say that children should not learn to read, but rather that they should be freed to learn about other aspects of the curriculum while they are still learning to read. This oracy work raises achievement for all, because it enables all children to clarify and build on their conceptual understanding, as already happens in many middle-class homes (Vygotsky 1962).

GROUPWORK SKILLS

The development of inclusion skills is based on the ideas embedded in groupwork skills training (Johnson and Johnson 1975; Schmuck and Schmuck 1977; Stanford 1977; Kingsley Mills *et al.* 1992). Many teachers have found that, when they try groupwork, the children appear to have difficulties with it, the task is not completed, the children are negative and disruptive to each other and chaos ensues. Not surprisingly, teachers are then reluctant to use groupwork in future. But groupwork progress can be analysed in the careful way that reading progress is, and a small-steps approach can be applied to the groupwork problems that children usually have, such as the inability to:

- take your turn;
- share ideas;
- build on previous contributions;
- include silent members;
- share out tasks.

A programme similar to that advocated in this chapter would probably then be devised by many practitioners. Such attention to group process skills, however, is rare, as many teachers assume that the choice of a suitable task is sufficient to ensure that the kinds of interaction they expect will happen automatically. This means that teachers are unlikely to get to the stage of cooperative groupwork, and witness the learning that children go through in this setting. This learning has been well documented (Slavin 1983; Jaques 1984; Sharan and Kussell 1984).

If teachers could be persuaded to engage in a skills training approach to groupwork, they could start to reap some of the benefits documented by others who have used it successfully to integrate and include students with special needs (Thousand and Villa 1991; Thousand *et al.* 1994; Stainback and Stainback 1992, 1995).

These benefits are summarised below:

1 Groupwork helps each person to feel that they are a part of what is going on, and individuals begin to feel genuinely integrated.
2 Working as part of a group ensures that each person has access to the same broad and balanced curriculum. Differentiation by outcome can then be built in through the assessment procedures and these can be shared with individuals and groups in an open manner.
3 Groupwork allows children to increase their ability to include everyone and to make statements about themselves. It facilitates a more constructive system of feedback for the student with special educational needs than feedback based on academic ability.
4 There is a potential to increase children's self-esteem by encouraging them to identify positive qualities in one another and to find constructive ways of giving negative feedback. Realistic feedback raises academic self-esteem (Burns 1982; Coopersmith 1967).
5 There is a clear link in the research between academic self-esteem and academic achievement (Hamachek 1986; Burns 1982). It is possible, therefore, that groupwork may well be more effective in getting academic improvements than direct one-to-one teaching by adults (Lawrence 1988).

For a more detailed programme of teaching these techniques see McNamara and Moreton (1993, 1995, in press).

COOPERATIVE GROUPWORK

Cooperative groupwork is a more sophisticated development of basic groupwork. As Johnson and Johnson (1975) point out, the skills needed for cooperative groupwork are numerous. McNamara and Moreton have found in their own teaching that it does takes time to teach these skills – about three weeks for three-year-olds, three months for five and six-year-olds, nine months for ten and eleven-year-olds, and eighteen months for fifteen and sixteen-year-olds. However, their experience showed that, once the youngsters are proficient in these skills, cooperative groupwork is relatively easy for them.

The evidence of student-improved achievement through cooperative groupwork is voluminous. Slavin produces reviews of the research evidence about once every five years, and there are always hundreds of studies that have been carefully structured with control groups which show that, provided you teach pupils the skills for groupwork, set group goals and demand individual participation within the group, the pupils of all abilities will achieve better academic results then when working alone (Slavin 1995). This is particularly true for pupils with special educational needs in mainstream classrooms (Slavin *et al.* 1991; Smith *et al.* 1994; Slavin *et al.* 1994).

PEER TUTORING

Peer tutoring is a powerful tool for enabling those with special needs to receive help in a way that does not emphasise their difference so much. It also enables them to give help to others and so experience the rise in self-worth that usually accompanies such an act. In the peer tutoring example in China quoted on page 68, for example, the tutor was the bright and able child. Topping's research shows that, while both tutor and tutee gain from the pairing, it is the tutor who gains most, and peer tutoring therefore has enormous potential for enhancing both self-worth and academic achievement for the child with special needs. Many of the typically 'special needs practices', such as teaching a phonics approach to reading, target setting, or breaking the task into small steps, can be used by students with special needs to teach to younger pupils or those whose difficulties are more profound than their own.

The problem with the small steps approach is usually that of motivation, but in peer tutoring the motivational issue is overcome by the fact that the two children decide together the approach they will take.

It is also the case that children who themselves have experienced difficulties in reading over a long period are often 'experts' in reading strategies, because they themselves have experienced every possible technique. For example, in one school an eleven-year-old boy with a sight vocabulary of thirty words came running back from his first peer tutoring session in the nursery shouting, 'Miss, miss, we've got to do a phonic puppet show – they don't know their sounds!'

When pupils start to teach other pupils they give each other attention instead of demanding it from adults, and the need for more adults starts to be reduced. In addition, peer tutoring research shows that children are often better than adults at structuring the learning for one another (Topping, 1988; Goodlad and Hirst 1989).

CONCLUSION

The evidence from some small-scale research carried out by this author is that, when these skills training programmes are put into place and the self-esteem of all pupils – but especially those with special needs – starts to rise, the support teacher becomes someone in great demand. In this situation it is possible to imagine all the students in the class as a matter of course identifying their own strengths and weaknesses, target setting around those areas of weakness and, in peer tutoring pairs, writing their own individual education programmes using the consultative help of class teacher and special needs support teacher. This is a very different job description to the one currently envisaged by many support teachers, faced with a workload of twenty and more IEPs to devise as part of their weekend's work.

In any one country or district, or even in any one school, there are likely to be different approaches to the education of children with special needs, but the traditional view is still largely predominant and is working with varying degrees of effectiveness. The challenges to this traditional view give rise to innovatory practices, often resulting from school-based research projects. Meeting special educational needs demands creative responses, but when such responses are developed into new teaching styles and strategies, we get the best practice, not just for those with special needs, but for all our children.

REFERENCES

Abrahmson, L. Y., Seligman, M. E. P. and Teasdale, J. (1978) 'Learned Helplessness in Humans: Critique and Reformulation,' *Journal of Abnormal Psychology*, 87, 49–74.

Ainscow, M. (ed.) (1991) *Effective Schools For All*, London: David Fulton.

—— (1994) *Special Needs in the Classroom: A Teacher Education Guide*, London: Jessica Kingsley/UNESCO.

Ashman, A. F. (1995) 'The education of students with an intellectual disability in the People's Republic of China: some observations', *European Journal of Special Needs Education*, 10(1), 47–57.

Audit Commission/HMI (1992) *Getting the Act Together. Provision for Pupils with Special Educational Needs. A Management Handbook*, London: HMSO.

Borba, M. and Borba, C. (1978) *Self Esteem a Classroom Affair. 101 ways to help children like themselves*, San Francisco: Harper and Row.

Burman, L., Farrell, P., Feiler, A., Heffernen, J., Mittler, H. and Reason, R. (1983) 'Redesigning the School Curriculum', *Special Education: Forward Trends*, 10(2),

Burns, R. B. (1982) *Self-Concept in Education*, London: Holt, Reinhart and Winston.

Burt, C. (1921) *Mental and Scholastic Tests*, London County Council.

Clarke, A. M. and Clarke, A. D. B. (1976) *Early Experience: Myth and Evidence*, New York: The Free Press.

Clarke, A. D. B. and Herman-Fleiss, B. (1955) 'Adult imbeciles, their abilities and trainability', *Lancet*, 2, 337–9.

Clarke, C., Dyson A. and Millward, A. (eds) (1995) *Towards Inclusive Schools?*, London: David Fulton.

Clarke, C., Dyson, A., Millward, A. and Skidmore, D. (1995) 'Dialectical Analysis, Special Needs and Schools as Organisations', in C. Clarke, A. Dyson and A. Millward (eds) *Towards Inclusive Schools?*, London: David Fulton.

Coopersmith, S. (1967) *The Antecedents of Self-Esteem*, San Francisco: Freeman Press.

Craske, M. L. (1988) 'Learned Helplessnes, Self Worth, Motivation and Attribution Retraining for Primary School Children', *British Journal of Educational Psychology*, 58, 152–64.

Croll, P. and Moses, D. (1994) 'Policy making and Special Educational Needs; a framework for analysis', *European Journal of Special Educational Needs*, 9(3), 275–87.

DES (1975) *A Language for Life* (The Bullock Report), London: HMSO.

—— (1978) *Special Educational Needs* (The Warnock Report), London: HMSO.

—— (1989) *English for Ages 5–16* (The Cox Report), London: HMSO.

Dessent, T. (1987) *Making Ordinary Schools Special*, Lewes: Falmer Press.

Dweck, C. S. (1975) 'The Role of Expectations and Attributions in the Alleviation of Learned Helplessness', *Journal of Personality and Social Psychology*, 31, 674–85.

Fish, J. and Evans, J. (1995) *Managing Special Education, Codes, Charters and Competition*, Buckingham: Open University Press.

Gardner, H. (1993) *The unschooled mind. How children think and how schools should teach*, London: Fontana.

Gold, M. W. (1973) 'Factors affecting production of the retarded: base rate', *Mental Retardation*, 11(6), 41–5

Goleman, D. (1996) *Emotional Intelligence, why it can matter more than IQ*, London: Bloomsbury.

Goodlad, S. and Hirst, B. (1989) *Peer Tutoring: A Guide to Learning by Teaching*, London: Kogan and Page.

Gurney, P. (1988) *Self-Esteem in Children with Special Educational Needs*, London: Routledge.

Hamachek, D. E. (1986) *Encounters With Self*, New York: Holt Reinhart and Winston.

Hopkins, D. (1995) 'Essential Conditions for Effective Classrooms', *Times Educational Supplement*, 6 October 1995.

Horner, R. D. and Keilitz, I. (1975) 'Training mentally retarded adolescents to brush their teeth', *Journal of Applied Behaviour Analysis*, 8, 301–9.

Jaques, D. (1984) *Learning in Groups*, London: Croom Helm.

Johnson, D. W. and Johnson, F. P. (1982) *Joining Together Group Theory and Group Skills* (2nd edn), Englewood Cliffs, NJ: Prentice Hall.

Johnson, D. W., Johnson, R. T. (1975) *Learning Together and Alone: Co-operation, Competition and Individualisation*, Englewood Cliffs, NJ: Prentice Hall.

Johnson, D. W., Johnson, R. T. and Howbec, E. J. (1986) *Circles of Learning Co-operation in the Classroom*, Edina: Interaction Book Company.

Kingsley Mills, C., McNamara, S. and Woodward, L. (1992) *Out From Behind The Desk*, Leicester: Leicestershire LEA.

Lawrence, D. (1973) *Improved reading through Counselling*, London: Ward Lock.

—— (1988) *Enhancing Self-Esteem in the Classroom*, London: Paul Chapman.

McNamara, S. and Moreton, G. (1993) *Teaching Special Needs*, London: David Fulton.

—— (1995) *Changing Behaviour*, London: David Fulton.

—— (in press) *Understanding Differentiation – a guide for primary teachers*, London: David Fulton.

McNamara, S., Moreton, G. and Newton, H. (1996) *Differentiation*, Cambridge: Pearson.

Mittler, P. (1995) 'Special needs education: an international perspective', *British Journal of Special Education*, 22(3), Sept., 105–8.

Mosley, J. (1993) *Turn Your School Around*, Wisbech: LDA.

—— (1994) *You Choose*, Wisbech: LDA.

Newcomer, P. L. and Hammill, D. D. (1975) 'ITPA and academic achievement', *Reading Teacher*, 28, 731–42.

OECD/CERI (1981) *The Education of the Handicapped Adolescent. Integration in the School*, Paris: OECD.

—— (1981) *The Integration of the Handicapped in Secondary Schools. Five Case Studies*, Paris: OECD.

Pijl, S. J. and Meijer, C. J. W. (1991) 'Does integration count for much? An analysis of the practices of integration in eight countries', *European Journal of Special Needs Education*, 6(2), 100–11

Piskin, M. (1996) *Self esteem – a cross cultural study*, unpublished PhD thesis, Leicester University.

Potts, P. (1995) 'Reforming special education in China', in P. Potts, F. Armstrong and M. Masterton *Equality and Diversity in Education: 2. National and International Contexts*, London: Routledge and The Open University.

Purkey, W. (1970) *Self-Concept and School Achievement*, New York: Prentice Hall.

Reynolds, D. (1995) 'Using School Effectiveness Knowledge for Children with Special Needs – The Problems and Possibilities', in C. Clarke, A. Dyson and A. Millward *Towards Inclusive Schools?*, London: David Fulton.

Schmuck, R. A. and Schmuck, P. A. (1977) *Group Processes In The Classroom*, Iowa: W. C. Brown.

Sharan, S. and Kussell, P. (1984) *Co-Operative Learning In The Classroom; research in desgregated schools*. Hillsdale, NJ: Lawrence Erlbaum.

Skaalvik, E. M. and Hagtvet, K. A. (1990) 'Academic Achievement and Self-Concept: an Analysis of Causal Predominance in a Developmental Perspective', *Journal of Personality and Social Psychology*, 58(2), 292–307.

Slavin, R. E. (1983) *Co-Operative Learning*, London: Longman.

—— (1995) *Cooperative Learning: Theory, Research and Practice*, Boston, MA: Allyn and Bacon.

Slavin, R. E., Karwait, N. L. and Wasik, B. A. (1994) *Preventing Early School Failure: Research on effective strategies*, Boston, MA: Allyn and Bacon.

Slavin, R. E., Madden, N. A., Karwait, N. L., Dolan, L. and Wasik, B. A. (1991)

'Neverstreaming: Prevention and Early Intervention as alternatives to special education', *Journal of Learning Disabilities*, 24, 373–8.

Slee, R. (1995) 'Inclusive Education: From Policy to School Implementation', in C. Clarke, A. Dyson and A. Millward *Towards Inclusive Schools?*, London: David Fulton.

Smith, L. J., Ross, S. M. and Casey, J. P. (1994) *Special Education Analyses of Success For All in Four Cities*, Memphis, TN: University of Memphis, Center for Research in Educational Policy.

Stainback, S. and Stainback, W. (eds) (1992) *Curriculum Considerations in Inclusive Classrooms: Facilitating Learning for all students*, Baltimore, MD: Paul H. Brookes.

Stanford, G. (1977) *Developing Effective Classroom Groups*, New York: Hart.

Thomas, G. and Feiler, A. (1992) *Planning for Special Needs*, Hemel Hempstead: Simon and Schuster Education.

Thousand, A. S. and Villa, R. A. (1991) 'Accommodating for Greater Student Variance', in M. Ainscow (ed.) *Effective Schools For All*, London: David Fulton.

Thousand, A. S., Villa, R. A. and Nevin, A. (eds) (1994) *Creativity and Collaborative Learning: A Practical Guide to Empowering Students and Teachers*, Baltimore, MD: Paul H. Brookes.

Topping, K. (1988) *The Peer Tutoring Handbook*, London: Croom Helm.

Tough, J. (1977) *The Development of Meaning*, London: Allen and Unwin.

UNESCO (1994) *The Salamanca World Conference Declaration*, Paris: UNESCO.

—— (1995) *World Conference on Special Needs Education: Access and Equality*, Paris: UNESCO.

Vygotsky, L. S. (1962) *Thought and Language*, Cambridge, MA: MIT Press.

Wade, B. and Moore, M. (1993) *Experiencing Special Education: What young people with special educational needs can tell us*, Buckingham: Open University Press.

Ware, J. (1990) 'Severe Learning Difficulties and Multiple Handicaps: Curriculum Developments, Integration and Prospects' in P. Evans and V. Varma *Special Education: Past, Present and Future*, Lewes: Falmer Press.

Ware, L. (1995), 'The aftermath of the Articulate Debate: The Invention of Inclusive Education', in C. Clarke, A. Dyson and A. Millward *Towards Inclusive Schools?*, London: David Fulton.

Wedell, K. (1995) 'Making Inclusive Education Ordinary', *British Journal of Special Education*, 22(3), Sept., 100–4.

Wells, G. (1985) *Language and Learning – an Interactive Perspective*, Lewes: Falmer Press.

—— (1986) *Meaning makers – Children Learning Language to Learn*, London: Hodder and Stoughton.

Welton, J. and Evans, J. (1986) 'The development and implementation of special education policy: where did the 1981 Act fit in?', *Public Administration*, 64, 209–27.

Wolfendale, S. (1987) *Primary Schools and Special Needs – policy planning and provision*, London: Cassell.

Chapter 5

Keeping track

Observing, assessing and recording in the learning relationship

Susan Cavendish and Jean Underwood

Assessment encompasses *'all methods customarily used to appraise performance of an individual pupil or a group. It may refer to a broad appraisal including many sources of evidence and many aspects of a pupil's knowledge, understanding, skills and attitudes; or to a particular occasion or instrument. An assessment instrument may be any method or procedure, formal or informal, for producing information about pupils: e.g. a written test paper, an interview schedule, a measurement task using equipment, a class quiz.'*

(DES 1988: Preface and Glossary)

INTRODUCTION

A key aim of this chapter is to support the reflective approach to teaching and learning which is discussed more fully in Chapter 7. In this we are encouraging teachers to move away from a competency-based or technician model of teaching towards a model which stresses the need for practitioners to monitor their own teaching behaviour and the ways in which that behaviour affects the pupils in their classrooms. Such reflection, we would argue, is best supported by the collection of evidence from the classroom.

ASSESSMENT

Decision-making is central to teaching, whether it is viewed as an art or a science. It includes decisions about what to teach, how to teach it and how to assess the effectiveness of our teaching strategies in relation to our initial teaching and learning goals. *Assessment* requires either *measurement* or *evaluation*, or both. The use of a spelling test to assess how many words a child has learnt is measurement. As a teacher, you may go on to reflect upon whether a particular child has performed as well as or better than you had expected: that is, you will evaluate their performance. However, evaluation need not always be based on measurement. We make 'value' judgements, such as 'Jane is not working well this morning', about individual pupils every day. It is not wrong to make such intuitive evaluations, and informal observation of our classroom is valuable. If, however, we view teaching as a decision-making activity, then the more information we gather the better, and measurement provides us with key information on which to make better-informed decisions in the future.

The assessment process has three key steps:

1 elicitation of evidence;
2 interpretation of that evidence;
3 actions consequent upon those interpretations.

A classroom is a complex place in which many individuals with different preferences and abilities work to accomplish a variety of personal, social and imposed goals. There is no one perfect way to assess children's development and learning. In planning and managing an assessment there will always be critical decisions, and we can begin by asking two basic questions – *why* are we assessing, and *what* are we assessing?.

Why is the assessment needed?

To inform classroom practice

Finding the starting point is one important role of assessment in education. It is recognised that teaching should start where the child is and develop onwards from that point. Another important role of assessment is to inform the teacher of the success or otherwise of their teaching, to help them to reflect on and review the strategies they employed.

> Assessments of pupils are not, nor can they be, statements of absolute ability. They are statements about achievements within the framework of educational opportunities that have actually been provided. In some degree every assessment of a pupil is also an assessment of the teachers and of the school.
>
> (Calouste Gulbenkian Foundation 1982: 82)

Such formative assessment is that which provides information which influences the organisation and structure of learning for both the individual and the whole class.

To inform the learner

Feedback to the pupils can take many forms. Whether the feedback is through praise or encouragement, comments on written work, or by giving a mark or grade, the effect is to inform the learner about where their future effort should be directed and enable them to become more autonomous. Hewitt and Bennett (1989) have argued that motivation and the feeling of ownership of learning are improved when pupils take responsibility for their own learning, understand what is required of them, set their own realistic goals and evaluate their own performance in the light of them.

To inform school policy

All schools need to develop clear, coherent educational goals and to evaluate their effectiveness in achieving those goals. Such summative evaluation focuses on outcome measures, such as the end of course or year exam results, and can act as a stimulus for staff development.

To inform outside agents

Teachers are being made increasingly accountable for pupil progress, and schools have to be aware of their performance in comparison with other schools, and to make that performance more public. In England and Wales, Standard Attainment Targets (SATs) have been developed to fulfil this role.

What are we assessing?

The relationship between the objectives of teaching and learning and their assessment is often taken as self-evident. The teacher teaches, the learner learns, and then we assess how much of the 'knowledge' the learner has acquired. But it is not as simple as that. Even if our objective is the acquisition of a body of knowledge, concepts and skills, the choice of measuring instrument may affect our results. For example, you could assess children's spelling by asking them to write down a standard list of words presented orally by the teacher, but you might get very different scores if children were asked to reproduce those words in a story. Measurement becomes even more complex if we not only want children to acquire knowledge, concepts and skills, but also to show an ability to apply them in new situations, or if our goal is to cause a shift in attitudes. (See Chapter 3 for a discussion of these issues.)

If we as teachers really want to reflect on the effectiveness of our practice, it is vital that we clearly specify our objectives. In our everyday teaching we measure children's performance using a range of formal and informal measuring instruments, from standardised reading tests through to creative writing exercises, but how can these instruments tell us whether or not our practice has been effective if we don't know what our objectives are? If our goal is to encourage children to transfer problem-solving skills, there is little point in developing a test instrument that merely replicates the original learning experience.

The form and method of assessment should vary with the activity and the type of information sought. How can we, as teachers, assess the effectiveness of our teaching and learning programme unless we know what the intended outcomes are? Equally, how can we select a measuring instrument if we cannot state what the outcomes of our teaching should be? The prerequisite of any assessment must be a clear definition of what is to be assessed, though in practice it is often easier to identify a high-quality piece of work than to say in detail why it is good. Assessment should be a continuous process of gathering and reviewing information, in order to help pupils succeed in the classroom.

Information can be collected by various means, including tests, questioning, written work and observation. Each of these methods has its own limitations. Using the end product of children's work, for example, may not be indicative of what they can do. Celia Hoyles *et al.* (1985) description of children programming in LOGO is a classic example of how the end product of a working session can sometimes reveal very little about the child's thinking. She noted that one pair of boys had produced a wonderful spiral across the computer screen. They were very proud of their efforts. When she returned again they had a second complex pattern, and this continued for several lessons. However, although the patterns were stunning, it became apparent that the boys had borrowed the initial short program from the boys working on the next computer. They had not created the program themselves. The wonderful patterns were a result of simple changes in the number of sides or the angle of turn in their program. The end product of such changes was spectacular, but the thinking behind it was very low level. The general conclusion is, therefore, that there should be more than one source of evidence for assessment purposes.

Types of assessment in the classroom

Bearing in mind the two questions of *what* and *why* are we assessing, we can now consider what types of assessment are available to teachers. According to Thomas (1990), there are three main forms of assessment used in primary schools:

- informal assessment;
- formal assessment;
- summary assessment.

Informal assessment is that continually undertaken during the normal course of the teaching day. The teacher monitors the children's performance and gets an impression of the successes and difficulties of each child. The learning relationship here may become one in which the child is constantly attempting to understand what the teacher requires of them and to react and behave accordingly. Feedback to these children is by means of the teacher's smiles, nodding of head and use of praise.

Formal assessment may take the form of tests produced by the teacher, or published 'standardised' tests which provide information on the child relative to other children of the same age. Observation may also be a formal measure if structured observation methods are employed. The role of the teacher here is that of a formal 'tester' and, as such, the relationship with the child changes. Here, the child has to work by itself, without the support normally available from the teacher. In schools where formal testing is commonplace the children become accustomed to this change in relationship and do not even attempt to initiate interaction with the teacher. However, where formal testing is not so common, the children may be rather bewildered at the sudden independence they have in their work. It is not surprising, therefore, that familiarity with the testing situation can exert some influence on the child's level of performance on the test. Feedback from these tests is in the form of a mark or grade indicating the child's achievement in relation to their peers. The teacher has to take a sensitive role here, to ensure that low-achieving children do not come to view themselves as failures. (See Chapter 4.)

Summary assessment draws together information from both formal and informal assessments to provide a record of the pupils' progress over a period of time. This information may be collated in the form of a Record of Achievement (ROA), providing a profile of a pupil's achievements and progress, both within and outside school. A key feature of an ROA is the involvement of pupils in their own assessment by means of dialogue between pupils and teachers. The learning relationship between teacher and pupil here is a partnership in which negotiated targets can be set and individual curricular needs and learning objectives identified.

Methods of assessment

No one form of assessment is capable of providing complete information. Quite often, teachers and researchers use a combination of methods to gather the evidence they need. Methods of assessment may include:

- oral questioning;
- written work;
- use of tests;
- observation.

Each of these methods can be used formally or informally. When gathered informally, the information may be largely intuitive, but because in the past many teachers have emphasised such informal assessment, the next section will focus on formal methods.

There are several important issues to consider when deciding on the form of assessment to use. We need to know that the assessment is *valid*: that is, that our assessment of the child's performance is a true measure of the knowledge or skill which we are intending to assess. We also need to take account of the *reliability* of the measure, or its consistency. Written tests are usually designed with high reliability, so that performance on one test is very similar to performance on a subsequent test. Written tests of this form have led to a lively debate as to their validity, and some researchers have argued that such tests are not useful (see, e.g., Holt 1964). Other researchers have argued that written tests can be devised to have high validity while retaining reliability (see, e.g., Schilling *et al.* 1990).

Schilling *et al.* devised a written assessment which was built into the general work activity within the classroom. This form of assessment can be treated as a normal part of the day's activities and helps to reduce the anxiety normally caused by testing. The researchers recognised that this form of testing does have problems of its own, putting added emphasis on the child's comprehension skills and powers of concentration. To overcome these problems the research team placed importance on observation as a means of assessing pupil performance. When a teacher is dealing with a class of over thirty pupils there are obvious advantages in using a written test for practical reasons. Yet the detail of information that can be acquired through observation makes it a valuable assessment technique. If a child succeeds on a written test then one can be fairly confident that the child has provided evidence of possessing the knowledge or skill being tested. If, however, a child fails on the written test, one cannot be sure that the child does not possess the knowledge or skill, or whether the child has difficulties with the form of the test. One strategy that can overcome this difficulty is to use a written test for the whole class, and on the basis of those results identify a few children for further investigation. These children can then be the focus of observation or the teacher can use an in-depth questioning technique (oral questioning accompanying a practical task), such as one used by Russell and Harlen (1990) for testing primary children's use of science processes. One might go further, given the time and human resources, to suggest that to obtain a complete assessment of development and learning, the ideal situation would be one in which the child is assessed by all three methods: that is, they have a written test, an in-depth practical test (of application) as well as being observed while working.

All teachers tend to use performance outcome measures because they are readily accessible and therefore more easily measured. However, the assessment of intellectual thinking, such as the development of science processes investigated by the STAR project (Cavendish *et al.* 1990), is problematic. For example, if we see children measuring the temperature of a cup of tea we might infer that they are investigating the rate of cooling. But if we watch again, they might re-measure the temperature using a second type of thermometer, because they are in fact conducting a survey into the ease of use of several different thermometers. Any assessment of intellectual processes, rather than knowledge and skills, depends on our ability to get at and to understand children's thinking, which is the concern of the opening three chapters of this book.

Since it is not possible to assess a child's thought processes directly, we have to collect evidence relating to the product of those thought processes. The most usual product is a piece of finished written work, but observation helps the teacher by providing information from ongoing interactions while the child is working. Indeed, the Primary Assessment, Curriculum and Experience Project (Broadfoot *et al.* 1991) found that observation of individuals was a major area of innovation in assessment practice. They also found that many teachers had experience of observation but not necessarily for assessment purposes, and generally conducted such observations in a general rather than a specific way. Because of the value of observation for assessment and the relatively limited experience of its use as a formal technique, the following section will focus on observation as a method of collecting evidence.

OBSERVATION

Formal and informal observation

Informal methods of observation involve the teacher in collecting information while working with children as part of their normal learning relationship, but it is on the basis of often very short interactions that teachers make judgements about a child's thinking, and there are pitfalls when using such informal observations (see Cavendish *et al.* 1990). Teachers often have preconceived ideas about pupils' motives behind their actions, and observations may be interpreted within that preconceived framework. They may instinctively protect their pupils, so that when failure occurs they look for external causes rather than 'blaming' the children. (Chapter 4 discusses how we attribute failure to different things.)

A further difficulty with informal observation is for it to be selective, because we can observe only what we are aware of. For example, when a group of teachers was asked to watch a lesson and make their own informal observations, they were amazed to find that all of their resulting observations were concerned with lesson management and organisation. There was no mention of the fact that it was a science lesson, or of its content, or of the scientific interactions that were taking place between the pupils in the video. When, however, the teachers watched the video for a second time, having been through a short science workshop themselves, the observations were far more detailed in terms of the science learning they thought was being demonstrated by the children. This example shows that awareness of what you want to know from the observation is a key issue. If, as teachers, we only make general observations, important detail may well go unnoticed.

Clearly, if accurate assessment about intellectual processing is required, then some more formal method would be appropriate. Post-task interview has been one method employed by several workers (see, e.g., Bennett et al. 1984). This method involved the pupils taking the interviewer back through the steps of working on a task so that the interviewer could identify where the pupils went wrong. This method, though useful and fruitful, is very time consuming and, while caution in the use of informal classroom observation is advised, the value of observation for assessing intellectual processes is widely accepted. In order to overcome some of the difficulties, researchers have developed several procedures which enable classroom observation to be valuable while at the same time being practical for teachers to use. Croll (1986) provides an extensive description of different observation methods, and Simpson and Tuson (1995) offer a useful introduction to using observation in small-scale research.

The two main types of observation methods which have been developed for classroom use are *systematic (structured) observation* and *participant observation*. In systematic observation, the observer first has to define the particular behaviours of interest and a method of coding the observed behaviours. This approach has been used by several classroom research projects, including ORACLE (Galton and Simon 1980), and the STAR project (Cavendish et al. 1990). In participant observation, the observer takes an active role in the proceedings, participating in activities with the people being studied. Structured observation has been criticised for failing to provide a full picture of the classroom, because the observer simply records ticks against a limited set of observed behaviours to get frequency counts. Participant observation has been criticised because, given that pupils are known to say what they think the teacher wants to hear, one cannot be sure whether the pupils are telling the truth to the teacher/interviewer. Both methods of observation, therefore, complement each other and should not be viewed as alternatives (Galton and Delamont 1985).

Participant observation

Participant observation is derived from anthropological and sociological research which involves the observer taking field notes over a period of time long enough to become accepted as a participant in the group being observed. Unlike systematic observation, where the observer remains outside the classroom interactions, the participant observer takes an active role. Advocates of this method of observation believe that actions and interactions only have meaning as a result of shared understandings of the participants. Triangulation procedures are important in this form of observation: i.e., observations are made and interpreted by more than one of the participants. In the classroom, then, the observer, the teacher and the pupils themselves would be asked their views about the same lesson.

Structured observation

Structured observation is the systematic recording on grids or checklists of specific behaviours. The main outcome of such recordings is how often such behaviours occur in particular situations or in different phases of an activity or lesson. The range of behaviours to be observed is pre-determined to minimise the level of inferential judgement about what is happening. Structured observation is a useful method for collecting quantifiable data for assessment purposes and will, therefore, be described at some length here.

In the STAR research project, the researchers and teachers were interested in assessing science processes used by primary children. A structured observation schedule was developed, the Science Processes Observation Categories (SPOC). Figure 5.1 shows a sample of the SPOC coding sheet. This section of the observation schedule contains the science processes which were the main concern of the STAR project. The work of Ennever and Harlen (1972) and the APU (1980, 1984) contributed to the development of the set of process skills to be observed. The final list of observation categories

> derived from consideration of the nature of science activities and of what skills it was useful for teachers to identify as separate foci for children's development, and hence for assessment and review.
>
> (Cavendish *et al.* 1990)

Individual pupils were observed for two-minute intervals, four times in each of four lessons. If, for the first round (two-minute interval) of observation, the pupil observed was actively involved in discussion about scientific observations, then a code of 1 was written into the box appropriate for the first observation round. If, however, the pupil was part of the audience to discussion, but not actively involved, then a code of 2 was written into the appropriate space. In addition, the researchers wished to know whether the teacher was involved in the interaction with the pupils, and if so a letter T was added to the box.

Once the observations were completed, the category codings were counted to obtain the frequency of occurrence over the whole observa-

	Pupil Name									
Observation round		1	2		3	4	1	2		3	4
Dialogue involves pupil in	9.1 discussing observations										
	9.2 interpretation										
	9.3 hypothesising										
	9.4 general planning										
	9.5 discuss specific plans/proc.										
	9.6 measurement										
	9.7 recording										
	9.8 raising questions										
	9.9 critical reflection										
Other pupil talk	10.1 recall of previous learning										
	10.2 recap of work done										
	10.3 read out/discuss instructions										
	10.4 about meaning of words										
	10.5 asking for help										
	10.6 organising task										
	10.7 non-task										

Figure 5.1 An extract from the SPOC Observation Coding sheet

tion period. In this particular example, the STAR team found that pupils were involved in discussing scientific observations for 33.5 per cent of the observed time, and of this the teacher was involved for 10 per cent. When frequencies are obtained across all of the categories, one obtains an indication of the pattern of science talk in that classroom. Further details of the entire observation schedule can be found in Cavendish *et al.* (1990).

Observation systems usually contain a range of *high inference* and *low inference* categories. Low inference categories are those easily identified, such as where a pupil is sitting, or whether the pupil is moving around the classroom. High inference categories are those which are less specific and require the observer to be somewhat more subjective and perhaps to observe for a time before being able to infer about the behaviour. When the activities are complex, as in observation of science processes, a system should be used in which the observer concentrates on a small number of behaviours/interactions and ignores others which are relevant to the whole lesson but not required continuously: e.g., one might be interested in the age or sex of the pupil or the social mix in which they are sitting, and this can just be recorded once at the beginning of the observation period.

The choice of who to observe depends on the purpose of the observation. If the purpose is for the assessment of particular children, then those children alone would become the targets for observation, and other children not recorded. If, however, the purpose is for feedback to the teacher on how effective was the organisation and management of the lesson, then it would be advisable to sample pupils who are representative of the whole class: i.e., a balance of achievement levels, age, etc.

Another method commonly employed by researchers is *time sampling*. In time sampling the observer records exactly what happens at an instant, with each observation taking place at, say, 25-second intervals or at whatever length interval is deemed appropriate. An observation schedule with many or complex categories would require longer time between observations for the observer to record all the information required at each instant. The result of these observations is a frequency count for each category, giving an overall impression of the lesson observed. Another method is to observe over an interval of time. This involves the observer recording all that happens over a short period, perhaps using a column for each second of observation. The results from this *interval observation* provide a more accurate picture of the classroom but the method requires intense effort and concentration on the part of the observer. A *continuous record* was used by Cavendish (1988) in her study of interaction and behaviour in mathematics lessons. In the majority of sessions, the continuous record was manageable, as behaviour while children are working through mathematics problems does not change quickly. The difficulties experienced were during quick-fire question-and-answer sessions – a teaching method often employed when teaching mathematics from the blackboard. The method usefully employed for observation, therefore, should be chosen to suit the classroom situation in which it is to be used and, in most cases, teachers are likely to want to develop their own observation schedule, tailored to their own assessment needs.

Developing your own observation schedule

Teachers have their own preferences for certain styles of teaching and classroom organisation. Their needs are likely to be different from those of educational researchers, and the method of assessing pupil progress and effectiveness of teaching, therefore, also needs to be individually designed. In order to develop an observation schedule, teachers need to:

- Be aware of exactly what they are looking for. The assessment of pupils needs to be focused.
- Collect evidence in a recorded form which is useful in providing information to others, whether they are colleagues, parents or the children themselves.
- Organise time to allow for observation – this may be by planning tasks of low teacher-intensitivity for the class of pupils, or by using other

people to help, for example student teachers or non-teaching head teachers.

Getting started

The simplest type of observation schedule is a blank piece of paper. Several teachers have reported the need to start in this way – taking notes of anything they observe during a lesson. It only takes one or two lessons to find that full notes are time-consuming, and also that some statements tend to recur several times during one session. A need for shorthand recording of the observations then becomes apparent. Figure 5.2 shows one possible next step for an observation schedule. Here, some basic information is collected at the top, followed by a list of categories for observation and blank spaces for comments or tallies as the teacher desires. A more detailed type of schedule is that of the SPOC, described earlier, but for most teachers this schedule would be far too detailed to manage while in charge of a whole class. An in-between type of schedule is one that includes detailed categories for some information, together with spaces for more open comments. Further examples of systematic observation schedules used by classroom teachers can be found in Hargreaves (1995).

Pupil Name .... Sex .... Age ....

Curriculum Area ....

Pupil talk	about the task	
	about resources	
	off-task	
Pupil listen	about the task	
	about resources	
	off-task	

Comments:

Figure 5.2 An example of a simple observation schedule

Finding time for observation

The biggest difficulty for teachers to overcome is finding the time and opportunity to observe in their own classroom. Each teacher has their own individual way of working and, while some work closely with others, as in team teaching, many teachers are in a solitary teaching environment. One of the STAR teachers was initially sceptical about the feasibility of observation in his classroom, yet, at the end of the project, he was helping other teachers by describing how he managed to do it successfully. What he did, in fact, was to analyse the demands on his time during a lesson and identify time-consuming periods. He subsequently changed his organisation and planned the tasks in such a way that the children could work more independently. More detail about this teacher's approach can be found in Cavendish *et al.* (1990: 85).

Teachers can be their own worst enemies in management of their time. Many like to feel wanted in the classroom. If children get on by themselves, teachers feel redundant, and so lessons are often managed such that the teacher is constantly in demand or busy with general classroom duties, such as handling resources or putting up displays. This desire to be needed makes it difficult for behaviour to change. Just like the sceptical teacher described above, teachers need to stand back and look at what is happening in the classroom, and to question their own role. Are there stages of a lesson which are less demanding on the teacher? Can the organisation of pupils be changed to allow more independence, and hence more efficient and focused use of the teacher's time?

When a teacher is the sole adult in charge of a class of 30 or more pupils, he or she will only be able to concentrate on a limited field of observation. Here, there is a choice: the teacher can limit the observation to very broad categories rather than very finely differentiated behaviours, or can concentrate on just one or two fine behaviour categories which have previously been determined as important for the purposes of the assessment. The number of pupils observed may also vary, according to what the teacher is trying to find out. It may be that only one child needs to be observed if the purpose is diagnostic, or a group of pupils may be observed. If the teacher requires feedback on how successful a whole lesson has been, then it is more likely that a sample of pupils across the classroom will be selected for observation throughout the lesson period.

Recording learning outcomes

We have discussed at length some methods for gathering information as evidence for assessment purposes, but the findings from this data-gathering need to be communicated to appropriate audiences. At the beginning of this chapter, the following reasons for assessment were given:

- to inform classroom practice;
- to inform the learner;
- to inform school policy;
- to inform outside agents.

This 'informing' necessitates the passing on of recorded information in a form that will be useful. Once written down, records of information can become the basis for reflection, comparison and discussion. The establishment of a National Curriculum in the UK and Australia, and the accompanying assessment procedures, have led to particular requirements in record-keeping to enable comparison of pupil performance not only from one year to the next, but also between one school and another. The detailed assessment required at a national level, for comparison of schools, is essentially different from that required by the classroom teacher. The form which the record takes, then, greatly depends on its purpose. If, for example, a school is interested in developing a particular curriculum area, teachers would need to keep detailed records with a definite focus, thus providing factual information as a basis for discussion about curriculum and staff development. If the progress of individual children is the main interest, a profile of achievement in different areas for each child would be more appropriate.

Systematic observation, when used in combination with teacher ratings and more formal written assessments, adds validity to the profiles of pupils' attainments. Based on these measures, the importance of formative assessments in demonstrating the current levels of achievement of pupils does not rule out the use of such profiles for diagnostic purposes. This process can be helped by the development of the Records of Achievement (ROA) approach into the primary school. This approach of recording achievement leads to the involvement of pupils in their own development, by means of negotiation in both teaching and learning. Not only does this fit in well with the philosophy of primary education, but it is also consistent with recent theories of how children learn, as discussed in the first three chapters of this book, and, for example, by Wood (1988). The findings from the evaluation projects associated with Records of Achievement Study show that, where this model of teaching and learning has been applied successfully, it has great impact on pupils' motivation and self-esteem.

The development of ROAs in the UK has gone hand-in-hand with two other developments – the rise in the availability of computer-based record systems and the move to local management of schools (LMS). The need for some form of computer-based management system in primary schools only became apparent with the 1988 Education Reform Act (DES

1988), while the move to LMS, with all that it implied for devolved budgeting, generated a ready – some might say a desperate – need for systems to support heads and governors facing a range of new responsibilities. The system known as SIMS (Schools Information Management System) has come to dominate the management market, but rival products are being developed, including KEY SOLUTIONS and PIMS (Primary Information Management Systems).

Computer Assisted Assessment covers:

- recording and analysing progress;
- reporting on student achievement;
- recording prior achievement and prior learning;
- all functions for the registration and certification of candidates;
- computer assisted or computer delivered tests and examinations.

As computer based assessment and recording methods become more widely available, the potential value of the information will increase. Where assessment and record-keeping are completed solely by the classroom teacher, the constraints of time and effort will limit the amount of detailed information entered on any assessment record and hence will impede the effective use of assessment evidence for changing and improving classroom practice. However, the first step towards effective use of assessment is the acceptance that formal, rather than informal, assessment can provide quantitative data which is more informative, more efficient and a more reliable form of evidence. This formal evidence complements informal assessment and contributes to raising the status of records on children's development and learning. If the status of the information increases, the recipients of that information are more likely to act upon the content and effect change.

SUMMARY AND CONCLUSIONS

It was stated at the beginning of this chapter that our key aim was to support a reflective approach to teaching and learning, where teachers monitor their own teaching behaviour and its subsequent effects on their pupils. Such reflection, we argued, is best supported by the collection of evidence from the classroom. The value of both informal and formal methods of collecting information is accepted and the methods viewed as complementary, but many teachers have in the past relied too heavily on informal intuitive assessment .

Assessing intellectual processes is problematic, since we can only really assess the end result and infer the process that has gone before. Observing both pupil behaviour and performance while on the task in hand is one method that helps to provide a more reliable assessment of processes. There are still limitations, however, as we rely on our interpretations of the observed behaviour to be valid, and they may not always be so. Even so, if data collected from several sources suggest the same results, then one can be fairly sure of a correct interpretation.

For assessment to be useful, the information has to be communicated in order to inform classroom practice, to inform the learner, to inform school policy or to inform outside agents. This communication is effected by means of assessment records, but the type and detail of record to be kept depends on the audience and the focus of interest. What is clear, however, is that a move towards formal methods of data collection and the establishment of written records of achievement can benefit children's learning by enabling and encouraging the reflective practice of teachers.

REFERENCES

Ainscow, M. (1988) 'Beyond the eyes of the monster: an analysis of recent trends in assessment and recording', *Support for learning* 3(3), 149–53.
APU (1980) *Great Britain: Assessment of Performance Unit. DES Primary Survey Number 1*, London: HMSO.
—— (1984) *Great Britain: Assessment of Performance Unit. Science in Schools Research Reports Nos 1, 2 & 3*, London: HMSO.
Bennett, N., Desforges, C., Cockburn, A. and Wilkinson, B. (1984) *The Quality of Pupil Learning Experiences*, London: Lawrence Erlbaum.
Broadfoot, P., Abott, D., Croll, P., Osborn, M., Pollard, A. and Towler, L. (1991) 'Implementing national assessment: issues for primary teachers', *Cambridge Journal of Education*, 21(2), 153–68.
Calouste Gulbenkian Foundation (1982) *The Arts in Schools*, London: Oyez Press.
Cavendish, S. J. (1988) *Sex Differences Related to Achievement in Mathematics*, unpublished thesis, Leicester: University of Leicester.
Cavendish, S. J., Galton, M., Hargreaves, L. and Harlen, W. (1990) *Assessing Science in the Primary Classroom: Observing Activities*, London: Paul Chapman.
Croll, P. (1986) *Systematic Classroom Observation*, Lewes: Falmer Press
DES (1988) *National Curriculum Task Group on Assessment and Testing: A Report*, London: HMSO.
Ennever, L. and Harlen, W. (1972) *With Objectives in Mind. Guide to Science 5/13*, London: Macdonald Educational.
Galton, M. and Delamont, S. (1985) 'Speaking with a forked tongue? Two styles of observation in the ORACLE project', in R. Burgess (ed.) *Field Methods in the Study of Education*, Basingstoke: Falmer Press.
Galton, M. and Simon, B. (eds) (1980) *Progress and Performance in the Primary Classroom*, London: Routledge and Kegan Paul.
Gardner, J. (1994) 'No pain, no gain', *Times Educational Supplement Update*, June, 4.
Hargreaves, L. (1995) 'Seeing clearly. Observation in the Primary classroom', in J. Moyles (ed.) *Beginning Teaching: Beginning Learning In Primary Education*, Milton Keynes: Open University Press.
Hewitt, P. and Bennett, N. (1989) *Assessment of learning. A Hertfordshire Primary Context. A Report Arising from the Secondment of two Primary Headteachers*, Hertfordshire LEA.

Holt, J. (1964) *How Children Fail*, New York: Pitman.

Hoyles, C., Sutherland, R. and Evans, J. (1985) 'Using LOGO in the mathematics classroom. What are the implications for pupil devised goals', *Computers in Education*, 12, 61–73.

Rowe, M. B. (1974) 'Wait time and rewards as instructional variable, their influence on languages, logic and fate control', *Journal of Research in Science Teaching*, 17, 81–94.

Russell, T. and Harlen, W. (1990) *Assessing Science in the Primary Classroom: Practical Tasks*, London: Paul Chapman.

Schilling, M. D., Hargreaves, L., Harlen, W., with Russell, T. (1990) *Assessing Science in the Primary Classroom: Written Tasks*, London: Paul Chapman.

Simpson, M. and Tuson, J. (1995) *Using Observations in Small-Scale Research*, SCRE.

Thomas, N. (1990) *Primary Education from Plowden to the 1990s*, Basingstoke: Falmer Press.

Tobin, K. (1984) 'Student task involvement in activity oriented science', *Journal of Research in Science Teaching*, 21(5), 469–82.

Wood, D. (1988) *How Children Think and Learn*, Oxford: Blackwell.

Chapter 6

Primary culture and classroom teaching
The learning relationship in context

Maurice Galton

INTRODUCTION – SCHOOL CULTURES: THEIR IMPACT ON THE PRIMARY CLASSROOM

Any visitor from a country such as the USA or the United Kingdom on a whirlwind tour throughout countries on and near the Pacific rim, from Myanmar to Japan and then on to Australia and New Zealand, would, if s/he ventured into schools, find much that was familiar but also much that was strange and puzzling. At primary level, in particular, there would be variations in the size of school and of classes. Some schools, in rural settings, would have fewer than fifty pupils, although they would not be a mere forty kilometres apart, as is often found in the UK. In conurbations such as Singapore, over 2,000 pupils would be the school norm, with many classes of over forty pupils. In Europe and the United States a big elementary school might have between 300 and 400 pupils and average class sizes of thirty children. In some cases, for example in the Scandinavian countries, class size is limited by law to below twenty-five pupils. Generally these pupils are placed in mixed gender groups and sit around tables or desks pushed together. A typical arrangement is shown in Figure 6.1. In those countries where class size is forty or greater, pupils usually sit in rows facing the teacher and are streamed by ability. Figure 6.2 shows a typical arrangement in a Singapore school for grade 1. A typical grade 6 classsroom in Singapore has rows of desks facing the teacher. Elsewhere, setting within a class is limited to certain subjects, such as Mathematics and Language. Much more common, however, is the trend for one teacher to cover the whole curriculum, apart from some specialist areas such as Music and Physical Education.

But if our visitor probes below these structural features, s/he will begin to identify more subtle variations in the way each classroom operates. Most important is the nature of the relationship between the teacher and the pupils. Do pupils view their teacher as 'the fountain of all knowledge', as a policeman, a facilitator, or a nursemaid? Does the teacher regard the pupils as friends, as empty vessels which need filling,

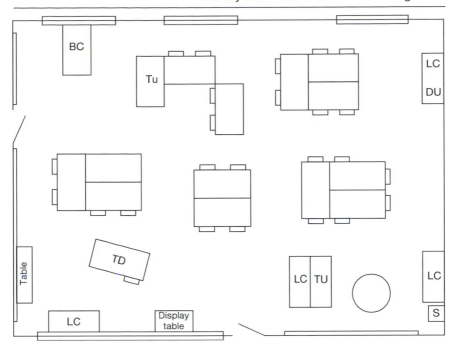

Figure 6.1 Typical arrangement of European classroom

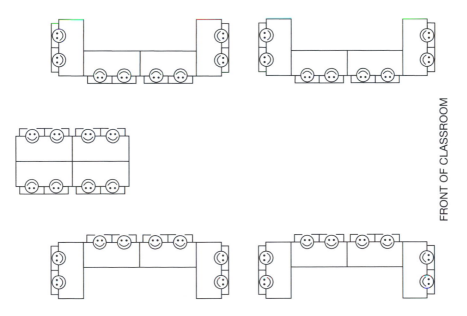

Figure 6.2 Typical arrangement in Singapore school for Grade 1 classes

tender plants needing nurturing, or a rabble which needs 'careful watching if they are not to gain the upper hand'? Such perceptions will manifest themselves in the way question-and-answer sessions are conducted, the form of classroom control exercised, the system of rewards and punishments meted out and, in particular, the degree to which pupils are permitted to exercise choice over what they learn. These aspects of the daily life of a classroom are often referred to as its 'ethos'.

Part of this classroom ethos derives from the structural features described above. Empty vessels tend to sit in rows, and to answer the questions put by the teacher rather than ask them. Tender plants will be encouraged to seek support from their peers, will exercise a degree of autonomy over what they learn, and will be more likely to be praised rather than criticised. These teacher behaviours, however, will also stem in part from the individual's personal belief system, their view of themselves and their openness to other people's ideas.

It is this interplay between ideas and structure that creates the life of the primary school and its classrooms; what is termed its culture, defined by Raymond Williams as depicting 'a way of life' of any group, be it a nation or a profession (Williams 1961). Others, such as Robin Alexander, describe the primary school culture in terms of its beliefs, concerns and distinctive language (Alexander 1992). Alexander argues there is an 'inescapable relationship' between ideas and structure within a culture;

> they do not exist independently of each other. Ideas generate structures; but structures also generate ideas in order to explain and sustain structures. In conjunction, ideas and structure secure collective cohesion and continuity, and confer identity and security on the individual.
>
> (Alexander 1992: 171)

Thus a culture not only serves to identify, but also to 'define, justify and control' its members (Alexander 1992: 169). This is because, as ideas, beliefs and values become identified with the group rather than the constituent individuals, as a manifestation of its cultural identity, they provide the ideological basis for action. In order to demonstrate membership of the cultural group, an individual is forced to enact the ideology, chiefly because the system of rewards, promotions, etc. is likely to be dependent on such demonstrations of 'cultural purity'.

Recognising the complex nature of this interplay between structure and ideas is crucial for any understanding of the typical patterns of classroom organisation which operate in any particular country. In recent years politicians and administrators have often sought to change educational structures through curriculum reform, in the expectation that school improvement would follow through a shift in teaching and learning strategies. In most cases, however, teachers have adopted the line of

least resistance to these curriculum changes and simply 'bolted' the innovation on to their existing practice. This appears to have happened in the
United Kingdom with the National Curriculum (Pollard *et al.* 1993;
Galton *et al.* 1995) and many Council of Europe (CDCC 1982, 1987) and
OECD studies confirm a similar trend. Before going on to look more critically at this apparent trend to *conservatism* among teachers, however,
some aspects of the primary school culture that give rise to certain patterns of classroom organisation, and their effects on teaching and learning, will be briefly described.

SOME MANIFESTATIONS OF PRIMARY SCHOOL CULTURE

In most countries, primary schooling, as it exists today, grew from the
need to provide mass education of a standard that allowed for the shift
away from an agrarian to an industrialised economy. In its minimalist
form, this elementary education required pupils to be able to read, write
and count. Although, during the course of the twentieth century, standards have been continually raised to meet technological advance, this
elementary tradition remains strong. Even in developed countries, the
bulk of curriculum time is still given over to these 'core' activities, which
nearly always take place at the beginning of the school day when pupils
are believed to be most attentive. Those responsible for early developments in mass primary education saw the teaching of language, in particular, as the key which opened up the cultural inheritance, in the sense
that the term was used by Matthew Arnold in *Culture and Anarchy* to represent all that was known to be best in our civilisation. Arnold's argument for inducting as many citizens as possible into this culture was that
only through the experience gained from the study of past achievements
could people be persuaded to turn away from the path of revolution as
the solution to the grave social problems that had arisen as the result of
industrialism. The view, as it developed, had important implications for
pedagogy in that it presupposed a 'transmission' model of teaching, and
a belief in the power of the educated mind to make decisions on behalf of
individuals whose education mainly consisted of acquiring practical
knowledge and skills. This led very early on to the creation of different
types of schools, and the search for ways of selecting each child for the
education to which s/he was best fitted.

Industrialism, however, also brought about a reaction which sought to
retain the perceived benefits of the agrarian way of life, particularly the
feelings and emotions resulting from close contact with natural surroundings. A crucial period in developing this awareness of nature was
seen to be early childhood, perceived as an age of innocence. From this
approach has flowed what Blyth (1989) has termed the developmental
tradition in primary education, giving rise to various stage theories of

learning, and culminating in the child-centred approaches which, in different countries, have been grouped under labels such as 'progressive', 'informal' and 'open education'. Central concepts within these approaches have been 'learning through doing', 'readiness', and a view of knowledge as 'integrated and personally constructed' rather than a collection of distinct disciplines consisting of universally agreed bodies of knowledge.

But, as Kliebard (1986) notes in his study of *The Struggle for the American Curriculum*, ideas, as they trickle down into the classroom, rarely retain their pure form. Partly because, as we have already seen, teachers often 'bolt' innovation on to existing practice, and partly because many classroom decisions are driven by pragmatism rather than theory, as a 'coping' response to immediate problems, new sets of ideas tend to get mixed up with existing ones. Kliebard refers to this mixing process as one of *hybridisation*, which frequently results in their being a gap between 'rhetoric' and 'reality'. Thus numerous studies of primary teaching in the UK and elsewhere, which will be summarised in a later section of this chapter, have found that those teachers, claiming to believe in experiential learning as part of a child-centred philosophy, nevertheless often spend considerable amounts of time teaching didactically, although in a classroom environment which emphasises individual learning (Galton 1989).

Curriculum hybridisation, therefore, serves to reinforce the common public culture of primary teaching, since the outwardly shared set of beliefs, often perceived as self-evident truths, creates a barrier which prevents too close an inspection of the disjunction between an individual teacher's aims and their practice. Alexander (1984) notes, for example, that research evidence is often reinterpreted to match the ideological perspective and those who challenge such views are accused of damaging teacher morale. Instead, critics are urged to celebrate what is good rather than dwell on weaknesses. It is for this reason that Hargreaves (1992: 217) argues that

> Physically, teachers are often alone in their own classrooms, with no other adults for company. Psychologically, they never are: what they do, their classroom styles and strategies – are powerfully affected by the orientations of the colleagues with whom they work now and have done in the past.

It is this psychological inter-dependency which is said to account for the strong resistance to change among primary teachers, and which led one commentator to describe the profession as characterised by *presentism*, *conservatism* and *individualism* (Lortie 1975). Teachers, according to Lortie, prefer to concentrate on short-term planning in their own classrooms where their efforts can be seen to bring immediate results (*presentism*);

avoid discussing fundamental issues concerning teaching and learning, for fear it might raise fundamental questions about their practice (*conservatism*); and shy away from forms of collaboration with colleagues, such as team teaching (*individualism*). For all these reasons schools, like living cells, seem to be largely impervious to outside pressures to change well established existing practices, and, as Chapter 9 of this book shows, the management of change must also be seen as part of a learning relationship.

This is particularly true of those countries which are in, or are about to enter, a post-industrial phase where there are many more competing rationales for curriculum building. Schools now face demands from a variety of sources that their pupils should be educated for *'employment'*, *'life'*, *'self-development'* and *'leisure'*, to name but several possibilities. Not surprisingly, given that the teaching approaches required to satisfy such demands often conflict, teachers tend to adopt a cautious approach to innovation, believing that, like trains and buses, if they miss the latest new idea someone will come up with another before too long. It is this scepticism which partly upholds the 'elementary tradition' in primary teaching and sustains existing patterns of classroom organisation.

PERSISTENT PATTERNS OF CLASSROOM ORGANISATION

During the late 1970s and throughout the 1980s a series of studies took place, mainly in the United States and the United Kingdom, which were designed to explore the consequences of existing patterns of organisation for students' learning. The general results of this research, nearly all of which involved pupils in the elementary school, has been summarised by Brophy and Good (1986) in the USA, and by Gipps (1992) in the UK. Typical of these studies was the Beginning Teacher Education Study (BTES) undertaken in California (Denham and Libermann 1985), and the ORACLE (Observational Research and Classroom Learning Evaluation) study undertaken in Leicester (Galton *et al.* 1980; see Chapter 5 of this book for a discussion of some of the observational techniques used in this and related studies).

The UK pattern showed a high degree of *asymmetry* between what teachers did with their time and what pupils did. Pupils spent nearly 80 per cent of their day working on tasks without interacting with the teacher or another pupil. For only 60 per cent of this time were pupils 'on task'. At other times they moved out of their place to get paper, sharpen a pencil or to watch what other students were doing. They would also wait in the queue to ask the teacher for help or to get their work marked. For some 12 per cent of the day pupils would be seated at the front of the class. These periods tended to take place at the beginning and end of sessions, when the teacher was giving instructions or sharing ideas and looking at the work produced. Towards the end of the school day class time would be used by the teacher to read a story. Most of these whole-class sessions consisted, therefore, of the students listening to the teacher giving instructions, commenting on work or reading aloud. Only a small proportion of the day, the remaining 8 per cent, involved pupils in collaborative activity, either in peer tutoring or cooperative groupwork. Even when pupils were asked to work together in this way, a substantial proportion of the conversations were not concerned with the task in hand. These results, a summary of the ORACLE findings, have been replicated with remarkable consistency by other researchers, such as Tizard *et al.* (1988) and Alexander (1992).

In contrast, teachers spent over 75 per cent of their time interacting with individual students, repeating instructions, marking and commenting upon work. These periods were very infrequent because, with thirty pupils in a class, each student received about six minutes a day of the teacher's attention if s/he distributed it equally. Often, however, more attention would be given to pupils who misbehaved, usually boys. Interactions involving the task tended to be of short duration. A follow-up to the ORACLE study found that over 40 per cent of these exchanges did not last for more than five seconds (Galton and Patrick 1990). Not surprisingly, therefore, these brief exchanges were not very challenging. The main task of the teacher was to keep everyone busy. For the most part the exchanges involved the teacher *as a resource* telling pupils where to find something (a book, a piece of equipment), how to do something (hints for solving a problem, demonstration of a a practical task), or whether something was correct (a spelling, a multiplication). From the teacher's perspective the classroom was a very busy, productive environment, while for some pupils with 'time on task' levels of around 50 per cent (Tizard *et al.* 1988) a considerable proportion of each day appeared to evaporate!

By way of contrast, consider the following description of a Singapore teacher's mathematics lesson to a class of ten-year-old students. The topic is the angles of a triangle.

> There are 45 children in the class. The pupils sit facing the teacher who stands at the front. Boys sit on one side of the room, girls on the other. The lesson begins by the teacher revising how to calculate the third angle of a triangle, given two angles. She then rapidly draws five triangles on the board marking two angles in each. Five children come out to the board to tackle these problems. While they are working out the answers she writes another five examples on another blackboard. When the first group have finished she asks the rest of the class to check if the suggested solutions for the third angle are correct. While this is taking place the second group of pupils are working on the next

set of examples. This sequence continues until all 45 students have had a turn at the board. The whole activity takes just 8 minutes.

When this task is completed each pupil is given a paper triangle with the centre of the paper cut away. They are told to tear off two corners and fit the pieces together. When they do so the pieces of paper form a straight line. The teacher tells them that this shows that the three angles of the triangle add up to 180°. They then go on to prove that the exterior angle equals the sum of the two opposite angles and again do examples on the board. They then move on to examples of right angles. By this time 40 minutes of the lesson has elapsed. For the remaining twenty minutes the students do examples from worksheets.

(Galton, personal observation)

Thus, for nearly 66 per cent of the lesson, class teaching was the preferred strategy, in contrast to the system operating in the UK in which, typically, the teacher would have started with a demonstration of the paper triangle, asked children what they could infer from the fact that the three corners fitted into a straight line, sent children to their table to work on examples from worksheets, and used the final ten minutes to point out the special properties of triangles with an angle of 90°. Perhaps 66 per cent of this lesson, in contrast to that of the Singapore teacher, would have consisted of what American researchers call *seat work*. Of greater interest is the way in which teachers from the two cultures might use the practical demonstration involving the paper triangle. The Singapore teacher uses it so that pupils can *confirm* what they have worked out previously: that the three angles add up to 180°. The UK teacher would use it so that pupils can *infer* this rule.

IDEOLOGY AND CLASSROOM PRACTICE

We saw earlier that classroom culture arises from the interplay between ideas and structure. All too frequently, critics of contemporary primary schooling tend to forget this fact and attribute perceived weaknesses in practice solely to the prevailing belief system. Thus the UK teacher chooses not to tell pupils that the three angles add up to 180° because s/he believes that 'finding out is better than being told', and that 'children should be left to discover things for themselves'. These maxims are, in turn, said to derive from the child-centred view of education which originally developed as a reaction to the worst excesses of the industrial revolution during the nineteenth century. Such views are reinforced in turn by theories of child development, such as Piaget's (see Chapter 2 of this book, and Wood 1988).

Clearly, such critics fail to appreciate the process of *hybridisation*, as described by Kliebard (1986), which explains why teachers who hold a constructivist view of knowledge in the manner of Piaget nevertheless spend most of their time interacting with individual pupils, providing them with information, or issuing routine instructions. Far from never telling pupils anything, teachers called *individual monitors* in the ORA-CLE study, who used the least amount of class teaching, were more likely to tell pupils what to do than were the *class enquirers*, who, as their name implies, frequently taught the whole class (Galton *et al.* 1980). All teachers strove to maintain the highest engagement levels, rarely taking the opportunity to stand and monitor the pupils' activity. Campbell (1993) attributes this high work rate to *conscientiousness*, a characteristic of the Protestant work ethic arising from the origins of mass elementary education within the Christian tradition of church schools, which was later transported to all parts of the globe through missionary activity. As a result, the primary culture includes a perception of teaching as a vocation requiring honest, hard-working, committed professionals.

Conscientiousness is certainly a common feature of both of the mathematics lessons described earlier in the chapter. Both teachers, during their training, will have had their attention directed to constructivist views of knowledge, but what will determine how they apply such theories will be structural features such as class size and ability groupings. For the Singapore teacher with forty-five children in the class, the proportion of time which could be devoted to individual pupils is too small to enable worthwhile exchanges. Given the homogeneity of the class, the tactic of checking on their work five at a time is both more efficient and more effective. In contrast, although a class of thirty still offers only limited opportunities between a teacher and each pupil, the wide range of ability found in most UK classrooms renders whole-class instruction problematic except for those tasks such as introducing activities and drawing conclusions from what different pupils have accomplished. Thus, equally important in an attempt to understand why teachers teach as they do is the concept of teaching as a pragmatic activity. Faced with a number of different problems – a difficult child, a rainy day requiring children to stay inside the classroom during playtime, limited numbers of the same text book – a teacher will select a course of action which s/he believes will allow the maximum number of children to engage in purposeful activity. The nature of that activity will vary according to the classroom ethos. The teacher with a class of difficult, unmotivated pupils, many of whom lack the self-confidence to learn, will be less concerned with the academic content of the task and more concerned that it should capture the pupils' interest. A teacher such as the one in Singapore, who had only to say 'Do you need me to put my finger to my lips?' to gain total silence, will naturally focus to a greater degree on the intended learning outcomes of each task she sets.

PEDAGOGY: A NEGLECTED ASPECT OF THE PRIMARY CULTURE

There is another factor which contributes to the strength of the prevailing view of the primary school culture. This is the lack of any coherent theory of pedagogy, in the sense used by Gage (1981) to describe a science of the art of teaching. In particular, as Eisenhart *et al.* (1991) argue, there is no expectation of progression or development within pedagogy, because 'there are no theories of how teachers learn to teach more effectively'. This view offers another reason why practice is so resistant to change. Namely, there is no *expectation* that it should change. As the final chapter of this book shows, there is a tradition that student teachers model their method on a more experienced classroom teacher's practice when acquiring basic teaching skills. If they find themselves with problems, they may modify these procedures by taking advice from other teachers, but otherwise, with minor modifications, they stick with the system that works. In teaching, therefore, there is no accepted notion of a progression on which to base professional development. When dealing with those aspects of pedagogy involving classroom discipline, teachers, as they gain experience, are rarely expected to consider the use of approaches that encourage pupils to exercise self-control. It is more often a case of having found one method that works and then sticking to it. This was true when, for example, one school principal offered courses on using less confrontational methods of classroom management. He was told by one teacher, 'You can't teach an old dog new tricks', to which he replied, 'But we are not dogs. We're people!' (Rogers 1990: 276).

Both Kagan (1992) and Reynolds (1992) have reviewed the extensive literature on teaching and professional development, and they concur with Berliner's (1992) view that probably the best available model for building a theory of pedagogy is one which seeks to differentiate between the cognitive states of teachers at different stages of their development. This is because appropriate training programmes can then be devised in the same way that different approaches are needed to move pupils to the point where they become 'independent thinkers'. This notion of needing to match INSET training to the teacher's cognitive development must be at the centre of any worthwhile theory of pedagogy.

TEACHING FOR UNDERSTANDING

As Good and Brophy (1994) note, one of the major shifts in thinking about teaching and learning during the past decade has been the increased emphasis placed on teaching for understanding, rather than for transmission of information. In this model, the main function of whole-class teaching is to provide a scaffold which will enable pupils to think productively (Nuthall and Alton-Lee 1993; Brown and Campione 1994). In science, for example, the teacher needs to provide a framework which enables a group of pupils to decide which hypotheses are plausible explanations of the facts and which are not. Part of this framework will involve developing the necessary skills to apply procedures in ways which aid productive thinking. For example, Galton (1989) describes how a group of nine-year-old pupils, when asked to time a twenty-five second interval between two sounds on a tape recorder using a stopwatch, obtained results within a range of fifteen and ninety-five seconds. Yet, the day previously, the same pupils had been asked to explore the relationship between the angle of incline of a wooden plank and the time it took for a toy car to travel down its length using the same stopwatch. Others, such as McNamara (1995 and Chapter 4 of this book) have argued that it is the teacher's failure to train pupils adequately in communication skills which accounts for the lack of effective groupwork in primary classrooms.

The evidence from research studies (Brophy and Good 1986) suggests that the use of direct instruction, of the kind employed in the example of the Singapore mathematics lesson, is most appropriate for teaching pupils to solve relatively simple problems involving procedural routines, content knowledge and factual information. The teacher's role in this kind of problem-solving is very similar to that of the computer programmer who provides the machine with the procedures necessary to work out a solution. As well as the actual calculation, this also involves routines for accessing, storing and retrieving information and rules for making decisions (e.g., how to proceed if a result is higher or lower than a given value). Decision-making in a computer consists of answering lots of 'yes or no' questions very quickly. The efficiency of the computer depends on this speed of processing and its capacity to store large amounts of information in chunks. The effectiveness is also increased by the use of 'sub-routines'. These are regularly-used procedures which can be automatically called up when needed rather than starting from scratch each time.

When this information model of 'man as a computer' is applied to learning by direct instruction, there are strong parallels. The pupils are given new information, they are shown how to remember it, and are taught how to use it in various procedures to solve problems. The pupils then practise these procedures until they can use them automatically. However, just as with the simple model of the computer in which, if the nature of the problem-solving changes appreciably, the computer has to be re-programmed, so too when we move from teaching multiplication of whole numbers to multiplying fractions or decimals, we have to begin the process of direct instruction again. Once we move to generalities, for example, understanding the principles of multiplication irrespective of the particular application, direct instruction appears to be less effective. This form of thinking, or concept development, involves the acquisition of new ideas (or the invention of them) and an ability to make appropriate use of them. In the process we may have to identify the nature of a problem, analyse its components, determine whether we have sufficient knowledge to solve it, and be able to monitor whether our efforts are likely to be productive. As we saw in Chapter 3, this ability to regulate our thinking processes, or to 'control the domain of cognition' (Meadows 1993: 78), lies at the heart of what Brown and Palincsar (1986) call 'learning as theory change'. The 'man as a computer' model is not very helpful for understanding these 'metacognitive' processes, but the ideas of Vygotsky, based upon cooperative learning, are (Cohen 1994). Here, those who are more competent help the less competent move to a position where they can become 'self-regulating' in their thinking. To assist the less competent learner, the more competent must provide a 'scaffolding' or framework by means of which these metacognitive processes can be internalised. Once this state is achieved, the pupil can become an independent thinker. Pupils still need to engage in the same metacognitive processes, but now 'talk to themselves' rather than with peers or an adult. The teacher's role is now primarily that of facilitator and 'friendly critic', as described in the Piagetian account of the thinking process. Thus Vygotsky and Piaget represent the ends of a continuum which moves from 'other' to 'self' regulation.

For example, part of the scaffolding for discussion during collaborative learning involves systematically considering all cases in support of the argument, then all counter-examples. Cases which are neither for nor against are then isolated and used to suggest possible alternative ways of presenting the original proposition (Brown and Palincsar 1986: 39). Groups are taught to apply this strategy until the process becomes automatic. These procedures, therefore, along with more fundamental skills, such as learning to listen carefully, to communicate views and to handle conflict of views within the group, need to be taught initially through direct instruction. Whether the teacher or peer provides the scaffolding depends on contextual factors. Brown and Palincsar (1986) argue that the more abstract the problem, the more dominant will be the teacher's participation. Much will depend on the extent to which the more competent pupils within the class have internalised the scaffolding procedures.

Decisions about classroom organisation should then follow from this analysis. In direct instruction, class teaching will be most effective because it maximises teacher contact. Thus, when teaching procedures or skills such as listening, the whole class can be involved. When new information is being offered, including demonstrations of relatively simple problem-solving using this information, ability groups are likely to be preferred. Once, however, thinking processes involving metacognition are required (e.g., getting ideas for story writing, hypothesis generation, evaluating historical evidence), the research evidence suggests that mixed ability groups may be more appropriate (Bennett and Dunne 1992).

However, even with this strategy in place, there remains a question of motivating pupils to participate enthusiastically in these activities. Studies show that, even when pupils have the necessary prior knowledge, they appear reluctant to engage in more demanding cognitive activities, preferring, instead, to feign dependency (Pintrich *et al.* 1993). For such pupils, too rigid a scaffolding of the kind offered in the example of group discussion can become a prison, so that thinking never operates outside the teacher's chosen framework. There will be apparent gains in learning, but creativity may be stifled as a consequence. Chapter 4 of this book suggests that it is only possible to use collaborative approaches if the pupils' self-image and self-esteem (both academic and social) are high. If pupils feel confident enough in their learning, so that they do not fear failure, they will be more willing to initiate exchanges with teachers in which they are open about the difficulties they have encountered and the solutions they have used in attempting to solve a problem (McNamara and Moreton 1995).

IMPROVING EDUCATIONAL PRACTICE

In a recent review of the field of research on teaching, Good (1995) argues that the study of student cognition, how pupils perceive learning and its relation to their social development, has not received the attention it deserves. One important factor has to do with the way that teachers regulate pupils' behaviour so that, as Galton (1989) argues, pupils are required to '*do as you think*' when learning is involved, but '*do as the teacher says*' when a behaviour problem arises. Pupils often find it difficult to interpret the teacher's dual role of learning facilitator and behaviour manager, and play safe by adopting dependency strategies which, in extreme cases, take the form of '*learned helplessness*' (as discussed especially in Chapter 4). Reviews of expert teaching (Sternberg and Horvath 1995) note that experts are less prone to create this kind of classroom environment, since they avoid the use of maxims such as '*don't smile until Christmas*', preferring instead to deal with each problem as it arises on the principle that '*circumstances alter cases*'. This suggests that one of the key elements in changing the culture of schooling, so that teaching for understanding rather than for knowledge transmission occurs, is the development of a comprehensive model of pedagogy which includes a shift from behaviourist models of classroom management to ones based on negotiation, of the kind advocated by Rogers (1990). Part of the teacher *conservatism* remarked on by Lortie (1975) stems not so much from an in-built resistance to change for change's sake, but from a feeling that experts are 'born, not made'. Too many teachers report, while admiring the way that a colleague dealt with a pupil, that 'I couldn't possibly do the same. I don't have his/her personal qualities.'

SUMMARY

As long as the profession continues to argue that teaching quality arises from personality traits, rather than from the consistent application of pedagogic theory, teaching effectively for understanding rather than for knowledge transmission will remain an elusive goal. This is a goal which is no longer restricted to the countries of the Northern hemisphere, but one which increasingly commands the attention of policy makers within the rapidly developing economies of Asia and the Pacific rim. There, the desire of China and India to participate fully in the global economy requires existing industrialised countries to equip their workforce with new skills if their competitive edge is not to be eroded. Furthermore, the marriage of communication and computer technology now results in the power of computer networks doubling every eighteen months or so, and this makes it difficult to visualise the demands of the workplace a generation further on. Since schools cannot predict the kinds of knowledge and skill their pupils will need, there appears to be no alternative but to

> shift the emphasis of the duration system away from mastery of content to the acquisition of thinking skills that will last the lifetime. Creativity and innovation skills will be at a premium as we move into higher value-added knowledge and technology-based industry. Our students must be encouraged to think independently and develop the habit of dealing with the unpredictable and the open ended.
>
> (Singapore Ministry of Education 1995)

Such goals provide a formidable challenge to both educators and researchers, who must provide the necessary pedagogical frameworks within which a new generation of teachers can be inducted into the profession, and existing members provided with the necessary incentive to adapt their existing practice.

REFERENCES

Alexander, R. (1984) *Primary Teaching*, London: Holt, Reinhart and Winston.
—— (1992) *Policy and Practice in Primary Education*, London: Routledge.
Bennett, N. and Dunne, E. (1992) *Managing Classroom Groups*, Hemel Hempstead: Simon and Schuster.
Berliner, D. (1992) 'Some Characteristics of Experts in the Pedagogical Domain', in F. Oser, A. Dick and J. Patry (eds) *Effective and Responsible Teaching: The New Synthesis*, San Francisco: Jossey-Bass.

Blyth, W. (1989) *Development and Experience in Primary Education*, London: Routledge.

Brophy, J. E. and Good, T. L. (1986) 'Teacher Behaviour and Student Achievement', in M. C. Wittrock (ed.) *Handbook of Research on Teaching* 3rd edn, New York: Macmillan.

Brown, A. and Campione, J. (1994) 'Guided Discovery in a Community of Learners', in K. McGilly (ed.) *Classroom Lessons: Integrating Cognitive Theory and Classroom Practice*, Cambridge, MA: MIT Press in association with Bradford Books.

Brown, A. and Palincsar, A. (1986) *Guided Cooperative Learning and Individual Knowledge Acquisition*, Technical Report 372, Cambridge, MA: Bolt, Beranak and Newham.

Campbell, R. (1993) 'A Dream at Conception: A Nightmare at Delivery', in R. Campbell (ed.) *Breadth and Balance in the Primary Curriculum*, London: Falmer Press.

CDCC (Council for Cultural Co-operation) (1982) *Primary Education in Western Europe: Aims, Problems, Trends*, Report of a Council of Europe Project No. 8 Seminar, held at Vaduz, Liechtenstein. Strasbourg: Council of Europe (DECS/EGT [83] 647).

—— (1987) *Development in Practice*, Report on Education Centres as a means of Introducing Innovation in Primary Education, by A. Strittmatter (Switzerland). Strasbourg: Council of Europe (DECS/EGT [87] 18).

Cohen, E. (1994) 'Restructuring Classrooms: Conditions for Productive Small Groups', *Review of Educational Research*, 64, 1–35.

Denham, C. and Libermann, A. (eds) (1985) *Time to Learn*, Report of the Beginning Teacher Education Studies, Washington, DC: National Institute of Education.

Eisenhart, L., Behm, L. and Romagnano, L. (1991) 'Learning to Teach: Developing Expertise or Rite of Passage?', *Journal of Education for Teaching*, 17(1), 51–71.

Gage, N. L. (1981) *Hard Gains in the Soft Sciences: The Case of Pedagogy*, a CEDR Monograph, Bloomington, IN: Phi Delta Kappa.

Galton, M. (1989) *Teaching in the Primary School*, London: David Fulton.

—— (1995) *Crisis in the Primary School*, London: David Fulton.

Galton, M. and Patrick, H. (1990) *Curriculum Provision in the Small Primary School*, London: Routledge.

Galton, M., Hargreaves, L. and Comber, C. (1995) *Implementation of the National Curriculum in Rural Primary Schools*, Final Report to the Economic & Social Science Research Council, Report No. R00023 3383, Slough: ESRC.

Galton, M., Simon, B. and Croll, P. (1980) *Inside the Primary Classroom*, London: Routledge and Kegan Paul.

Gipps, C. (1992) *What we know about Effective Primary Teaching*, London: Tufnell Press.

Good, T. (1995) 'Teaching Effects and Teacher Evaluation', in *Handbook of Reseach on Teacher Education* 2nd edn, New York: Macmillan

Good, T. and Brophy, G. (1994) *Looking at Classrooms* 6th edn, New York: HarperCollins.

Hargreaves, A. (1992) 'Cultures for Teaching: A Focus for Change', in A. Hargreaves and M. Fullan (eds) *Understanding Teacher Development*, London: Cassell, in association with Teachers' College Press, Columbia University, New York.

Kagan, D. (1992) 'Professional Growth among Preservice and Beginning Teachers', *Review of Educational Research*, 62(2), 129–70.

Kliebard, H. (l986) *The Struggle for the American Curriculum 1893–1958*, New York: Methuen.

Lortie, D. (1975) *Schoolteacher*, Chicago, IL: University of Chicago Press.

McNamara, S. (1995) 'Let's Cooperate! Developing Children's Social Skills in the Classroom', in J. Moyles (ed.) *Beginning Teaching: Beginning Learning in Primary Education*, Buckingham: Open University Press.

McNamara, S. and Moreton, G. (1995) *Changing Behaviour*, London: David Fulton.

Meadows, S. (1993) *The Child as Thinker: The Development and Acquisition of Cognition in Childhood*, London: Routledge.

Mortimore, P., Sammons, P., Stoll, L. D. and Ecob, R. (1988) *School Matters: The Junior Years*, Wells: Open Books.

Nuthall, G. and Alton-Lee, A. (1993) 'Predicting Learning from Student Experience of Teaching: A Theory of Student Knowledge Construction in Classrooms', *American Educational Research Journal*, 30(4), 799–840.

Pintrich, P., Marx, R. and Boyle, R. (1993) 'Beyond Cold Conceptual Change: The Role of Motivational Beliefs and Classroom Contextual Factors in the Process of Conceptual Change', *Review of Educational Research*, 63(2), 167–200.

Pollard, A. with Osborn, M., Abbott, D., Broadfoot, P. and Croll, P. (1993) 'Balancing Priorities: Children and the Curriculum in the Nineties', in R. Campbell (ed.) *Breadth and Balance in the Primary Curriculum*, London: Falmer Press.

Reynolds, A. (1992) 'What is Competent Beginning Teaching? A Review of the Literature', *Review of Educational Research*, 62(1), 1–36.

Rogers, B. (1990) *You Know the Fair Rule: Strategies for making the hard job of discipline in school easier*, Hawthorne, Victoria: ACER (Australian Council for Educational Research).

Singapore Ministry of Education (1995) Opening Address by the Minister of Education, Mr Lee Yock Suan, at the 5th MIT–NTU Conference, Shangri-La Hotel, Singapore, 30 June 1995.

Sternberg, R. and Horvath, J. (1995) 'A Prototype View of Expert Teaching', *Educational Researcher*, 24(6), 9–17.

Tizard, B., Blatchford, D., Burke, J., Farquhar, C. and Plewis, I. (1988) *Young Children at School in the Inner City*, Hove: Lawrence Erlbaum.

Williams, R. (1961) *Culture and Society*, London: Penguin Books.

Wood, D. (1988) *How Children Think and Learn*, Oxford: Basil Blackwell.

Chapter 7

Look back and wonder

The reflective practitioner and the learning relationship

Neil Kitson

> Excellent teacher preparation and superior teaching demands continuous attention to problems of teacher self-evaluation and its avowed goal – teacher self-improvement. Mere teaching experience will not guarantee improvement.
>
> (Simpson 1966: 1)

INTRODUCTION

The role of a classroom teacher involves a complex web of skills and relationships. The development of educational issues and teaching practice means that a teacher's work is never finished. When this is coupled with the wider demands placed upon the practitioner, such as meeting the prevailing ideology or dealing with less than perfect surroundings, it may seem that the job is one where the conflicts can never be reconciled. Yet the reality is that teachers cope to varying degrees of success in the situations that they find themselves. To help them cope, there are a range of strategies, but for many years writers (Zeichner 1982; Costello 1990; Whitty and Willmott 1991) have begun to develop the notion of reflective teachers who can view their own practice within the broader context of teaching and, through reflecting on it, can then improve and enhance their own work.

THE REFLECTIVE TEACHER

The notion of the reflective teacher is not, however, a new one; it originates with the work of Dewey (1933) who, when looking at the learning of skills, developed the concept of 'routine action' and 'reflective action'. Dewey suggests that routine action is somewhat fixed and static and governed by such things as tradition, habit and authority, by institutional structures and expectations. Conversely, reflective action is characterised by engaging in constant self-appraisal and development. Among other things, as Pollard and Tann (1987) suggest, it implies flexibility, rigorous analysis and social awareness.

Pollard and Tann have developed and extended Dewey's notions, applied them to teaching, and extrapolated four basic characteristics of reflective teaching (1987: 4–5). These are:

1 Reflective teaching implies an active concern with aims and consequences, as well as with means and technical efficiency.
2 Reflective teaching combines enquiry and implementation skills with attitudes of open-mindedness, responsibility and wholeheartedness.
3 Reflective teaching is applied in a cyclical or spiraling process, in which teachers continually monitor, evaluate and revise their own practice.
4 Reflective teaching is based on teacher judgement, partly by self-reflection and partly by insight from educational disciplines.

The reflective teacher needs to be aware of the aims and consequences of their action. We can see that the child-centred philosophies developed in Britain during the 1960s and early 1970s had a significant effect on the general practice of teachers. The philosophy itself has a long history, taking support from such post-war child psychologists as Piaget (1950) and gaining official sanction in the Plowden Report (Central Advisory Council for Education 1967). These notions developed into an ideology or system of professional beliefs which has now been shattered. Where once there was certainty there is now confusion. What were taken to be answers now stand as debate. The arena of educational development is open to a wide range of competing and conflicting opinions.

The previous chapter discussed some of these wider issues in terms of ideology and change, and this chapter will now focus more on the primary school practitioner, standing within this confusion and attempting to make moral and political sense amid the social complexity. Teachers are trying to operate within a professional framework and to answer practical educational questions on the spot, whereas the broader concerns of educational and social aims are taken out of the school arena and placed firmly in the political domain. The result of this is an increase of professional tension between the practice within the classroom and the political debate. Costello (1990) alludes to the relationship between the issues and the practice as seen by the classroom practitioner, and highlights the difficult gap currently apparent between the theory and the practice. With the educational debate in such a volatile state, teachers are placed in a difficult position, in that they are now cast in the role of the interpreters of political policy (White 1978; Silcock 1994) rather than just the implementers. In order to do this effectively and bridge the divide, teachers need to be willing and able to consider for themselves both educational values and social consequences. Furthermore, they need to participate in the debate at the widest possible level. In order to do this effectively, and as a result operate as effective practitioners, they need to be reflective about the process of education and not merely reactive to it.

> Thus reflective teaching implies very serious considerations of ends as well as means. This is an issue which we feel has been relatively neglected in . . . teacher education . . . .
>
> (Pollard and Tann 1987: 6–7)

SKILLS, ATTITUDES AND THE REFLECTIVE TEACHER

Several previous chapters have shown the importance of the skills and attitudes which children bring to the learning relationship, and reflective teaching also focuses upon skills and attitudes rather than upon aims and objectives. It is about ownership and responsibility rather than dogma and authority. The ability to reflect constructively upon our teaching gives a degree of autonomy and empowerment by making the teacher in the classroom the agent of their own change. By becoming flexible and responsive to the needs of the children and the demands of the curriculum, optimal positions can be adopted. The teacher can become ever more effective within the classroom by assessing the learning relationship.

Pollard and Tann (1987) identify six types of skill which contribute to the cyclical process of reflection. These are:

1 Empirical skills – knowing what is actually going on and how people really feel.
2 Analytical skills – the ability to interpret the information gathered and to make sense of it.
3 Evaluative skills – making judgements about the effects of what has been seen and relating it to future judgements.
4 Strategic skills – planning what needs to be done as a result of the new information and deciding whether the action that needs to be taken should be at class, school or local authority level.
5 Practical skills – here the teacher must put into practice the ideas developed. It is not sufficient to be able to analyse and theorise without the skill of implementation.
6 Communication skills – necessary because the reflective teacher must test out his/her perceptions and viewpoints with others. Indeed Liston and Zeichner (1990) go further in suggesting that such communication is essential to the process of reflection.

These skills are necessary but not sufficient for teachers to develop as reflective practitioners, for they need to be placed within an attitudinal framework first identified by Dewey and developed further by Zeichner (1982), Pollard and Tann (1987) and Liston and Zeichner (1990). The framework consists of three elements: open-mindedness, responsibility, and wholeheartedness.

Open-mindedness

This is important as part of the reflective process, as it enables the practitioner to consider objectively 'what is going on'. If one is closed to the full range of possibilities then only that information that fits within the perceptual set will be attended to. Therefore the teacher will see only what she expects to see and will not fully attune to the evidence. As Dewey states, open-mindedness is an

> active desire to listen to more sides than one, to give heed to facts from whatever source they come, to give full attention to alternative possibilities, to recognise the possibilities of error even in the beliefs which are dearest to us.
>
> (Dewey 1933: 20)

But to be open-minded must lead directly to the consideration of where such *open-mindedness* may lead. Each observation made will have an associated course of action and related outcomes, so that if we are going to look for something we must be prepared to deal with what we discover. In order to deal with these outcomes, Dewey proposes the second attitude necessary for a reflective practitioner: that of responsibility.

Responsibility

In its intellectual sense, Dewey sees that responsibility enables us to consider the consequences of a projected step, which means that we must be willing to adopt these consequences when they follow reasonably: 'Intellectual responsibility secures integrity' (Dewey 1933: 30).

Clearly Dewey was concerned with the classroom and the wider context of the school. Yet, as indicated above and in the introduction to this book, the relationship between the teacher, the learner and the learning situation is dependent upon the wider social and political context. The teacher tends to relate to the learning environment in accordance with loose criteria set out by a society. These criteria have a political and cultural underpinning which needs to be understood by the reflective practitioner. Liston and Zeichner (1990), writing from an American perspective, expand upon this notion by examining the relationship between teachers and learners.

> Lately, the sense within teacher education seems to be that as long as teachers 'reflect' on their action and purposes, then everything is all right. When this is the case, calls for further reflection become

groundless, that is, such proclamations lack any substantial basis for discerning what will count as good reasons for educational action. We sense that teacher education ought to aim directly at developing teachers who are able to identify and articulate their purposes, who can choose the appropriate means, who know and understand the content to be taught, who understand the cultural and cognitive orientations of their students, and who can be counted on for giving good reasons for their action. . . .

[T]eachers' educational rationales should take into account the activity of teaching, the larger community of educators, and the greater understanding of the social and political context of schooling. Furthermore such reason-giving should provide some basis on which to discern good from bad, and better from worse, educational rationales.

(Liston and Zeichner 1990: 236)

Quite clearly, Liston and Zeichner are asserting that moral, ethical and political issues will be raised, and indeed this must be so if teachers are to make professional and personal judgements about what is educationally worthwhile.

Wholeheartedness

The third of Dewey's attitudes necessary for a reflective practitioner is that of wholeheartedness. This refers essentially to the way in which decisions based upon intellectual responsibility are made. It was Dewey's contention that teachers should be dedicated, single-minded, energetic and enthusiastic.

There is no greater enemy of effective thinking than divided interest. . . . A genuine enthusiasm is an essential attitude that operates as an intellectual force when a person is absorbed. . . . The subject carries him on.

(Dewey 1933: 30)

On their own, each of these attitudes is admirable enough, but, as Pollard and Tann (1987) state, it is only when they work in conjunction that the teacher is enabled to become truly reflective.

REFLECTION AND ITS RELATION TO COMPETENCE AND ACTION RESEARCH

There is a number of strategies that teachers can employ in developing their practical skills through reflective processes but, for the purposes of this chapter, we will consider two, both of which hold the notion of reflection as central. The first involves teachers reflecting upon their skills and practice, relating them to specified criteria defined in terms of *competencies*; the second, based on the concept of *action research*, is the engagement in the process of actively asking questions of their work in the classroom. We will now consider both of these strategies in order to evaluate their effectiveness for practitioners in the classroom.

Competency-based teacher reflection

In changing times, unchanging schools are anomalous. Competency based [teacher] education promises the thrust necessary for adaptation to meet the challenge of a changed and changing society. The emphasis in competency-based teacher education on objectives, accountability and personalisation implies specific criteria, careful evaluation, change based on feedback, and relevant programs [of learning] for a modern era.

(Houston and Howsam 1972: 1)

A great deal has been written about the use of competencies within the professional development of teachers (McNamara 1990; Baird 1991; Bennett *et al.* 1992; Carter, *et al.* 1993), and what Howsam and Houston described back in 1972 has become increasingly significant today for teachers, as our schools, and the educational system they operate within, experience major changes.

But what, then, are competencies and what is their function in the development of the reflective practitioner?.

The notion of competency was originally conceived by industry and the world of employment from the ideas developed by behavioural psychologists. What theorists attempted to do was to break down the specific activities relating to a job into their basic component parts – the basic skills which would enable an individual to carry out the job successfully. Competency initially considers all the elements that would be needed, and then groups them into specific, manageable skills. By working through these skills the individual learner, be they a surgeon, an electrician or a teacher, can assess what they have already achieved, what they have still to do, and then what they must begin to work on next. It means that, through reflection, the learner can focus upon those areas that are important to them and pay less attention to those where improvement has already taken place or those areas that the individual brings with them from another part of their previous learning. In this respect it is more like real-life learning, as opposed to the traditional, academic kind where all learners must follow the same set of instructions and be presented with the same body of knowledge to ensure that they have all received equal amounts of the same instruction. This 'traditional' method clearly fails to take into account the fact that everybody is different and that their life experiences vary considerably. Competency-based learning attempts to be more efficient by acknowledging the strengths of individuals and allowing the greater expending of energy on those areas where development is needed.

Unlike the traditional models of teaching/learning which concentrate on the transmission of a body of knowledge, kept secret until the point of transfer, here the skills needed to complete the task are presented at the outset. The individuals have knowledge of the range of skills and understanding that is required. They are able to become active participants within the learning process and are no longer the passive recipients. Here reflection plays a key role. Through the reflective process they are enabled to identify their previously acquired strengths, their areas of deficiency, and then to select those new skills which they wish to develop. Once they have engaged with the reflective process, they become aware not only of what needs to be covered but also of their responsibility for the learning. No longer can they blame others for being ineffective! If competency-based learning has been correctly established, the learners have the responsibility to ensure that they are gaining access to the knowledge, skills, and understanding that they require.

Now we will consider how this way of working can be used to help develop the skills of a teacher.

Competencies within teaching and professional development

Teachers' professional enhancement can be seen to fit this structure because it is the process for the preparation and continued development of those individuals who want to practise in the teaching profession. In common with the majority of professions, this process involves:

- the acquisition of knowledge and the ability to apply it;
- the development of a specified repertoire of critical behaviours and skills.

To the extent that the knowledge, behaviours and skills can be identified, these become the competency-objectives for the training of teachers.

Learning objectives are commonly classified according to one of five criteria that can be applied in the assessment of our performance as teachers. These criteria are:

1 cognitive objectives;
2 performance objectives;
3 consequence objectives;
4 affective objectives;
5 exploratory objectives.

What, then, are these objectives, and how do they relate to teaching, the matter under consideration?

Cognitive objectives   specify knowledge and intellectual abilities or skills that are to be demonstrated by the learner. In the professional development of teachers, such objectives need to include knowledge of the subject matter to be taught, knowledge of pedagogy, the ability to analyse the curriculum area being taught, etc.

Performance objectives   require the learner to demonstrate the ability to perform a given activity – one must not only know what to do but also how to do it. For teachers, such an objective could be identified as the development of higher-order reading skills, the development of group-work, or the instigation of a personal skills programme.

Consequence objectives   are seen as the results of the learner's actions. The teacher may need to develop, for example, a programme of phonics to help an individual's reading progress, or to show that she can enable the class to engage in independent collaborative groupwork. Teachers need to be able demonstrate the *effect* of their teaching, not simply to have *knowledge* of it.

Affective objectives   deal with the area of attitudes, values, beliefs, and relationships. Difficult to define, these objectives normally relate to the social health of the learning group: i.e., the way that the children interact with and relate to each other.

Exploratory objectives   seen as processes of self-learning or investigation. Here, teachers will find out more about a specific issue or topic in order to develop their own teaching.

All five of these learning objectives are important in the professional development of teachers who are flexible enough to meet the challenges of today's teaching. When we look at competencies for teaching we must make the greatest possible use of the *consequence objectives*. The knowledge alone of how to do something is only of limited use (McNamara 1990). What we must strive towards is the *knowledge*, the *skill* of being able to put it into practice, and the *ability* to evaluate its effectiveness through the result seen in the children's work. The key to the success of this, however, is the teacher's ability to reflect constructively on their own work.

Characteristics of competencies for teaching

'Teaching acts are an observable performance' (McDonald 1974). This performance is linked to situations that vary in terms of the underlying purposes of the teaching, the materials that are to be used, the children who are being taught and how they are responding to the specific situation. Such 'performances' have two main elements within them:

1   a behavioural component
2   a cognitive component.

The first of these, the behavioural component, is a set of observable actions, while the second is a combination of perceptions, interpretations and decisions. (See Chapters 2 and 3 for a discussion of these cognitive elements and how they develop.) Proficiency in both areas is needed in order to produce a competent performance, and, conversely, any set of competencies that might be established needs to take both components into account.

As part of a learning relationship, teaching is an ongoing learning process of developing skills, knowledge and understanding, of appraisal and re-evaluation. Teachers need constantly to examine their practice, assess and alter their approach with every new child and every new situation that they meet. To this end, as already demonstrated, teachers need to become reflective practitioners, the sense of which is built into the competency model in the way in which it looks at the professional development of teachers as an ongoing process. As McNamara (1990) shows, it is not enough just to have the facts necessary to teach; the best ways of putting those facts across are also needed. In order to help children learn effectively we need to identify attainable goals, and we also need to feel that we are succeeding, not that we are being constantly de-skilled by discovering that there is yet more and more that we don't know. When using a competency approach, the learner is given access to the range of skills at the outset, and it is her responsibility to select those areas that she feels she would like to work on. It is then clearly implicit within the structure of the competencies approach that the learning will never be complete, only that a higher level will have been achieved.

Over recent years the UK government has become increasingly interested in this competency-based approach to the education of teachers. In 1992 the Department of Education published a list of competencies for newly-qualified teachers, and interest has been shown in looking at how this can be related to practising teachers (Earley 1992a). Indeed a considerable amount of work has been done linking the notion of competencies to that of appraisal and to teachers' individual action-planning for their professional development (Earley 1992b, 1993).

The way forward?

Everybody is talking about competence. It is an El Dorado of a word with a wealth of meaning and the appropriate connotations for utilitarian times. The language of competency-based approaches to education and training is

compelling in its common-sense and rhetorical force. Words like 'competence' and 'standards' are good words, modern words; everybody is for standards and everybody is against incompetence.

(Norris 1991: 331)

Despite their apparent simplicity, the concepts of competence and standards have had a troubled history. The tacit understanding of the words,
Norris suggests, has been overtaken by the need to define concepts precisely and to operationalise them. What has previously been seen as
practical has become shrouded in theoretical confusion, and what was
apparently simple has become profoundly complex.

This developing commitment to competencies, however, is not
straightforward. As yet the definition of individual competencies is far
from clear and, when it has been defined, how will it be assessed? There
would seem to be a tension here in that a definition of competency that
lends itself to assessment will not find favour among the values of those
professionals engaged in teacher education (Carr 1993). But as
McCulloch (1994: 129–30) shows:

> [T]his is being challenged by those who argue that the true definition
> of competence implies the kind of understanding and values which
> underpin a liberal higher education and . . . these higher order char-
> acteristics can be specified, defined, observed and assessed.

McCulloch extends this debate by suggesting that the notion of competence is often used in two different ways: first, in a theoretical way which
can indicate enhanced performance; and second, by theorising about
competence as the underlying structure which is responsible for observable performance. If we wish to study *competence* we will be studying a
working model of the development of expertise. If, on the other hand, we
are to look at *performance*, we are caught up in the methodological problem of how to relate what a person can do to what they really understand. In other words, as McCulloch (1994) indicates, competence
concerns what people know and can do in ideal circumstances, while
performance is what they do in reality under existing circumstances.
Competence includes the structure of knowledge and abilities, whereas
performance also includes the process of 'accessing and utilising those
structures and a host of affective, motivational, attentional and stylistic
factors that influence the ultimate response' (Messick 1984, quoted in
McCulloch 1994).

Throughout all of this we are concerned with what the reflective practitioner is able to do within the learning environment. Many within
teacher education have resisted the whole concept of competencies. They
feel that it is a reductionist model with an over-emphasis on skills and
techniques, ignoring what informs teaching performance. Such theorists
as Whitty and Willmott (1991) propound the 'Gestalt' notion of educa-

tion, arguing that the process of teaching and learning is far more than the sum of its parts – the process cannot be reduced to a series of functions to be carried out by the teacher. To Whitty and Willmott, the reflective qualities that are so important in the continuing development of a teacher are lacking in the competency model. Others have argued that the competency-based approach does allow for the major elements within the complex and dynamic process of teaching – evaluation, research and experimentation. Authors such as Hextall *et al.* (1991) are able to define a range of reflexively-based competencies. Evaluation, research and experimentation

> are not value-added features of teacher quality; they constitute the very bases of competence in teaching – that is reflectivity. . . . The quality of reflectivity can be formulated as a series of competencies which can be observed, developed and monitored.
>
> (Hextall *et al.* 1991: 5)

There is, however, a suggestion from McCulloch that this may be a somewhat politically-based response which attempts to fit traditional concepts of teacher education into the vocational model which is currently in vogue. Hextall and colleagues are challenging the simplistic competency-based approaches to the development of teacher skills without appearing to challenge the skills-based model being promoted at this time by the government (McCulloch 1994). This confusion about the nature of the process underpinning the competencies is further complicated by fact that the language of descriptors is so vague.

Despite the complexity of the task, there is a number of advantages which can be seen when following this form of professional development for teachers. The first is that the whole process of teacher education is demystified (its critics might even say over-simplified!) by the definition and description of the competencies, and the second is that, as schools move to a more criteria-based assessment of their children, they have a shared experience with which to inform their practice.

Disadvantages

When attempting to relate the concept of competencies to the professional development of teachers there remains, despite the work of Earley (1993), a number of difficulties. We need to consider definitions of competency that go beyond skill but, by doing so, we come to the difficulty of assessment (McCulloch 1994). It is for this that we need to re-establish the concept of the teacher as a reflective practitioner, because herein lies the opportunity for self-assessment across a range situations.

The compromise here is the association of specific definitions with range statements which detail the different contexts within which the competencies must be displayed. There remains the problem of where a 'pass' occurs, whether comparative judgements can be used instead . . . or whether the identification of novice skills as compared with an expert can give our absolute 'pass' – norm referenced as it inevitably is.

(McCulloch 1994: 138–9)

The advantages to the reflective practitioner of competency-based professional development remain to be proven, while the difficulties of definition and specification, and the associated identification of realisable assessment criteria, still dominate the debate. As Norris (1991: 337) concludes:

> What is wrong here, as I see it, is the assumption that the assessment of knowledge or performance, taken separately or together, can cope with the range of context dependent and contingent nature of professional action. It is not the standards of performance that are required since these are beyond our capacity to specify. What is needed are standards of criticism and principles of professional judgement that can inform action in the context of uncertainty and change.

We are left, then, with an *impasse*. There is a growing move by centralised training bodies towards the notion of competencies for both the development of initial teacher training and for the professional development of teachers. Yet there is considerable evidence to suggest that there are problems with this method of teacher development. Not least there are the problems regarding definition and terminology. Clearly we are partway along the road, and much still needs to be examined. While the notion of competencies might be seen as an ideal solution to teacher development, there still remains a number of unanswered questions. What if, instead of looking outwards to a set of external competences, we look inwards for teacher development, towards action research?

ACTION RESEARCH AND THE REFLECTIVE PRACTITIONER

One area of work which has looked at the notion of teachers' professional development through reflection on practice has become known as 'action research', the name given to an increasingly popular study within educational research originated by Lewin (1946). It sets out to encourage the teacher to reflect on her own practice in order to improve its quality, and to this end it is a self-reflective enquiry which is now being used widely in school-based curriculum development, professional development, school-based improvement schemes and, to some limited extent, initial teacher training. This growing movement is now being seen as a real alternative to more academic, theory-based educational research, which has often looked at issues within the educational debate rather than focusing on the practical concerns of the teacher. Unlike the action-based method of enquiry, this larger-scale educational research is often seen as being imposed upon classroom teachers and not dealing with their own specific priorities. It sees the educational process as a holistic structure rather than a series of independent autonomous areas of study, and views the teacher as being central to the process.

> Action research approaches education as a unified exercise, seeing a teacher in the class as the best judge of his total educational experience.
>
> (McNiff 1992: 1)

Action research is an effective tool for unifying the divide between educational theory and practice, for it is the teacher herself who is encouraged to develop her own theory based upon her *own* practice.

> Action research might be defined as *'the study of social situations with a view to improving the quality of action within it'*. It aims to feed practical judgements in concrete situations, and the validity of the 'theories' or hypotheses it generates depends not so much on 'scientific' tests of truth, as on their usefulness in helping people to act more intelligently and skilfully. In action research, 'theories' are not validated independently and then applied to practice. They are validated through practice.
>
> (Elliott 1991: 69)

Lewin's (1946) model of action research was a model for change based on action and research. It involved teachers and researchers in a cyclical process of planning, action, observation and reflection: on the basis of reflecting upon the observations, a new planning cycle is then begun. As with the competency model of professional development, teachers are encouraged to observe their own practice and to reflect upon it. The most significant difference is the autonomy placed upon the individual practitioner. With the competency model the teacher is fitting her practice into previously determined criteria which then become the 'benchmark', whereas with the action research model the teacher is empowered to investigate those areas of concern as she perceives it within her own teaching situation.

The model originated by Lewin (1946) was further developed by Stenhouse (1975), and has since been elaborated by Elliott and Adelman (1976), Ebbutt (1985) and others, who developed the term 'teacher-as-researcher' to refer to the participants in the movement they helped to create. This encouraged teachers to assume the position of researchers within their own classrooms, as part of their professional reflective role.

But as Pollard and Tann (1987) indicate, this approach has been criticised for encouraging a focus on practical classroom ideas while the wider issues are accepted and left unchallenged. Despite this, Carr and Kemmis (1986) postulate that such work provides a means for the teacher to become 'critical'. They suggest (1986: 165) that action research involves:

- the improvement of practice;
- the improvement of the understanding of the practice by the practitioners;
- the improvement of the situation in which practice takes place.

As with Stenhouse (1975), they see the potential for the action research model as being emancipatory, releasing teachers from the straitjacket of habit, precedent, assumption and entrenched ideology.

Lewin described action research as series of steps in a spiral and, put simply, each step had four stages; planning, acting, observing, and reflecting. The scheme in action is represented in Figure 7.1.

The enquiry would then move on to the next step of the process, the replanning of the action. The model would thus be extended as shown in Figure 7.2.

Stenhouse took Lewin's ideas, which were not intended specifically for an education setting, and developed the concept of the teacher researcher. His theoretical notions came out of his work on the Schools Council Humanities Curriculum, which aimed at establishing a liberating environment in which pupils could learn, and his central premise was that teachers should regard themselves as researchers and see themselves as the best judges of their own practice.

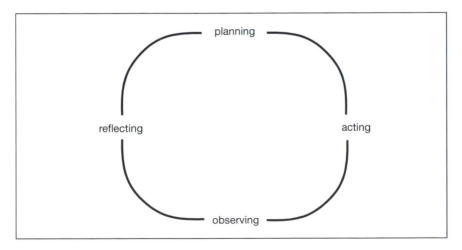

Figure 7.1 The four stages of action research
Source: McNiff (1988)

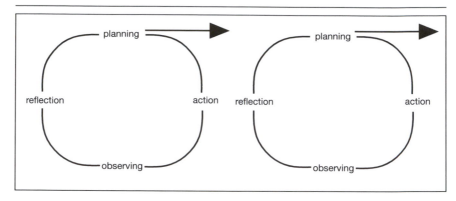

Figure 7.2 The action research model extended to include replanning of the action

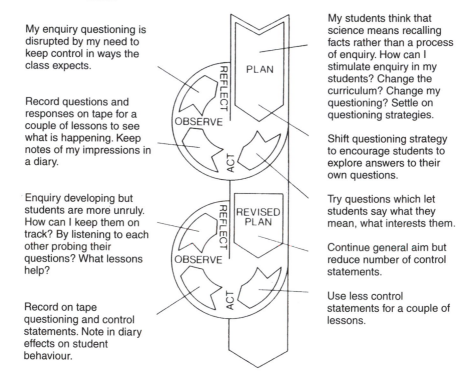

My enquiry questioning is disrupted by my need to keep control in ways the class expects.

Record questions and responses on tape for a couple of lessons to see what is happening. Keep notes of my impressions in a diary.

Enquiry developing but students are more unruly. How can I keep them on track? By listening to each other probing their questions? What lessons help?

Record on tape questioning and control statements. Note in diary effects on student behaviour.

My students think that science means recalling facts rather than a process of enquiry. How can I stimulate enquiry in my students? Change the curriculum? Change my questioning? Settle on questioning strategies.

Shift questioning strategy to encourage students to explore answers to their own questions.

Try questions which let students say what they mean, what interests them.

Continue general aim but reduce number of control statements.

Use less control statements for a couple of lessons.

Figure 7.3 The 'action research spiral'
Source: based on Kemmis and McTaggart (1988: 14)

This basic notion has been developed, both in this country and abroad, by Kemmis, Elliott, Ebbutt, McNiff and others, and a range of models of the process has been suggested, some of the key ones being illustrated in Figures 7.3 and 7.4. While the proposers of the various

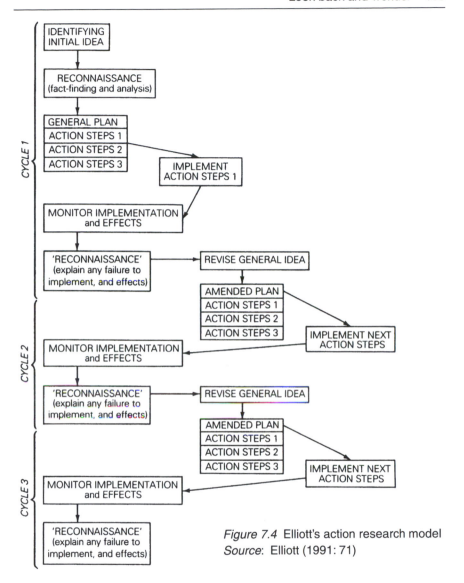

Figure 7.4 Elliott's action research model
Source: Elliott (1991: 71)

models may disagree about the accuracy of the spiral or the linear structure, what is significant for us here is that they all have within them the central notion of reflection. The learning about practice does not come from the setting of a focus, nor does it come from the observation of the practice. It comes about through reflecting on the practice – from thinking about what has occurred in relation to what was previously assumed to have occurred, and about how the learning environment might be altered to improve the experience for the children.

Much has been talked about the benefits of action research for the classroom practitioner, but writers have voiced a note of caution. There are three main areas of concern. First, classroom action research has moved a long way from how Lewin originally saw the concept, which was externally implemented, very functional, and prescriptive. Today it is more usually seen as problem-solving and eclectic in orientation, yet much energy has been expended in trying to intellectualise the basis for action research as it is derived from Lewin's original work.

> We should take care that what began as a useful label to describe teacher research for professional development does not assume a different character as a result for intellectual credibility.
>
> (Hopkins 1993: 54)

Second, no model can ever mirror reality, and great effort continues to be expended by the theoreticians in developing and refining the models. There is a danger that teachers may become entrapped by the tight steps of the various models, rather than liberated by them. At best, the models provide a starting point for the work and a guide thereafter. At worst they will become a straitjacket, confining teachers within a set of assumptions.

Action research frequently focuses upon words such as 'difficulty', 'problematic' and 'improvement'. Thus, professionally we are offered an image of a deficit model of teacher development. We need to talk positively about classroom research, and to encourage teachers to reflect evenly upon what they do rather than to dwell on the negative elements of what they have got wrong.

> Action research is one way of restoring and enhancing professional confidence . . . the importance of action research is not to be underestimated. Action research provides teachers with a more appropriate alternative to traditional research designs and one that is, in aspiration at least, emancipatory.
>
> (Hopkins 1993: 56)

TEACHERS ARE ALSO REAL PEOPLE!

When we consider ourselves as teachers, we must also consider those elements that make us what we are. We must recognise our social, cultural and educational backgrounds, for all of these have a significant influence upon a teacher's work within the classroom. It is our personal biography that goes to make what, in psychological terms, is known as the 'self', and it is this that makes us the people that we are. This is as true for teachers and children as it is for anyone else (Hargreaves 1992). The reflective teacher needs to consider her own values and beliefs carefully, and to be conscious of their implications for teaching. It is this value structure that will underpin the way that other ideas and decisions are dealt with. Much of this is bound up with what is traditionally thought to be the role of the teacher. Often what is done within the school is done in the way that it is because that is how the role of the teacher is perceived – this in turn being a leftover from the training process that teachers have undergone (Dewey would term this 'routine action' rather than 'reflective action'). There are considerable pressures placed upon teachers to conform to a range of roles, all invariably constructed by 'others' and not by the teachers themselves (such as, for instance, competences). The UK government has a notion of the role of the teacher, parents have a view, as do school governors, children and the media. No two views are the same, and each brings with it a set of pressures which are external to the real task of teaching. In order to free themselves from these imposed roles, teachers need to be able to interpret the pressures, make sense of them within the context of their own work and then make appropriate judgements. This can only be helped by encouraging teachers to reflect on themselves, as individuals and as practitioners within the classroom.

> Thus, knowing oneself as a person, establishing a clear set of values, aims and commitments, and understanding the situation one is in, are three essential elements in any reflective consideration of teaching.
>
> (Pollard and Tann 1987: 38)

DEVELOPING A SENSE OF 'SELF'

Studies of primary teachers indicate that those people entering the profession have a strong sense of professional identity and personal values. Nias *et al.* (1992) further indicates that this feeling is so strong that many individuals see themselves as 'persons in teaching' rather than as 'teachers'. Many were looking for personal fulfilment through teaching, over and above 'the job'. Clearly teachers must recognise this and resolve any differences between their perceived role – 'what teachers do' – and their concepts of self – 'how I see myself'. Chapter 4 showed how changing children's learning must involve a consideration of their feelings about themselves as learners; similarly, the ability of teachers to change through reflection is dependent upon how they see the relationship between their role and themselves. Therefore there is a need to be open and willing to change, and the teacher must feel comfortable with the 'self'. We must encourage teachers to develop self-awareness and self-knowledge. By doing this we are equipping them to cope with the wide and ever-changing problems that are part of the learning relationship.

CONCLUSION

Effective teachers need to be reflective teachers. They need to develop a sense of openness with themselves, with other staff and with pupils, in order to get feedback. In this way they can find out more about how they perform in the professional setting in order that informed development can occur. Teachers must be encouraged to work collaboratively with colleagues and to develop open and trusting working relationships. It is important not only that these professional relationships offer a different perspective on practice but that they also offer support so as to deal with whatever is revealed. (For further discussion of this, see Chapter 9).

It is important that teachers should identify how they feel about the learning process, rather than fall into assumptions or habitual practices: 'we've always done it like this' is a weak position from which to integrate new concepts into teaching practice. If we are not careful, we will be swept along by the prevailing ideologies. It is important that, as teachers, we are aware of and develop our own pedagogy.

> Changes in the professional role of teachers may make considerable demands on our personal and social attributes, as well as on our pedagogic skills. They also make demands on our willingness and capacity for change. We need, therefore, to consider our aims in the light of the many demands which are made upon us.
>
> (Pollard and Tann 1987: 45)

REFERENCES

Baird, J. R. (1991) 'Individual and group reflection as a basis for teacher development', in P. Hughes (ed.) *Teachers' Professional Development*, Melbourne, Australia: ACER.

Bennett, S. N., Wragg, E. C., Carré, C. G. and Carter, D. S. G. (1992) 'A longitudinal study of primary teachers' perceived competence in, and concerns about, national curriculum implementation', *Research Papers in Education* 7, 1.

Carr, D. (1993) 'Guidelines for teacher training: the competency model', *Scottish Education Review*, 25(1), 17–25.

Carr, W. and Kemmis, S. (1986) *Becoming Critical*, London: Falmer Press.

Carter, D. S. G., Carré, C. G. and Bennett, S. N. (1993) 'Student teachers' changing perceptions of their subject matter during an initial teacher training programme', *Educational Research*, 35, 1.

Central Advisory Council for Education (1967) *Children and their Primary Schools*, London: HMSO.

Copeland, W. D., Birmingham, C., De La Cruz, E., and Lewin, B. (1993) 'The Reflective Practitioner in Teaching: Toward a Research Agenda', *Teaching and Teacher Education*, 9(4), 347–59.

Costello, P. J. M. (1990) 'Philosophy, reflective teaching and educational reform', *Curriculum*, 11(2), 86–95.

Dewey, J. (1933) *How We Think: A Restatement of the Relation of Reflective Thinking to the Educative Process*, Chicago, IL: Henry Regnery.

Earley, P. (1991) 'Defining and assessing school management competences', *Management in Education*, 5(4), 31–4.

—— (1992a) 'Using competencies for school management development', *British Journal of In-Service Education*, 18(3), 176–85.

—— (1992b) 'Initiation rites', *Education*, 180(21), 412–13.

—— (1993) 'Developing Competence in Schools: A Critique of Standards-based Approaches to Management Development', *Education Management and Administration*, 21(4), 233–43.

Ebbutt, D. (1985) 'Educational Action Research: Some General Concerns and Specific Quibbles', in R. Burgess (ed.) *Issues in Educational Research*, Lewes: Falmer Press.

Elliott, J. (1991) *Action Research for Educational Change*, Milton Keynes: Open University Press.

Elliott, J. and Adelman, C. (1976) 'Innovation at the Classroom Level: a case study of the Ford Teaching Project', Unit 28, Open University Course E203, Milton Keynes: Open University Educational Enterprises.

Hargreaves, D. H. (1992) 'The New Professionalism', paper presented to the *Fourth International Symposium in Teachers' Learning and School Development*, University of New England, New South Wales, July.

Hextall, I., Lawn, M., Sidwick, S. and Walker, S. (1991) *Imaginative Projects: Arguments for a New Teacher Education*, London: Goldsmiths' College.

Hopkins, D. (1993) *A Teacher's Guide to Classroom Research* (2nd edn), Buckingham: Open University Press.

Houston, W. R. and Howsam, R. B. (1972) *Competency-Based Teacher Education*, Chicago, IL: Science Research Associates.

Lewin, K. (1946) 'Action Research and Minority Problems', *Journal of Social Issues*, 2.

Liston, D. P. and Zeichner, K. M. (1990) 'Reflective Teaching and Action', *Research Journal of Education for Teaching*, 16(3), 235–53.

McCulloch, M. (1994) 'Teacher competences and their Assessment', in M. McCulloch and B. Fidler (eds) *Improving Initial Teacher Training*, London: Longman.

McDonald, J. F. (1974) 'The Rationale for Competency Based Programmes', in W. R. Houston (ed.) *Exploring Competency Based Education*, California: McCutchan.

McNamara, D. (1990) 'Research on teachers' thinking: its contribution to educating student–teachers to think critically', *Journal of Education for Teaching*, 16, 2.

McNiff, J. (1992) *Teaching as Learning: an Action Research Approach*, London: Routledge.

Messick, S. (1984) 'The Psychology of Educational Measurement', *Journal of Educational Measurement*, 21(3), 215–37.

Munby, H. and Russell, T. (1989) 'Educating the reflective teacher: an essay review of two books by Donald Schön', *Curriculum Studies*, 21(1), 71–80.

Nias, J., Southworth, G. and Campbell, P. (1992) *Whole School Curriculum Development in the Primary School*, London: Falmer Press.

Norris, N. (1991) 'The Trouble with Competence', *Cambridge Journal of Education*, 21(3), 331–41.

Piaget, J. (1950) *The Psychology of Intelligence*, London: Routledge and Kegan Paul.

Pollard, A. and Tann, S. (1987) *Reflective Teaching in the Primary School*, London: Cassell.

Silcock, P. (1994) 'The Process of Reflective Teaching', *British Journal of Educational Studies*, 24(3), 273–85.

Simpson, R. H. (1966) *Teacher Self-evaluation*, London: Macmillan.

Stenhouse, L. (1975) *An Introduction to Curriculum Research and Development*, London: Heinemann.

White, J. (1978) 'The Primary Teacher as Servant of the State', *Education 3–13*, 7(2), 18–23.

Whitty, G. and Willmott, E. (1991) 'Competency-based teacher education: approaches and issues', *Cambridge Journal of Education*, 21(3), 309–18.

Zeichner, K. (1982) 'Reflective teaching and field-based experience in pre-service teacher education', *Interchange*, 12, 1–22.

Chapter 8

Classroom talk

Communicating within the learning relationship

Martin Cortazzi

INTRODUCTION

The language used by teachers in the classroom is a major element of a vital communication system: classroom discourse. This chapter will discuss some of the many ways in which classroom discourse frames learning. Teacher–pupil talk is the medium through which learners encounter so much of the curriculum. It is the medium for classroom organisation, management and control; a medium for socialisation into schooling and culture. Teacher–pupil talk is the major means through which children develop their literacy skills which, in turn, they will use for so much other learning.

The talk of teachers, therefore, has a far-reaching influence. It can be a model of how to use language for learning and thus the means for pupils to learn how to learn. Teacher talk can implicitly convey the norms and expectations of classroom behaviour, of teachers' and pupils' roles, of how to attain knowledge and understanding. It can show how to express and explain what one knows, or even that one may come to know something through trying to express what one thinks it might be. Teacher talk can convey a hidden curriculum of all these things. Together with the interaction of learners' talk to each other, teacher talk can be the foundation of cultures of learning. In all these areas, teacher talk can be a bridge or a barrier, either facilitating learning relationships or limiting them.

During class time, classroom discourse is practically continuous. It is rare to find sustained silence in primary schools. Teachers – and pupils – are constantly creating this medium for learning, yet it is easy to take it for granted. Precisely because it seems so normal, especially for more experienced teachers, we may overlook some of the ways in which it works and ignore aspects of its complexity. This means it is difficult to change (if change is desired), but easy to become a victim of it – to find that we only use language in certain ways because (we believe) those are the ways of talking in classrooms.

This chapter will elaborate on these ideas, first outlining some of the ways in which teacher talk functions on various levels. Then it will examine some of the patterns of the language exchanges between teachers and learners. Some of these exchanges are designed to conform to a plan or to reach an outcome known in advance by the teacher. However, many exchanges are not pre-structured or formulaic. They cannot be predicted because children's responses cannot be easily predicted. Rather, classroom exchanges are negotiations of meaning in which participants respond to each other's on-going talk. The chapter therefore also examines talk intended to create a learning relationship for children – an environment of communication with teachers, linked to thinking and experience, in which children will learn and develop.

ORAL COMMUNICATION IN THE CURRICULUM

Language is, of course, an important *subject* of the curriculum and it is vital for teachers to present an appropriate model of language. Until recently, the language area of the primary curriculum in many countries gave priority to literacy and literature, but now it is increasingly common to give more emphasis to children's talk. There are good reasons for this: children in the primary phase are still acquiring their mother tongue, and in many cases a second or other language. This means that they are still developing areas of grammar, pronunciation, and, most clearly, vocabulary (Durkin 1986); but, more than this, they are also developing sociolinguistic skills of appropriate use (Andersen 1990) and their awareness of language itself and the ability to reflect on it and deliberately control its use (see Chapter 2 of this book and, e.g., Gombert 1992). Also, the development of fluent talk can be seen as being important for children's social and psychological development, e.g. for self-confidence and self-esteem, as seen earlier in this book.

For pupils in British primary schools, this means that English is a core subject, taught and used by virtually all teachers. (Two exceptions are when a foreign language is taught and when a teacher switches languages to support bilingual pupils' learning.) This means that teacher talk is an important model of language, both as a source of input for children's language development and as an example of appropriate target language. This is the reason why teacher training programmes in many countries stress the use of clear speech by teachers, a wide but appropriate use of vocabulary and, in general, a high standard of talk.

There is another dimension or level to this: language is the *medium* for learning all subjects in the curriculum, including language (English or another language). Many linguists and educators emphasise the importance of talking for children's learning (see, e.g., Britton 1970; Stubbs 1983; Tizard and Hughes 1984; Wells 1986; Edwards and Mercer 1987;

Corson 1988; Meadows and Cashdan 1988). They have emphasised these kinds of linked propositions:

- language develops primarily through purposeful use;
- expressing ideas is a means of understanding them;
- talk with parents and teachers is making meaning;
- oracy is a bridge to literacy;
- talking is a foundation for learning;
- language use contributes to cognitive development.

Therefore the ability of teachers, and learners, to express themselves verbally – and understand other's talk – is crucial for the teaching–learning relationship.

Language is a symbol system. Through names, technical terms, subject-specific phrases and expressions, the knowledge and concepts involved in all subjects are encoded. It is difficult to discuss art, science or music without relevant terms. Language labels concepts and encodes ways of thinking: the language of maths *is* maths. Hence, it is difficult for teachers not to be involved, directly or indirectly, in language teaching, whatever they are teaching. The example below shows how older children have internalised this idea of subject registers: each subject involves learning a different way of talking because the subject embodies its own way of thinking. However, younger learners still have to learn how to handle these differences of register. The speaker is a secondary school student:

> When you're speaking with each other, you're practising your English. Geography is a different language, you don't speak that. When you're speaking about Maths, that's English, but when you write, you have to write Maths. You have to use words like 'thus', and 'hence' and 'implies that'. History has a completely different set of words, like 'bitterly hostile', and there are some words that you can't use in Geography – like 'mardy' and 'beautiful'.
>
> **Transcript 1 (from Harold Gardiner 1980; personal communication)**

This presents teachers with a paradox: there is a need to simplify their talk to children because they are still acquiring language, yet there is a need to provide a language-rich environment to facilitate their development. This is heavily reinforced by another paradox: the need to use language as a medium for learning subject content when children are still developing that medium. English is both a target and the means to reach that target. It is also the means that teachers have to use to help children attain these.

ORAL COMMUNICATION IN SOCIAL INTERACTION AND CLASSROOM ORGANISATION

A further level of complexity is the fact that teacher talk is the means for organising and managing children's learning. Teachers need to give instructions, set up activities, or organise groups of learners. Teachers need to inform children about what to do, how to go about tasks, and they need to assess and evaluate learning. All of these teacher roles are predominantly carried out through language. The language used for controlling and disciplining pupils is also part of this dimension.

Consider these questions asked by primary teachers:

- Can you play the guitar?
- Can you get into groups?
- Can you get on with your work?

All of these could be answered by *yes* or *no*, without further action by the children, i.e. they could be interpreted as requests for information about the ability to do these things. This depends on the context, however. If the first is said to a child holding the guitar, it could be a request for action, a polite command to play. The second example is clearly a classroom instruction. The last example could be an instruction, but is more likely to be a reprimand; yet, if said by a teacher who wants to know if children need help, it is a request for information. Teachers know that the context and tone of voice make all the difference, that utterances are not only *saying* something but are also *doing* something. Older pupils also know that speech performs actions and they can decode the underlying meaning.

TEACHER What are you laughing at?
PUPIL Nothing.

Here the pupil understands the question as a reprimand – one is not supposed to laugh in class – and so replies 'Nothing'. This is clearly not literally true, and can be taken to mean *Nothing that I can tell you about*, i.e. it is unofficial laughter, not part of the classroom agenda. While older pupils realise and respond to such indirect requests and controls by teachers, they are a challenge for some younger learners and second language users.

TEACHER Before noon it is ante-meridian, or a.m. If it's after, it's post-meridian. What does that mean? Can you guess . . . post-meridian? Yes, Simon.
CHILD 1 Afternoon.
TEACHER Afternoon. That's right. Good boy.

CHILD 2 It's like when somebody's having a baby. It's post-mature if it's after . . .

TEACHER It's post-natal and ante-natal, not mature.

CHILD 2 I know, but . . .

TEACHER That's right. Good girl. Yes, post. Good.

CHILD 3 My mummy told me about the p.m. and the a.m. and I worked it out. In the mornings it's a.m. and if it's in the afternoon it's p.m.

TEACHER Good. Well, I want you to practise doing it with these cards that I've made you. Alright, shush the rest of you! If you want to get bottle tops to draw round for clocks then do so. Could you just get on quietly for a minute, Anna? Just a minute, Donald, please. Any time after 12 o'clock at night, midnight, until 12 o'clock noon – which is our lunch time isn't it? – we say ante-meridian or a.m.

Transcript 2 (quoted in Francis 1977: 78; my interpretation)

The management role of teachers can often conflict with a teaching role, especially under pressure of time. This is illustrated in the example of Transcript 2, which occurred with eight-year-old pupils who were about to practise some work with clocks.

The teacher starts by explaining and asking about the terms a.m. and p.m. and one child provides an acceptable answer. The second child then offers an unsolicited comment which includes the term *post-mature*. The teacher interrupts this with a correction. (The social rights of speaking in classrooms include the norm that teachers may interrupt pupils at any time, but not vice versa.) This would normally stop such an exchange but here Child 2 acknowledges the teacher's correction: '*I know, but . . .*'.

The *but* shows that the child has more to say. At this point the teacher again cuts in, apparently acknowledging, now, Child 2's original contribution by focusing on the word *post*. The teacher's praise also seems to enforce control, preventing Child 2 from continuing. Child 3 now offers another comment which effectively repeats the teacher's original explanation. The teacher acknowledges this, then moves into management talk in order to set up the task. This is obviously not too easy. Most children need to be quietened, and some (Anna, Donald) are obviously bidding for individual attention from the teacher. The extract shows how the teacher wants to get the class working on the task and tries to avoid being switched off course by children's comments. An explanation from one pupil, Child 3, cannot be taken to imply that the whole class understands. The teacher seems to be aware of this trap, since, after quietening the class, she returns to summarise the basic point.

The extract analysed so far shows conflicts between three of the functions of teacher talk: explanation, organisation and control. But there is more. There is also a conflict between organisation and social expression. Child 2 is apparently offering a comment from personal experience. This use of language for social interaction is not reciprocated by the teacher, who apparently sees it as a distraction and maintains the instructional focus of the talk by correcting, then praising, Child 2's terms. This is a pity: Child 2 has more to say and, in fact, she is using *post-mature* correctly. The teacher does not seem to know that it refers to a child born after the normal nine-month term of pregnancy and is thus an antonym of *premature*. This is likely to have emerged in a subsequent sharing of experience by Child 2, but we will never know, since the teacher cut her off, prematurely. Had the teacher made a more socially-oriented comment after Child 2's '*I know, but* . . . ', and allowed her to explain, an exchange between teacher and pupils similar to the one described in the diagram in Figure 8.1 might have been the result.

		Before	After
TIME	-noon	*ante-meridian*	*post-meridian*
BABIES	-birth	*ante-natal*	*post-natal*
	-a full term pregnancy	*premature*	*post-mature*

Figure 8.1 A diagram of the teacher–pupils exchange in Transcript 2 as it might have been

This would have reinforced the meaning of *post* and consolidated the meaning of *ante* by associating it with *pre*. This would have been closely related to the chief concept of the lesson and it would have helped the children see the language systems involved. As was illustrated in Chapter 2 by Hargreaves and Hargreaves and Chapter 3 by Merry, such a continuation could have shown the pupils the value of personal expression and sharing experience, relating new concepts to what they already know.

The example shows that, potentially, the social dimension of teacher–pupil talk can intersect powerfully with content-centred talk. Talk is a crucial social mode of learning. In this case, the teacher could have been learning from the child. Unfortunately, the learning relationship was, on this occasion, dominated by the need for control and organisation. All teachers face such dilemmas.

TEACHER TALK AS METACOMMUNICATION

There is one function of teacher talk which links language learning with classroom organisation and control. This is a *metacommunicative* function (Stubbs 1983) in which teachers communicate about classroom communication. Generally, this means teachers use talk to control the pupils' talk, but it can be used to make learners aware of language and how to use talk in different ways. Examples of primary teachers' metacommunication are:

- Can you give me an example of that?
- Don't shout out. Wait till I ask you.
- Has anybody got a question to ask this group about their experiment?
- Daniel, I like the way you said that. You expressed it very well.

Like so many other aspects of classroom talk at primary level, metacommunication is assymetrical: teachers use it frequently but it is very rare for children to use it. One reason for this is that metacommunication often has a strong control function. It regulates pupil talk and reflects the social rights and power of the classroom.

Metacommunication can be used with much less intervention than these comments indicate. It can be used to suggest, or model, ways of talking and thinking. This is shown in the example of Transcript 3, in which a group of eleven-year-olds are discussing where a new road should be built. Each pupil has a role and is arguing a case.

For most of the time the teacher is observing and listening but does not interrupt, although it must have been tempting to intervene after Marcia's second or after Steve's third comment. When the teacher does speak, she skilfully steers the discussion by eliciting Marcia's reasons.

MARCIA I want route A.

STEVE Well, I don't, I want route C, cos . . .

MARCIA I don't care what you want.

STEVE Route A will destroy my golf course.

TERRY What about Elkin Hall? . . . It'll . . .

TRACY What about the people who live in Lawstown . . . the kids having to cross the road?

MARCIA What about it . . . it's falling down anyway.

STEVE You're not coming through my golf course and that's that.

MARCIA Oh yeah . . . we'll see about that . . . we're having route A.

TEACHER Perhaps Marcia would give us her reasons for so strongly supporting route A?

TERRY There aren't any, she's just being awkward.

> **TEACHER** I think we should listen to what Marcia has to say in favour of route A and then put forward any questions or queries or worries that we have.
>
> **MARCIA** Route A is the cheapest . . . it doesn't go through the town so it won't be a danger or a nuisance to the residents of Lawstown . . . and it won't mean having to destroy an area of beauty where there's lots of wildlife.
>
> **STEVE** Yeah, route A has some good things about it . . . but the golf . . . the golf course provides for lots . . . of people . . . their recreation.
>
> **TRACY** But couldn't the golf course be rebuilt . . . I mean it's better to build a golf course than to have a busy road through the middle of the town.
>
> **TERRY** Yeah, but Elkin Hall . . . I know it's old but that's the point, isn't it? . . . You could take it down and move it . . . rebuild it, but it wouldn't be the same . . . it wouldn't be got like real any more, would it?
>
> **Transcript 3 (from Corden 1992: 176; my interpretation)**

The teacher's brief comments focus on content, but indirectly on argument (*'give us her reasons . . .'*) and discussion procedure (*'listen . . . then put forward any questions or queries or worries . . .'*). Another teacher might have reprimanded the pupils or focused on their social relations and a brewing quarrel. In fact, these teacher's comments are metacommunication which draw the pupils back to the task, focusing on their talk and including the group rather than Marcia alone (*'Give us her reasons . . .'*, *'we should listen . . .'*).

There is a paradox with metacommunication. Teachers use it to control pupil talk by clarifying, expanding, rephrasing, summarising and directing discussions. For many children this facilitates language and interaction by prompting and explaining talk. However, if it is always the teacher who does this, there are severe restrictions on the opportunities for children to develop independence in controlling their own talk and in managing and interpreting discussion – someone else is always the chairperson. As the example shows, activities such as drama and role play, or group discussions with a pupil as chairperson, may encourage pupil metacommunication. Yet teachers need to use metacommunication to maintain control and to organise classroom events, and they need metacommunication to organise children's drama, etc.

The argument so far is that the teaching–learning relationship is built up in teacher–child exchanges of talk. As outlined here, this classroom communication functions on several interrelated levels, and involves paradoxes. As demonstrated by Kitson in Chapter 7 of this book on the reflective practitioner, it is a major point for professional development to be aware of these levels of communication in one's own classroom, and to reflect upon such paradoxes, even if there does not seem to be an immediate solution to them.

Given the importance of teacher talk and pupil expression for the subject, content and medium of learning, for social interaction, control and classroom organisation, it would not be an exaggeration to say that the curriculum is born and carried on the tip of the tongue. However worthy the policy documents, syllabuses, textbooks and materials which are used to plan and carry through classroom activities for learning, ultimately what primary children learn is crucially dependent on teacher–pupil exchanges of talk.

THE STRUCTURE OF CLASSROOM EXCHANGES

Classroom exchanges are stretches of interaction between two or more participants in which the talk is jointly constructed to achieve a purpose. In those exchanges which involve the teacher, the teacher's contribution is usually to inform learners or to question them. Pupils respond, and this in turn is followed up by the teacher. Such exchanges have been more intensively researched than other aspects of classroom communication (see, e.g., Sinclair and Coulthard 1975; Mehan 1979; Coulthard and Montgomery 1981; Sinclair and Brazil 1982; Willes 1983; Lemke 1989; Willis 1992; Hoey 1993; Tsui 1994).

One can see how this works from the example of Transcript 4, which contains sequences of two- or three-part exchanges. The teacher is asking an early-years class about a picture of a christening, as part of a project about festivals. Each exchange is initiated by a teacher question which a pupil answers, with the teacher taking every alternate turn. This gives *question–answer* exchanges. However, the teacher frequently repeats the answers, giving a three-part exchange structure: *question–answer–repetition*.

> **TEACHER** Listen, one at a time. John, you tell us what he's doing.
> **JOHN** Making a cross on his hand.
> **TEACHER** What is he doing? What is it? What is it that's in the picture? What is it called?
> **PUPILS** He is being christened.
> **TEACHER** He is being christened. What happens when you're christened?
> **DAVIN** You get a name.
> **TEACHER** You get a name. What's your name?

> **DAVIN** Davin.
>
> **TEACHER** Davin. Where do you think this is taken from? Who do you think they are?
>
> **PUPILS** From the church.
>
> **TEACHER** In a church. What makes you think it's in a church?
>
> **PUPILS** (*inaudible*)
>
> **TEACHER** Wait. Listen, one at a time, shall we? Steven?
>
> **STEVEN** And you have a christening cake.
>
> **TEACHER** And you have a christening cake. Where do you have a christening cake? In church?
>
> **PUPILS** No.
>
> **TEACHER** When do you have christening cake? At home? Afterwards or before?
>
> **PUPILS** Afterwards.
>
> **TEACHER** Afterwards. What do we call this here?
>
> **SEAN** I know.
>
> **TEACHER** What is it?
>
> **SEAN** A font.
>
> **TEACHER** A font. That's a good boy, Sean. That's a font . . .
>
> (*the exchanges continue is this way for some time*)
>
> Transcript 4 (from King 1978: 44–6; my interpretation)

The teacher did not want to simply inform the children about christenings. She assumed they could use their background knowledge to interpret the picture and that her role was to elicit this through questions. When a child gave a 'correct' answer she repeated it for emphasis; 'wrong' answers were ignored.

Some teachers say that they repeat pupils' answers in this way so that the rest of the class can hear. This seems strange, given that an aim of language education is to help children to speak audibly, confidently and fluently. With constant repetitions, children learn not to listen to each other; they need only wait to hear the teacher's repetition. They also learn to direct their answers only to the teacher, not to their peers. There are probably stronger reasons for the repetitions: first, they serve to punctuate the discourse, keeping the regulation of speakers' turns within the teacher's control; second, the repetition is actually *evaluation* – it signals the correctness of the pupil's response. If a teacher does not repeat, or otherwise evaluate a response, this is generally interpreted by learners to mean that the response is wrong, so other pupils give different responses. With the repetition, other pupils do not give further responses because they know that the repeated item was correct. This illustrates the power of the third move in classroom exchanges.

A complication in this interpretation of teacher's repetition is that it depends on intonation: rising intonation generally means a questioning repeat, throwing doubt (or surprise) on the response; falling intonation signals acceptance that the response is correct. This is illustrated in the next example, where a teacher and some eight-year-olds are examining building materials and artefacts. The teacher here uses incomplete sentences with rising intonation – these are essentially slot-filling questions for children to supply the final words.

> TEACHER So this is a corner . . . ?
> CHILD 1 Of the . . . er . . .
> CHILD 2 Someone's house.
> TEACHER Co . . . so what do we call it? . . . It's a corner . . . ?
> CHILD 2 Slab.
> TEACHER Slab?
> CHILD 1 Corner Tile.
> TEACHER Corner Tile.
>
> Transcript 5 (from Corden 1992: 174; my interpretation)

The teacher's repetition of 'Slab?' with rising intonation is taken as negative feedback by the children – otherwise it is doubtful if Child 1 would continue to offer 'Corner Tile'. The teacher repeats this response with falling intonation to indicate approval and the exchange is over.

Younger children and those learning in a second language can have problems in interpreting such delicate cues, as in the following example where a teacher is helping a nine-year-old bilingual pupil with prepositions.

> TEACHER Where is the cup?
> CHILD On top of the box.
> TEACHER Right, the cup is on top of the box. (*moves cup*) Now where is the cup?
> CHILD In the box.
> TEACHER The cup is . . . ?
> CHILD In the box.
> TEACHER The cup is in . . . ?
> CHILD The cup is in the box.
> TEACHER Right, very good, the cup is in the box.
>
> Transcript 6 (from Johnson 1995: 9–10; my interpretation)

Here the answer '*In the box*', although parallel to the previously accepted answer of '*On top of the box*', is not accepted. We know this, as the child does, because the teacher does not repeat or otherwise evaluate the answer, but instead gives an incomplete sentence cue with rising intonation. The child interprets this as a slot-filling question and completes it, '*In the box*', although this means repeating the previous answer. Again, there is no evaluation from the teacher, which signals that this is not the reply she wants. Instead, she repeats the incomplete sentence, which the child now re-interprets as a cue for a long answer, '*The cup is in the box*'. The teacher now signals acceptance: '*Right*'; praise: '*very good*'; and repeats the sentence – a triple positive evaluation.

In fact, the *question–answer–repetition* pattern is a particular example of a more general pattern which has an opening move or *initiation* (I) from the first speaker, then a *response* (R) from the second speaker and finally a *follow-up* move (F) from the first speaker. This is shown in Figure 8.2, with indications of other realisations of the same general pattern. Variations of this basic pattern are common: I–R; I–R–I–R–F; I–R–F–F; and other elements can expand the basic pattern: *question*–(pupils raise hands, bidding to answer)–teacher *nominates* one pupil–*answer*–*follow-up* . . . .

In classrooms, the *initiation* is usually, but not always, from the teacher. *Responses* tend to come from pupils in answer to teachers' questions or to follow instructions or explanations. The *follow-up* is virtually the prerogative of the teacher.

Such exchanges are constructed by the joint effort of the teacher and pupils: it is the teacher who initiates and responds, while the pupil's role is to be a respondent, sandwiched between the teacher's two-thirds of each exchange. This would explain at the micro level Flanders's (1970) well-known finding that teachers talk for two-thirds of class time.

To understand the system, it is useful to look at the I–R–F exchanges as *question–answer–evaluation*. Teachers' questions generally evoke answers: when the answer comes the teacher knows both *that*, and *how*,

Initiation	Response	Follow up
question	answer	repetition
elicitation	query	acknowledgement
request	temporisation	evaluation
directive		elaboration
informative		reinterpretation
		refocus

Figure 8.2 Examples of I-R-F patterns

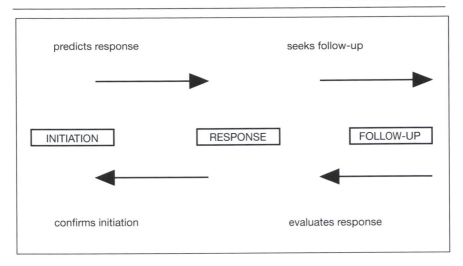

Figure 8.3 The structure of a common classroom exchange

the question was understood, besides being able to evaluate the answer. This makes the I–R–F exchange very useful for teachers to check children's understanding (see Figure 8.3). This is also useful for the children: when the teacher repeats, evaluates or praises the answer this gives pupils feedback, and in fact pupils' answers are often designed to elicit such feedback. The three parts of classroom exchanges can thus be seen as two overlapping pairs of moves – or *adjacency pairs*, to use Schegloff's and Sacks's (1973) terms – I–R, and R–F, in which the first predicts or seeks the second, while the second confirms or interprets the first.

IMPROVING THE EXCHANGE

The research literature suggests two ways of improving the learning and communication involved in classroom exchanges. The first is to wait. This means teachers should wait an extra second or two at one of several possible points in the exchange: before asking, after asking but before a response (i.e., before calling on a pupil to reply), and after a response but before giving feedback. Basically, the pause gives extra thinking time for both teacher and pupils. Rowe (1986) summarises the consequences of increasing the wait time:

For pupils

- There are fewer failures to respond;
- There is an increase in the length of responses;
- Responses become more confident (shown by intonation);

- There is an increase in unsolicited responses;
- There is more pupil–pupil discussion;
- There are more questions from pupils.

For teachers

- There are fewer questions;
- Questions are more varied; more of them are cognitively demanding;
- A wider variety of pupil responses are accepted;
- Follow-up moves are more flexible;
- There are fewer self-answers by teachers;
- Expectations of certain pupils (previously less noticed) improve.

A second way to improve the exchange is vary the *initiation* element by improving questions or using alternatives to questions. While questions are powerful prompts for learning, there is evidence that they are over-used or mis-used (see, e.g., Hargie 1978; Richards 1978; Dillon 1988; Galton 1989). There are generally too few questions which demand reasoning or evaluation, for instance. Dillon (1990) and Brown and Wragg (1993) suggest:

- *preparing* questions: planning and sequencing key questions in advance;
- *putting* questions: distributing, prompting, *listening* and *responding;*
- *pondering* the question–answer exchanges to seek improvements next time.

Alternatively, other sorts of *initiations* could be tried which are not teacher questions:

- A 'state of mind statement': '*I don't quite follow*';
- An invitational statement: '*I'd like to hear more about . . .*';
- A statement of interest: '*I was interested in your . . .*';
- Reflective re-statement (of a pupil's comment) to encourage clarification;
- Pupil questions to teacher, giving systematic opportunities to ask;
- Group questions, other pupils ask one pupil questions.

CREATING A LEARNING RELATIONSHIP THROUGH TALK

A second general approach to overcome the disadvantages of classroom exchanges is to use alternative teaching strategies. A basis for developing these is suggested by recent work which builds on insights from Vygotsky (1986 [1934]), who stressed the socio-cultural foundation of learning. The teaching–learning relationship, in this view, thrives in sharing knowledge and meanings through talk in interactive tasks. The growth point for learning lies within the child's *zone of proximal development* (ZPD). As we saw earlier in this book, this refers to the distance between *actual* development (seen by the child's ability to solve tasks independently) and *potential* development (determined by the child's ability to solve tasks with adult guidance or in cooperation with more advanced peers). The goal of the teacher is to ascertain the point of potential development for any particular area of learning (ZPD) and to help the child actualise it.

This has led to a surge of research and development (see, e.g., Edwards and Mercer 1987; Meadows and Cashdan 1988; Tharp and Gallimore 1988; Newman *et al.* 1989; Moll 1990; Wertsch 1991; Daniels 1993). Within this neo-Vygotskian tradition are the following selected propositions:

• learning is internalisation of concepts mediated by experience and talk
• such verbalisation must be two-way, teacher *and* child;
• learning is not simply transmission but is *construction*, a joint building up;
• a teacher's mentoring role is helping a child to learn how to do something;
• the teacher draws attention to significant features of an activity;
• the teacher engages in *scaffolding*, giving temporary help;
• scaffolding is later removed and initiative is handed over to the learner;
• the aim of scaffolding is to move the child towards independence;
• teacher talk and task-setting must challenge children at times;
• this challenge should be within a child's ZPD;
• the teacher must continually ascertain this ZPD for any given concept;
• the teacher must be learning about the child's learning.

POINTS FOR REFLECTION

In keeping with the notion of the reflective practitioner, outlined in Chapter 7, this chapter concludes with some suggestions aimed at practising teachers, to help the ideas discussed here to be taken further into professional practice by consideration of the following:

• Teachers can use language to change classroom contexts, e.g. from a serious to a humorous tone; from off-task to on-task; or vice versa. How do you yourself use language to change classroom contexts? When do you do so?
• The I–R–F pattern has been identified as the basic pattern of teacher–pupil exchanges. When do you use this pattern? Do you over-use it? Can you extend the F element so that children make comments, suggestions and their own evaluations?

- Extending 'wait time', and using alternatives to questions, seem potentially useful. If you tried these in the classroom how would you monitor the effect? Would you ask the children about their perceptions?
- The 'zone of proximal development' seems a vital idea for teachers to have in mind when talking to individual children. Could it be applied to pairs? Or to small groups? Or to a whole class?
- Teachers' metacommunication could help children to reflect on tasks, learning and language. How do you use metacommunication in the classroom? How might it be used more effectively?
- The transcript examples in this chapter were recorded over a period of twenty-five years. Looking back over them, with the dates in mind, do you detect any shifts in patterns of communication over this period? Do you think they are reasonably representative of primary classrooms? One example is actually from a secondary school: does this of itself make any difference? How would these transcripts compare with one made in your own teaching context?
- Classroom communication and the various patterns of teacher–pupil talk are crucial channels for children's learning. If teachers wish children to take responsibility for their own learning, and to be aware of language around them, then arguably we should teach children explicitly about classroom discourse. How would you do so?

SUMMARY

Teacher talk is a paradox. It is by nature transient, but in its passing it can create enduring learning relationships. At its best, it is temporary in the sense that some of its characteristics will have been handed over to a learner who, having learnt, no longer needs the same support and is moving towards independence. To paraphrase Vygotsky, what children can only say today with their teacher's help they will be able to say alone tomorrow. They will be able to think through those words to make them their own, if we encourage a culture of learning which provides such tools for thinking.

REFERENCES

Andersen, E. S. (1990) *Speaking with Style, the sociolinguistic skills of children*, London: Routledge.
Barnes, D. (1986 [1969]) 'Language in the Secondary School', in D. Barnes, J. Britton and M. Torbe *Language, the Learner and the School* (3rd edn), Harmondsworth: Penguin.
Britton, J. N. (1970) *Language and Learning*, London: Allen Lane.
Brown, G. and Wragg, E. C. (1993) *Questioning*, London: Routledge.

Corden, R. (1992) 'The Role of the Teacher', in K. Norman (ed.) *Thinking Voices, the work of the National Oracy Project*, London: Hodder and Stoughton.

Corson, D. (1988) *Oral Language across the Curriculum*, Clevedon: Multilingual Matters.

Coulthard, M. and Montgomery, M. (eds) (1981) *Studies in Discourse Analysis*, London: Routledge and Kegan Paul.

Daniels, H. (ed.) (1993) *Charting the Agenda; educational activity after Vygotsky*, London: Routledge.

Dillon, J. T. (1988) *Questioning and Teaching: a manual of practice*, London: Croom Helm.

—— (1990) *The Practice of Questioning*, London: Routledge.

Durkin, K. (ed.) (1986) *Language Development in the School Years*, London: Croom Helm.

Edwards, D. and Mercer, N. (1987) *Common Knowledge, the development of understanding in the classroom*, London: Methuen.

Flanders, N. (1970) *Analysing Teacher Behaviour*, Reading, MA: Addison-Wesley.

Francis, H. (1977) *Language in Teaching and Learning*, London: Allen and Unwin.

Galton, M. (1989) *Teaching in the Primary School*, London: David Fulton.

Gombert, J. E. (1992) *Metalinguistic Development*, Hemel Hempstead: Harvester Wheatsheaf.

Hargie, O. (1978) 'The importance of teacher questions in the classroom', *Educational Research*, 20(2), 99–102.

Hoey, M. (1993) 'The case for the exchange complex', in M. Hoey (ed.) *Data, Description, Discourse*, London: Harper Collins.

Johnson, K. E. (1995) *Understanding Communication in Second Language Classrooms*, Cambridge: Cambridge University Press.

King, R. (1978) *All Things Bright and Beautiful? A sociological study of infants' classrooms*, Chichester: John Wiley and Sons.

Lemke, J. L. (1989) *Using Language in the Classroom*, Oxford: Oxford University Press.

Meadows, S. and Cashdan, A. (1988) *Helping Children Learn, contributions to a cognitive curriculum*, London: David Fulton.

Mehan, H. (1979) *Learning Lessons*, Cambridge, MA: Harvard University Press.

Moll, L. C. (ed.) (1990) *Vygotsky and Education, instructional implications and applications of sociocultural psychology*, Cambridge: Cambridge University Press.

Newman, D., Griffin, P. and Cole, M. (1989) *The Construction Zone, working for cognitive change in school*, Cambridge: Cambridge University Press.

Richards, J. (1978) *Classroom Language: what sort?*, London: George Allen and Unwin.

Rowe, M. B. (1986) 'Wait time: Slowing down may be a way of speeding up!', *Journal of Teacher Education*, 37, 43–50.

Schegloff, E. A. and Sacks, H. (1973) 'Opening up Closings', *Semiotica*, 7(4), 289–327.

Sinclair, J. McH. and Brazil, D. (1982) *Teacher Talk*, Oxford: Oxford University Press.

Sinclair, J. McH. and Coulthard, R. M. (1975) *Towards an Analysis of Discourse, the English used by teachers and pupils*, Oxford: Oxford University Press.

Stubbs, M. (1983) *Language, Schools and Classrooms*, London: Methuen.

Tharp, R. G. and Gallimore, R. (1988) *Rousing Minds to Life, teaching, learning and schooling in a social context*, Cambridge: Cambridge University Press.

Tizard, B. and Hughes, M. (1984) *Young Children Learning, talking and thinking at home and school* , London: Fontana.

Tsui, A. B. M. (1994) *English Conversation*, Oxford: Oxford University Press.

Vygotsky, L. (1986 [1934]) *Thought and Language* (trans. A. Kozulin), Cambridge, MA: Cambridge University Press.

Wells, G. (1986) *The Meaning Makers, children learning language and using language to learn*, London: Hodder and Stoughton.

Wertsch, J. V. (1991) *Voices of the Mind, a sociocultural approach to mediated action*, London: Harvester Wheatsheaf.

Willes, M. J. (1983) *Children into Pupils, a study of language in early schooling*, London: Routledge and Kegan Paul.

Willis, J. (1992) 'Inner and Outer: spoken discourse in the language classroom', in M. Coulthard (ed.) *Advances in Spoken Discourse Analysis*, London: Routledge.

Chapter 9

Managing primary schools
Facilitating the learning relationship

Paul Ryan

INTRODUCTION

It seems a rather obvious statement to make that primary schools are staffed by individuals with characteristics. However, this rather obvious statement is often forgotten when questions of management are being considered. The push to develop an organisation can often result in the individual being forgotten. This need not be the case however. Hargreaves (1994) places great emphasis upon the individual within educational organisations. In his analysis, there has to be a recognition of the differences between individuality and individualism. Individualism is normally associated with selfishness, when individuals behave in a manner that is inconsiderate to others. Individuality, on the other hand, is individual behaviour characterised by expressions of opinion, creativity and thought, with regard to maintaining relationships with other people. He argues that management in schools should find room for both individualism and individuality.

Management in primary schools involves working with teachers and other adults, and the establishment of relationships. While it is not possible to legislate for the types of relationships, management involves consideration of people's wide variety of beliefs, actions and related responsibilities.

How this responsibility is exercised will depend upon the relationships that are created. It is also reasonable to conclude that the nature of relationships will depend upon the views held by those who manage in connection with the relationships they create, maintain and develop with colleagues. For example, if a person with management responsibility perceives that a colleague is behaving in a manner which is characterised by individualism, it would normally be considered negative behaviour. Alternatively, if a person is displaying a degree of individuality, then it may not necessarily be regarded as negative behaviour. The deciding factor in both scenarios would be the people involved and their perceptions of appropriate and acceptable behaviour.

The task of management in primary schools involves working with individuals and the building of relationships. The number and types of behaviour that can be expressed among any group of people are wide, varied, and often unpredictable. It is not easy to predict what the behaviour of individuals will be and always maintain a working relationship. Management in primary schools is more effective if relationships are based on trust, honesty and openness, where individuals feel they can express their opinions, beliefs and concerns freely. Effective management must involve listening, considering and acting in recognition of individual factors; not an easy task.

When considering management based on relationships, what can theoretical perspectives and research evidence provide in terms of possible strategies? What might these strategies look like in practice? Finding answers to these and other fundamental questions begins with a consideration of management in educational and non-educational organisations, and then in primary schools in particular.

THE CONTEXT FOR SCHOOL MANAGEMENT

Management in primary schools raises significant issues related to the management of educational organisations in general. Such management involves recognising the national and global context within which schools operate. In the UK, this has been characterised as:

> An increase in institutional autonomy, with commensurate accountability, operating in the context of increased client choice balanced by increased central direction of the curriculum.

> (West-Burnham, *et al.* 1994: 5)

These changes have been described in terms of the need for self-managing schools.

> A self-managing school is a school in a system of education where there has been significant and consistent decentralisation to the school level of authority to make decisions related to the allocation of resources. . . . The school remains accountable to a central authority for the manner in which resources are allocated.

> (Caldwell and Spinks 1992: 4)

Within this context, the need for more effective management practices is paramount, but what exactly is educational or school management? Management has been described by Murgatroyd and Morgan (1993: 27) as:

> [T]he ability of the staff to provide an appropriate service mix; . . . the internal organisational structures, roles and management working processes; and . . . delivery of the chosen strategy.

It can also be viewed from a different perspective, one that recognises schools as places where there is a lack of certainty, where the quality of the management depends upon the personal and professional qualities of those who *lead* and *manage*, and where managerial effectiveness is based upon the capacity to make judgements.

Bush and West-Burnham (1994) have suggested that the management of schools involves consideration of both theory and practices. The practices of managers serve as a useful starting point for a third consideration of educational management. Managers *do* something; to assess the quality of management we need to know what they do, how they do it, why they do it, when they do it, and who they do it with. To summarise: we need to know about managers' aims, styles and practices.

TO MANAGE OR TO LEAD?

The behaviour of educational managers is not, however, morally neutral. Managers in schools must be clear about the purposes of management, which can be defined as the need to facilitate student learning and, in so doing, serve as a model for the learning process, demonstrate a degree of integrity and consistency, practise what is preached, and recognise a tension between decision-making and managerialism. In this analysis, decision-making equals autonomy, and managerialism equals control.

Management in primary schools also requires some form of leadership. This is not the implementation of appropriate procedures but discrimination, selection and prioritisation, followed by implementation, reflection and adaptation. It is reasonable to assume, then, that educational management involves a moral, logical and instrumental relationship with the staff who work in a school and the pupils who attend it.

> The management of schools has changed from an emphasis upon control, to leadership to bring out the best in people and the ability to respond quickly to change . . . .
>
> (Lofthouse 1994: 125)

Educational management has been heavily influenced by general or business management theory and practices. To judge whether business management practices are appropriate to the primary school context we must consider whether educational management is different from other forms of management. Bush and West-Burnham (1994) highlight seven factors where education differs from industry. Education differs in terms of objectives, measurement, evaluation, children and pupils, professional issues, fragmentation, and time.

Handy and Aitken (1986: 32, 33) offer an alternative view. They outline some of the key management functions where education is seen as similar to industry. The function of managers is to:

- decide upon key tasks and constituencies to be served (strategy);
- divide the work up (structure);
- monitor (systems);
- recruit (staff);
- train (skills);
- work out the best way to lead and relate to people (leadership style);
- create a sense of mission (shared values).

The place of theory in the management of schools provides a rationale for decision-making. Bush and West-Burnham (1994) put forward three factors to support the place of theory in educational management, interpretation, experience and context. Managers have to interpret events, use their own and other managers' experiences, and make judgements and decisions taking into account the context of their particular institution. However, there should be a recognition that:

- there is no one, all-consuming theory;
- there is no one, best way;
- there is no recipe for success;
- theories of education and the social sciences are different to scientific theories;
- there are different views and interpretations, not necessarily a search for the *'truth'*;
- managers adopting one approach can exclude others;
- a manager's choice is a way of understanding events;
- managers adopt a particular perspective;
- managers use *'frames'* for influence upon practice.

Educational management theory is usually characterised as observational, selective and normative. Researchers observe what they perceive as successful or effective practices, they select what they feel may be of relevance, and they advocate particular approaches based on generalisable data. Educational management theory must help managers understand the practices of other managers who have been more successful or effective. It is up to each individual manager to use, adapt and relate management theories to their particular institutional context. It is also important to recognise that there are different models of educational management. However, most models have four main elements: goals, structures, environment, and leadership.

One of the significant differences between education and industry is the issue of professionalism. School managers work with teachers who can be regarded as professionals. If teachers are regarded as professionals, then their place in the management of a school has to be considered.

This could be regarded as a rhetorical question, but that is not my intention. Consideration of professional issues in relation to teachers implies that they can exercise a degree of responsibility. If management responsibility is the sole preserve of the headteacher, teachers do not need responsibility, only to be controlled. This is not a management practice that I would wish to advocate. If effective relationships are to be established, maintained and developed, responsibility must be shared. Responsibility allows for individuality and, as such, presents a managerial perspective that is based on sharing, which involves creativity, spontaneity and some degree of innovation.

It has also been argued by Lofthouse (1994) that credibility in school management rests upon the nature of bureaucratic structures and the degree to which teachers are regarded as individuals (with autonomy). The tension between managerialism and decision-making is again highlighted. Is the best style of management in primary schools a controlling one, or a management style based upon individuality?

MANAGEMENT IN PRIMARY SCHOOLS

One style or theory of management that can help with the management of tensions between control and autonomy has been described as collegial or collaborative management. Collegiality and collaboration fall within democratic theories of educational management; they are characterised by shared decision-making.

The major factors associated with collegiality and collaboration are normative; they suggest a 'normal' way to behave, and they value authority of expertise, emphasise common sets of values, formal representation within structures, and consensus.

Collegiality and collaboration involve schools in democratic decision-making where authority of expertise is valued and consensus is aimed for. However, this model of educational management is not common, as headteachers have ultimate responsibility; which implies the question, why use a participatory style? Justification for a collegial or collaborative style assumes that staff want to be involved, that such a style will improve the quality of decision-making, and make for more effective implementation of decisions.

Hargreaves (1994) argues that it has become heresy to suggest that collaboration and collegiality are not pivotal to educational change. In his analysis, collegiality fosters teacher development, school improvement, school effectiveness, implementation of imposed change, school based curriculum development, and leadership development. Collegiality also caters for context, commitment, understanding, raising of morale, teacher satisfaction, raising of teaching standards, and teacher growth.

Arguing that collaboration and collegiality are the keys to educational change, Hargreaves (1994) also examines some of the difficulties with this approach. There is often a lack of time for collaboration, a lack of clear boundaries for collegial roles, and a lack of clear definitions of meaning. Hargreaves goes on to argue that there is no one 'real' or 'true' thing that we can call collegiality or collaboration. There are different forms of collegiality and collaboration.

> Whose culture is it anyway? If teachers are told what to be professional about, how, where and with whom to collaborate, and what blueprint of professional conduct to follow, then the culture that evolves will be foreign to the setting. They will once again have 'received a culture'.
>
> (Hargreaves 1994: 189)

In this analysis, there is no one 'best' or 'correct' perspective. The micropolitical perspective takes the view that teachers may be interested in each other's ideas, beliefs and practices, but would not necessarily want to belong to teams because their own ideas, beliefs and practices are different. It also questions professionals' rights to individuality, individualism and solitude.

The micro-political perspective encourages us to discriminate between different forms of collegiality and collaboration – 'bottom up' and 'top down'. It recognises a distinction between a collaborative culture and contrived collegiality. Collaborative cultures are spontaneous, voluntary, development oriented, pervasive across time and space, and unpredictable. Contrived collegiality is administratively regulated, compulsory, implementation oriented, fixed in time and space, and predictable.

Collegial models are viewed by Bush (1995) as incomplete because they underestimate the official authority of the head and because they present bland assumptions of consensus. However, it is widely recognised (Wallace 1988; Nias et al. 1989; Ryan and Bush 1995) that a collegial or collaborative style of management is an appropriate style for managing primary schools. The numbers of staff involved, the informal culture and flat management structures, make collaboration more achievable. Advocates of a collegial or collaborative style also argue that decisions are more likely to be implemented (Fullan 1991).

Having considered the management of primary schools in general, I now turn to a consideration of issues related to effective primary school management in action, using management of the curriculum as an example.

MANAGING THE CURRICULUM IN PRIMARY EDUCATION

Management of the curriculum is obviously part of management in primary schools. The management style that is adopted in matters related to the curriculum should fit with the overall management style. The management perspective for management of the curriculum that is advocated here involves many of the functions already outlined in a collaborative or collegial style of management.

Lofthouse (1994) argues that management of the curriculum is based upon study of the curriculum. Study of the curriculum involves an appreciation of perspectives that highlight a distinction between liberal and illiberal studies. The distinction between liberal and illiberal studies lies in a consideration of the values and priorities underlying the curriculum delivered, as well as of what is actually delivered. There also has to be a consideration of the relationship between the planned and the received curriculum in relation to race, class and gender issues.

The management of the curriculum involves what has beeen called 'ground-clearing', the process whereby different curricular perspectives are considered with a view to establishing clear or agreed understandings about the nature of the curriculum. Effective management of the curriculum is difficult to establish without managers engaging in such a ground-clearing process. Ground-clearing involves consideration of the most effective practices for bringing about effective learning, and what constitutes effectiveness has been the subject of detailed research.

Mortimore (1993), in his review of research into school effectiveness, begins with a consideration of what the research contributes to the debate about the management of effective teaching and learning. School effectiveness research highlights how effective schools can make a contribution to teaching and learning. Schools do make a difference and add value. However, there are likely to be differences in the average progress of pupils, and these differences are not affected by home factors to the same degree as other facets of pupils' progress. Schools have a crucial role to play in this respect; if they are to help pupils to progress, effective management practices are essential.

Mortimore (1993: 300-305) outlines a range of factors related to school effectiveness:

- strong, positive leadership;
- high expectations; an appropriate challenge for students thinking;
- monitoring of student progress;
- student responsibilities and involvement in the life of the school;
- rewards and incentives;
- parental involvement in the life of the school;
- the use of joint planning and consistent approaches towards students;
- academic press and learning.

When these factors are related to a ground-clearing process and a collaborative style of management, definitions of strong purposeful leadership, for example, can be arrived at. It is important to recognise that effectiveness factors are open to a degree of interpretation, based upon a consideration of school-specific contextual characteristics. Mortimore (1993) has also considered the research conducted into effective teaching. Teaching is regarded as an overt activity, something that can be observed and judged. The research regarding effective teaching dates back to the work conducted by Bennett published in 1976, referred to in Mortimore (1993) and his later work published in 1987. Bennett argued that a formal style was best in order to achieve the 'match' between a task and the ability of the child. Bennett's ideas have since been modified, and he now accepts that assessing effective teaching is more complex.

In research carried out before 1993, Mortimore et al. (1988) also found that defining effective teaching was 'far too complex' to be assessed easily, and that effectiveness depended on the task being set to pupils. Research has emphasised some of the factors related to effective teaching. These include relationships with pupils, classroom management, planning and preparation, aims, objectives and their achievement, choice of teaching materials, marking, the 'match' of work to pupils, and question-and-answer techniques.

Subsequent research has re-defined effective teaching in terms of classroom organisation, planning and preparation, 'match' of work to pupils, classroom interactions, mastery of subject, and competence in teaching skills. Mortimore (1993) also considers forms of knowledge and skills that can aid more effective teaching, curriculum knowledge, pedagogical knowledge, presentation skills, psychological knowledge, sociological knowledge, process knowledge, understanding how learners learn, understanding how subject knowledge can be transferred, organisational skills, analytical skills, assessment skills, management skills, and evaluative skills.

Mortimore (1993: 296) contends that teachers also bind and blend these forms of knowledge and skills together with:

- imagination;
- creativity;
- sensitivity.

In the same paper, Mortimore examines the research related to effective learning. The work of psychologists is used to highlight the links between effective teaching and learning since, as Chapter 2 of this book in particular emphasised, learning is not directly observable. We cannot be certain what has been learnt, and we can only infer that something has been learnt.

Theories of self-efficacy hold that learners' belief in themselves can be reinforced or reduced, and the effects of achievement noted. In this respect schools and teachers can have an effect. Adaptive instruction, on the other hand, suggests that learning must be considered in relation to the individual and the learning environment. A better 'match' between the two would lead to optimum learning.

Learning is therefore affected by its intellectual, linguistic and social context. As a result, learning in school should not be confused with general learning. Learning in school is pure rather than applied thought; school involves individual rather than collaborative thought. When school and life are related it draws upon attribution theory, whereby girls and boys attribute failure to different causes. In this respect teachers provide differential feedback.

In summary, effective learning is active rather than passive, covert rather than overt, complex rather than simple, affected by individual differences among learners, and influenced by a variety of contexts.

Learning is more than the simple aquisition of facts.

[The] curriculum is to be thought of in terms of activity and experience rather than knowledge to be acquired and facts to be stored.

(Lofthouse 1994: 128)

Managers guide the defining process and act as gatekeepers of core values. As Chapter 6 of this book has shown, teachers left to their own devices will understandably drift towards the comfort zone of safe methods. Managers need to know the range and quality of learning experiences being offered, and the gathering of such knowledge involves monitoring, curriculum and learning reviews, staff development and a focus on the pupil.

CURRICULUM MANAGEMENT IN ACTION

One of the central problems in managing primary schools is how to link the drive for organisational development and the establishment of effective practices with considerations of individual development, expressions of individuality and the occasional expression of behaviour that can be described as individualistic. An examination of curriculum management practices and the research conducted into effective schooling, effective teaching and learning, highlights the complex nature of the difficulties inherent in primary school management.

Put more succinctly, one may ask what the nature of a collaborative or collegial management style looks like when applied to the primary school. It is obviously not possible to provide examples of curriculum management that encompass all aspects of the curriculum, but a specific example of an aspect of curriculum management in action can be demonstrated with the use of case study research data.

THE CASE OF CLABRIX PRIMARY SCHOOL

Context

Clabrix primary school is a junior, mixed and infant school with a nursery class attached. At the time of data collection the number on the roll was approximately 350 children, with a new intake of reception-aged children to be admitted after the Easter break. Clabrix is staffed by eighteen teachers. Of these, fourteen teachers are class-based, one is on maternity leave, the Head and Deputy are not class-based, and one teacher is employed for supporting children with language difficulties and children whose first language is not English. In addition to the teaching staff the school employs two nursery nurses, five primary helpers, seven learning support assistants for children with statements of special educational needs, ten midday meal supervisors and two administrative staff.

The racial mix of the children attending Clabrix primary school is approximately 65 per cent Afro–Caribbean origin, 20 per cent white, 10 per cent African origin and 5 per cent from other racial backgrounds. The majority of the children live in local authority accommodation with a small number living in privately owned property. Clabrix school has a policy of integrating children with special educational needs and children who have a physical or mental disability. At present, Clabrix primary school has nine children who have statements of special educational needs, with a further eleven at various stages of the statementing process.

The organisation of posts of responsibility for the Clabrix teaching staff in respect of curriculum management is as follows:

- Head teacher – overall responsibility for management of the curriculum;
- Deputy head – responsible for staff development, including INSET (In Service Education and Training) courses, mentoring, INSET budget and whole-school planning, record keeping and assessment;
- Five 'B' allowance holders who hold coordinating responsibilities for English, Maths, Science, Special Educational Needs, and Key Stage One;
- Four 'A' allowance holders who hold coordinating responsibilities for History, Geography, IT, and Art, Design and Technology;
- Five teachers have no curriculum responsibility.

The current curriculum management focus

A review of the INSET plans of Clabrix primary school for the Autumn and Spring terms of 1994/95 reveals that the teaching staff of the school were involved in devising a whole-school assessment profile. The key factor in determining INSET plans was the school's development plan. This stated that the main focus of the INSET work for the period was intended to be the devising of a Maths scheme throughout the school. However, a change in post-holder had resulted in postponement of the Maths scheme and the bringing forward of an assessment focus that had been scheduled for the Summer and Autumn terms of 1995.

The decision to focus on assessment was made by the Head and the Deputy for two main reasons. The first came from an evaluation of the school's current status with respect to assessment and the recording of children's achievements. This revealed an inconsistency in practice and the perception that this was due to excessive workload and lack of expertise by some members of staff. The second motivating force was the review of the National Curriculum that was taking place in the UK.

Guidance related to the National Curriculum review was seen to offer the opportunity of easing the workload of teachers by them taking advice and not attempting to collect evidence and assess every single aspect of the curriculum. In addition, teachers were also being advised that they did not have to devise and keep detailed and complicated record-keeping systems. Such systems generated huge amounts of paperwork and involved long hours of teachers' time on administrative detail away from the classroom. The Head and Deputy felt that they had the opportunity not only to ease teachers' workloads but also to attempt to help teachers develop their confidence and expertise in assessing children's work.

For the Spring term, teachers were given a total of seven after-school group meetings with the focus of each group as follows: Group 1: Writing; Group 2: Maths; Group 3: Science. The groups were led by the relevant subject coordinators, and staff were able to choose which group they wished to join.

Observations

The group of teachers with a Maths work focus decided against collecting samples of children's work. Through discussions about the nature of current maths work samples, teachers felt that a true assessment of a child's understanding of a mathematical concept could only be attempted if a specific task or set of tasks was set by the teacher. Teachers needed the opportunity to observe, evaluate and plan for the next stage of a child's learning. What the teachers seemed to be interested in was the process of children's learning as well as the product.

The maths post-holder had a crucial role in the process of devising what they called 'assessment tasks'. She advised on the nature of tasks and what their focus would be. In this case, the group began with number and the use and application of mathematical concepts. At times she provided individual teachers with set tasks that would be appropriate to a specific age range, and provided an overview of the tasks in an attempt to achieve progression across the age range taught. The role adopted by the post-holder was a facilitating one where she judged it to be appropriate, and became more directive when she felt the group had reached an *impasse* or when a consensus could not be achieved. She also acted as a subject specialist when she advised and provided ideas or activities that would help the group achieve their aim of assessing the processes of children's learning. The post-holder kept the group on task by asking for class-based work to be undertaken within deadlines, and led the discussion with regard to the final presentation of the group's work to the whole staff.

The Science-focused group also decided to use 'assessment tasks' in an attempt to assess the process of children's learning in this subject. The group proceeded in a different manner to the maths group, with each teacher working in their own class on a science activity of their own choice and then reporting back their findings to the group. This led to the group discussing and agreeing upon the need for an activity structure to which all staff would need to adhere, to achieve consistency in assessment. An agreed structure would, it was felt, also allow children to progress within an activity or develop it further, and allow the teacher to assess current understanding and how that understanding is applied.

This process highlighted a weakness in teachers' science teaching. Mainly, teachers were not requiring children to make a prediction when engaging in a science activity. This flaw in teaching led the group to conclude that teachers throughout the school needed to make sure that they taught what they thought was important, what the National Curriculum required, and what they thought it important to assess. Essentially the group was asking for teachers to evaluate their practice on a continual basis.

The post-holder's role in the group's work was slightly less successful than in the maths group. She did lead discussions, act as a facilitator and subject specialist and provide a structure to the group's activities. However, she was hampered by staff absence and, at times, by her own inability to direct when she judged it necessary. As a result the group did not provide concrete examples of work for the whole-school presentation. They did, however, have some valuable insights to offer about the type of teaching that was taking place within the school and how effective assessment could be achieved with respect to science.

When observing the group which focused on Writing, it immediately became apparent that they were finding their tasks a lot simpler than the previous two had done. This was due to three main reasons. The first was the fact that the Autumn term group had provided a structure to their work that only needed minor adaptation. The second was that the group decided that the main way of assessing childrens' writing would be to get them to write, to collect the work, and then to assess and moderate it. It was the group's view that writing was a mental process and that it was extremely difficult, if not impossible, to assess a child's thought processes. The third and final reason for the ease of the group's work was the contribution of the post-holder, who acted as the leader of the group. She set a clear structure, led discussions effectively, ensured people carried out agreed tasks, encouraged the group to keep to deadlines, and when necessary she made decisions. Her style was businesslike and efficient, while not allowing herself to become dictatorial. Honesty and openness were apparent, as well as the confidence to let teachers act and make judgements without the fear of losing control.

Overall, the teaching staff of the school identified the need for the school's curriculum planning framework or scheme of work to be broken down into subjects. This would allow the teaching staff to devise detailed schemes of work for Maths, Science and Writing (the school had already devised a scheme of work for the teaching of Reading). Coupled with the schemes of work, the staff felt that time should be allocated to allow them to devise directly related 'assessment tasks'. Following a lengthy discussion, the whole staff clearly expressed a wish for the curriculum to remain firmly focused upon the process of children's learning.

Schemes of work with 'assessment tasks' and a whole-school profile of children's work assessed would, they hoped, begin to raise standards of teaching and, as a result, children's learning throughout the school.

One crucial discovery by the groups was that work which teachers assessed to be average or above average came out at a lower level in relation to National Curriculum levels. The reasons for perceived low standards of work were identified as weaknesses in teaching, omission of the teaching of key skills such as making predictions, the previous absence of any moderation of children's work, and inconsistencies in what was taught, and when, throughout the school.

The roles of the Head and the Deputy in this process of curriculum management were to decide upon the original focus, devise the structure of tasks, monitor the groups' progress over the weeks, and offer and give advice as it was required. Essentially this was a process whereby groups met once a week to plan, organise and structure their own work, while the Head and Deputy took an overview of the whole process. When individual groups made their presentation, the discussions were lead by the Deputy with contributions from the Head. Evaluation of the whole process and plans for the following term's INSET were drawn up by the Deputy. The Head was consulted upon final INSET plans for the following term.

CONCLUSIONS: IMPLICATIONS FOR PRIMARY SCHOOL IMPROVEMENT AND THE MANAGEMENT OF CHANGE

Hopkins (1994: 14) uses the concept of a 'journey' as a metaphor for school improvement. Identifying two key factors that assist in the task of improving a school, he writes:

[S]chool improvement efforts appear to include:

- reconstructing externally imposed education reforms in the form of school priorities;
- creating internal conditions that will sustain and encourage change in schools.

The case study outlined on pp. 165–8 clearly fits into Hopkins's model of school improvement, which in turn assists in the management of change. Staff were engaged in a reconstruction exercise within what appeared to be conditions for bringing about sustainable change. The management style that has been conceptualised in this chapter is best summarised as a 'learning style', and it can be seen from the case study evidence that the conditions for change were fostered around the concept of this 'learning style' of management. The work of Fullan (1991) presents a learning-centred approach to the management of change in educational organisations. Fullan argues that changes in goals, skills, philosophy, beliefs and behaviour are multi-dimensional, and involve people's basic conceptions of education. In addition, he contends that individual values in relation to change have a dynamic relationship with multi-dimensional innovation, which involves materials, teaching approaches and beliefs. Some effect upon the factors mentioned above has to take place before change can happen in practice. When considering a style of management that is 'learning-centred', managers need to consider various aspects of the change process. These include the soundness of proposed changes, an understanding of the failure of well intentioned change, guidelines for understanding the nature and feasibility of particular changes, the realities of the *status quo*, the deepness of the change, and the question of valuing. In Fullan's analysis, educational change is *technically simple* but *socially complex*.

Fullan's perspective on the management of change has people as the central agents of change. If people are not convinced of the need for change, they are less likely to implement or even to begin to engage in change. The case study example highlights the complexities of and the time involved in managing curriculum change. However, the style of management adopted, while not totally collaborative, does have elements of collaboration. The teaching staff in the case study school had the freedom to decide what changes in assessment arrangements they would prefer to see and which area they wished to develop. In areas where freedom was restricted – for example, in the allocation of time and the central focus of the work to be carried out – it could be argued that the staff could accept a degree of imposition when it was balanced with other freedoms.

The central message that arises out of this review of management theories and related research is that people matter. The idea of learning relationships is just as important for managers as it is for classroom teachers, and managers should therefore engage in processes whereby they learn from colleagues and vice versa. Management in primary schools, conceptualised in this manner, is more effective when it is a shared, learned and collaborative process.

REFERENCES

Bush, T. (1986) *Theories of Educational Management*, London: Paul Chapman.
—— (ed.) (1989) *Managing Education: Theory and Practice*, Milton Keynes: Open University Press.
—— (1995) *Theories of Educational Management*, revised edition, London: Paul Chapman.
Caldwell, B. J. and Spinks, J. M. (1988) *The Self-Managing School*, London: The Falmer Press.
—— (1992) *Leading the Self Managing School*, London: Falmer Press.
Fullan, M. G. (1991) *The New Meaning of Educational Change*, London: Cassell.
Handy, C. and Aitken, R. (1986) *Understanding Schools as Organisations*, Harmondsworth: Penguin.
Hargreaves, A. (1994) *Changing Teachers, Changing Times*, London: Cassell.
Hopkins, D. (1994) 'Follow the Yellow Brick Road', in *Managing Schools Today*, 13(6).
Lofthouse, M. (1994) 'Managing Learning', in T. Bush and J. West-Burnham (eds) *The Principles of Educational Management*, Harlow: Longmans.
Mortimore, P. (1993) 'School Effectiveness and the Management of Effective Learning and Teaching', *School Effectiveness and School Improvement*, 4(4), 290–310.
Mortimore, P., Sammons, P., Stoll, L., Lewis, D. and Ecob, R. (1988) *School Matters: the junior school years*, Wells, Somerset: Open Books.
Murgatroyd, S. and Morgan, C. (1993) *Total Quality Management and the School*, Buckingham: Open University Press.
Nias, J., Southworth, G. and Yeomans, R. (1989) *Staff Relationships in the Primary School*, London: Cassell.
Ryan, P. and Bush, T. (1995) *Managing the Curriculum in Primary Education*, Leicester: University of Leicester.
Wallace, M. (1988) 'Towards a Collegiate Approach to Curriculum Management in Primary and Secondary Schools', *School Organisation*, 8(1), 25–34.
West-Burnham, J., Bush, T., O'Neill, J., and Glover, D., (1994) *Leadership and Strategic Management*, Harlow: Longmans.

Chapter 10

Back to the future

The learning relationship in initial teacher training

Mark Lofthouse

Those who can, do. Those who can't, teach.
Those who can't teach become teachers of teachers.

INTRODUCTION

This is one contemporary British saying which needs little explanation, because its critical thrust is only too apparent. However flippant, cynical and unfair this saying may appear to those engaged in education, it sums up a peculiarly English contempt for both teachers and teacher training. Yet is this contemptuous attitude embedded only in the UK, or is it now being exported on a worldwide basis? The British have been exporting ideas in the name of trade for a very long time. A central theme developed in this chapter is the idea that what has been termed 'the unconscious imperialism of trade' was the means by which Britain exported far more than goods. Ideas followed exports and Britain gave to colonies and emerging countries alike her own circumscribed view of education.

Chapter 6 has shown how different cultures have different educational ideologies and thus different expectations about teachers, and this chapter will consider the origins of English ideologies and expectations in more depth. The English have for a long time suffered from an imperfect understanding of what might constitute a learning relationship. Elementary schooling in England was characterised by a pervasive belief in doing things *to* children rather than *with* children. Thus, examples from British history cited in this chapter are of significance because their export (conscious or unconscious) has played a part in determining the present development of others.

Against the background of this historical context, the first section of this chapter, *Policies, Politics and People*, provides a comparative historical summary illustrating how there has been a widespread tendency to devalue primary education, primary teachers and, by implication, primary training and trainers.

How this widespread devaluation currently impacts on policies and practice in initial teacher training is analysed in the second section, *The Consequences of Competencies*. Here the proposition that teacher training is currently reverting to a process of social reproduction, rather than educational transformation, is explored.

The summary of the chapter argues that, in the UK and parts of the 'old Commonwealth', we are currently witnessing the bizarre spectacle of 'going back to the future', namely the imposition of nineteenth-century ideologies apparently as a means of solving twentieth-century dilemmas. Therefore, as our end is in our beginning, we start with a review of the historical and comparative cultural demands made upon primary teachers and their trainers.

POLICIES, POLITICS AND PEOPLE

Primary teacher training is viewed in a mirror composed of those reflections, values and attitudes which a society has of its teachers, schools and children. In 1597 John Lyly reflected the anti-intellectualism which prevailed at that time when he pronounced, 'If any man among all his servants shall espy one either filthy in his talk or foolish behaviour, him be committeth ye guiding and tuition of his sons' (Lyly 1597: 403). Such an evident contempt for tutors, teachers and teaching was deeply rooted in English society (Lawson 1967: 61). One dimension of this English problem was the reluctance of the state to become involved in the provision of either schooling or training (Harrison 1979: 63). While Napoleon in France and Bismarck in Germany vigorously used schooling to serve the needs of the state, successive British governments hung back, leaving schooling to the churches and charity (Cobban 1965: 9; Armytage 1969: 21). Thus, while French and German teachers soon became assimilated into the ranks of the bourgeoisie, in England a combination of voluntarism and *laissez-faire* policies ensured that anyone, however ineffectual, could teach. In a village school in Gloucestershire, during the year 1846, it was recorded: 'A shepherd being too infirm at eighty to look after the sheep, undertook instead the education of the children, to whom he taught very elementary writing' (Horn 1978: 79). With such limited expectations, teacher training was not required, much to the fury of Matthew Arnold, who found in Europe what he believed should be in England – systems and methods for training teachers.

In 1888 Arnold uncompromisingly told an Educational Commission of Enquiry that England was 'falling behind the continent in terms of our aspirations for elementary education'. In the field of teacher training, he bleakly concluded: 'we have barely begun to compete' (Arnold 1888: 95, 242; see also Arnold 1869, Smith and Summerfield 1969). The clash between Arnold and members of the Cross Commission is interesting because it raises fundamental questions about the nature and purpose of teacher training, questions which continue to reverberate:

• Teacher training or teacher education? – a debate often wrapped up in discussion as to the place of theory and practice within a course or programme.
• What is the purpose of the 'disciplines' within teacher training? – a debate now conducted between those who regard the 'disciplines' as curriculum clutter and those who regard academic 'disciplines' as safeguards of standards.
• What are the cultural and social expectations of teachers and their training? – an ongoing debate, uncomfortable and frequently acrimonious, as societies change but wish schools and teachers to remain static.

In addressing these questions, it can be noted that there is no need of training, if tasks are simple. For almost the first fifty years of the nineteenth century, informed opinion in England persisted in regarding teaching as such a simple, undemanding task that it required no training at all (Dent 1977: 2). The nub issue here is the need to separate the activity of teaching from that of child minding. The progress of early childhood education in England was blighted, from its earliest origins, by an arrogant belief by politicians and policymakers that little children needed 'minding' rather than 'teaching' (Whitbread 1972: 7). The continued low esteem in which work with young children is held stems from the erroneous beliefs that such work is easy and that anyone can do it.

Such views were rife in Victorian times, and therefore the debate concerning the role and place of theory and practice in teaching did not start in Britain until the 1880s. In sharp contrast, Germany and France had by this time embraced the concept of educating teachers. Both countries were 'theory friendly', and quickly established training systems which brought aspiring teachers into contact with academic knowledge and newly emerging disciplines, such as psychology (Barnard 1929: 27–32). Significantly, England did not follow the European pattern, being more interested in teacher training than teacher education. Early modes of English training, such as the pupil-teacher system, adopted apprenticeship methods where 'copy and do' predominated. When teacher training colleges finally limped into existence in England (James Kay-Shuttleworth being the founding father of one in Battersea, London, in 1840), the obsession with practice, rather than knowledge, was embedded. While Kay-Shuttleworth deplored the ignorance of his students, he and his successors tried to counter difficulties largely by concentrating on what today would be described as 'skills and dispositions' rather than by providing knowledge (Lofthouse 1992: xii). In short, the English teacher training system was all about 'doing' rather than 'thinking'. This might be regarded as of marginal significance if it were not for the fact that our Victorian predecessors were such busy 'doers' that they succeeded in creating the British Empire, an empire envied and emulated by others (Morris 1992: 5–7). Taking for granted the notion that what was right for Britain must be right for the colonies, the mother country exported to Australia, New Zealand, the West Indies and, more slowly, to India and Singapore, British attitudes to schooling and training. As empire building was, for the most part, left to the shock troops of merchants and missionaries, the latter in particular found no difficulty in setting up training systems and institutions which had served them well in the UK. Thus, as Martin has pointed out, the teacher training curriculum deployed in Jamaica in 1889 by the British and Foreign School Society was identical to that set down for the first of the Society's colleges founded in Borough Road in London (Martin 1989: 29–36). Inventories of cargoes carried by ships of the East India Company landing freight at Port Royal show that, intermingled with the iron and pottery goods, were steadily increasing supplies of school textbooks and teacher training manuals. The essential point from this is that both British and colonial students came into contact with a limited and utilitarian curriculum, where knowledge of God and salvation was more important than secular concerns. While the French strove to inculcate a love of French culture and traditions, the British offered fustian fare, at home and abroad. Dent has identified the foundation blocks of the teacher training curriculum which permeated Britain and the Empire:

> Firstly, a knowledge of English grammar sufficient to qualify them to speak and write their own language with correctness and propriety; secondly, the improvement of their own handwriting and knowledge of arithmetic; thirdly geography and history, and in addition, when time and other circumstances will permit other useful branches of knowledge.
>
> (Dent 1977: 7)

For those interested in curriculum studies, it is not difficult to detect that this is a timetable pretending to be a curriculum.

First announced in 1814, the sheer longevity of this rag-bag collection of subjects was as problematic in Britain as it was to be in the Empire and Commonwealth. In Britain custom and practice ensured continuity and conformity. When Jones conducted his monumental survey of teacher training in Britain in 1924, the 1814 timetable was still recognisably alive and well (Jones 1924: 84). Such a lack of interest in content strongly suggests that practice, and not knowledge, was the principal objective. Unsurprisingly, increasing numbers of teacher training students became dissatisfied with the perceived irrelevance and fatuity of their subject work. In the Empire and the Commonwealth, a different problem was caused by irrelevant knowledge being canonised as high-status knowledge, simply because it was irrelevant and thus mistaken for being academically desirable. The post-colonial legacy for many countries has been bound up with re-shaping imposed structures and knowledge (not least in teacher training), while finding an obstinate desire among some of the indigenous population to retain what is regarded as 'high-status' knowledge. The report of the Singapore Review Committee on Improving Primary School Education notes the problems associated with high-status academic work being conducted through the medium of English, compared with the low status accorded to vocational work undertaken in a variety of mother tongues. Apparently, 'Not made here' still has a powerful appeal, whether in terms of imported knowledge or imported cars (Singapore Review Committee 1995: 1–4).

As trade makes the world smaller, there is a global debate as to what constitutes appropriate social and cultural expectations of teachers and teaching. Often these debates are too specific to bear generalisation, except where history and culture coincide. In nineteenth-century Britain, teachers in elementary schools came to resent the lowly position accorded to them within society. A hunger for acceptance and respectability gave way in the early twentieth century to more forceful demands for better conditions, better pay and, mixed up in a bundle of hopes and expectations, better training (Eaglesham 1967: 71). Such an agenda is now recognisable in the developing countries. Indeed, what afflicted Victorian primary school teachers now assails their counterparts in the third world. The reasons cited to deny status and recognition for teachers of young children in nineteenth-century Britain are brought out and dusted off so as to dampen the expectations of teachers in the developed as well as the developing countries. These arguments may be summarised as follows:

- The age-range divide: knowing about how younger children develop and learn is somehow not proper knowledge; teaching subject-based knowledge to older children confers greater status.
- The expert–novice divide: the more specialised you are the more expert you are; as primary teachers do everything, they are not specialists.
- The gender divide: in many societies, caring for young children is seen as woman's work, and childminding is confused with teaching; as small children have little status, those who work with them have low status.
- The power divide: societies are divided into the 'haves' and 'have nots'; systems of schooling invariably service the needs of society as it is, rather than as it wishes to be. In this context, knowledge is power and therefore knowledge has to be distributed carefully. It is usually in

the interests of elite power groups to keep teachers of young children poor and relatively ignorant.

Summary

If this sounds harsh and bleak, a review of teacher training during the nineteenth century powerfully suggests that the whole process was severely *functional*. As Simon argues, the system was designed for *social reproduction* (Simon 1989: 77–84). In Britain there was a hysterical and protracted debate over whether the social reproduction system was going wrong, namely whether elementary school teachers were getting ideas above their station. Charles Dickens, a sensitive barometer of Victorian opinion, wrote a series of vicious portraits of elementary school teachers achieving social advancement which they did not deserve (Dickens [1865] 1938). Dickens's work and attitudes expose the issue of what constitutes gentlemanly knowledge as compared with skills and knowledge classified as utilitarian and vocational. The latter was suitable for 'trade', but not for 'gentlemen'. Elementary school teaching and teachers struggled to achieve 'trade' status during the nineteenth century, at home and abroad. The struggle was not helped by the *anti-theoretical, pragmatic* training they received, if they received any training at all. 'Doing' was everything, thinking and learning were luxuries. As Simon has demonstrated, there was no pedagogy in Britain (Simon and Taylor 1981: 124–45). Above all else, teacher training was amazingly *static*, showing minimal development over the century.

THE CONSEQUENCES OF COMPETENCIES

Historians currently argue as to when the shift from modernity to post-modernity took place. Kung contends that the real turning point was 1918, the end of the First World War, which signalled the end of the old European empires (Kung 1990: 3). Certainly at this time the old mould of a Euro-centric world disintegrated, and a new world order began to shift away from Europe and towards America and the Far East. In retrospect, while this began to happen visibly, the realignment was not accompanied in the field of teacher training by any paradigm shift in thinking or ideology (Kuhn 1962: 3). A debilitating combination of war-weariness and financial retrenchment ensured that, in Britain and much of Europe, primary teacher training during the inter-war period was conducted along pre-war lines. It was a case of old wine in very old bottles (Lofthouse 1992: 79). Only after the Second World War did Britain show signs of accepting post-modern concepts, and in the field of primary teacher training the paradigm shift finally occurred during the 1960s.

During this decade I was teaching in primary schools, and during the

1970s I was working in the field of initial teacher training. Applying Kuhn's model of paradigm shifts to what I experienced (personal and partial though this is) I would suggest that some of the shifts shown in Figure 10.1 occurred.

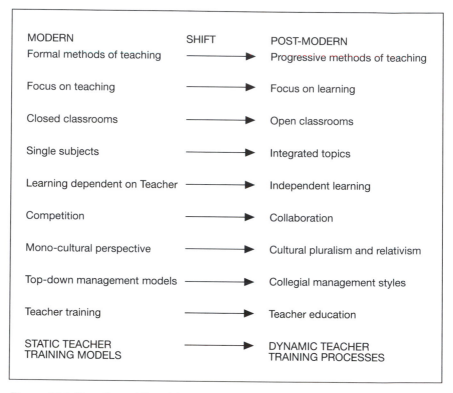

MODERN	SHIFT	POST-MODERN
Formal methods of teaching	⟶	Progressive methods of teaching
Focus on teaching	⟶	Focus on learning
Closed classrooms	⟶	Open classrooms
Single subjects	⟶	Integrated topics
Learning dependent on Teacher	⟶	Independent learning
Competition	⟶	Collaboration
Mono-cultural perspective	⟶	Cultural pluralism and relativism
Top-down management models	⟶	Collegial management styles
Teacher training	⟶	Teacher education
STATIC TEACHER TRAINING MODELS	⟶	DYNAMIC TEACHER TRAINING PROCESSES

Figure 10.1 Paradigm shifts which occurred during the 1960s and 1970s.

First, a disclaimer. Figure 10.1 does not pretend to be a comprehensive model. The modern–post-modern debate concerning teacher development has been more closely worked out by Hargreaves in his book *Changing Teachers, Changing Times* (1994). Second, Simon is right to suggest that the progressive revolution in British primary education was a revolution that largely never happened (Simon 1989: 381–2). However, enough happened to be of continuing interest and my purpose is to trace some of the key ideas and see how they impacted on initial teacher training.

Like the majority of British primary teachers, I entered teaching with a certificate in education. This was acquired at a teacher training college over a period of three years (the length of the course having just been raised from two years). Significantly, my final certificate commented on my abilities in practical teaching and professional studies, and referred to my 'main subject' without naming it. This quite accurately reflects the division of the course: two-thirds practical, one-third academic. Although the certificate was awarded by a university, most of us at our college knew little about the place and certainly never visited it. This was in sharp contrast to our colleagues in secondary schools, most of whom studied for a three-year first degree at a university and stayed on to complete a further one year Post Graduate Certificate in Education. The pallid 'Cert. Ed.' behind our name, compared with the status conferred by 'BA, PGCE' for our secondary colleagues, made the point forcibly. What it conveyed most particularly was that primary training was strictly for primary teaching. In a nutshell, the Cert. Ed. was a hermetically sealed product, which could only be cashed in for primary teaching.

The paradigm shift, when it finally came, was a belated but very welcome recognition of teacher education as opposed to teacher training. This was signalled in Britain by changes of title: teacher training colleges suddenly found themselves renamed colleges of education (Reid *et al.* 1994: 5). This change of title was the outward symbol; Reid has summed up the dramatic shifts which occurred within the colleges, as the Certificate Of Education was dropped and the new, four-year B.Ed. degrees were introduced:

> The importance of these changes . . . reflected a fairly profound change in the conceptualisation of the teacher from classroom crafts person, who needed to learn a trade, to the teacher as educated person, equipped with knowledge and the ability to apply this and his or her intelligence to the profession of teaching pupils. Hence the associated curriculum changes were of much greater depth . . . .
>
> (Reid 1994: 5–6)

For primary school teachers the curriculum changes were brought together in the Plowden Report. In higher education (which the newly named colleges of education strove to enter legitimately), curriculum change centred on planning degrees which had large elements of 'Education Studies', a bland title for the emerging educational disciplines – the philosophy, psychology, sociology and history of education. These disciplines were classically surveyed and promoted in 1966 by J. W. Tibble in his book *The Study of Education*. The list of contributors – Paul Hirst, Richard Peters, Brian Simon, William Taylor – is a roll-call of those academics who gave impetus to the new wave of thinking. In retrospect, it is possible to ask how far the new wave rolled, and to what effect. In the colleges of education the effects were mixed. The study of professional and educational issues became more open and intelligent, but it also became regrettably compartmentalised. In organisational terms, colleges tended to respond to the arrival of disciplines by creating departments of professional and educational studies. Invariably the latter became associated with high-status knowledge, where staff were properly expected to publish. In contrast, professional studies departments all too often took on a 'schools ghetto' role, characterised by staff who, rather than write articles, were expected to undertake an enormous burden of school practice supervision. Given this divisive context, it is not surprising that every new course proposal tended to degenerate into a dog-fight over the relative merits of professional knowledge versus education theory. The same questions rolled back and forth:

- Is teaching an art or a science?
- What do beginner teachers most need: skills, knowledge or appropriate attitudes?
- What is the role of school experience compared with school practice?
- Should students have greater freedom to plan their own course?
- Should 'education studies' become free-standing, independent of professional courses?
- What is the relationship between theory and practice? What do we mean by the term 'beginner teacher'?

As can be seen, the debate was cyclical and, of course, the questions were never really answered. As an Oxford tutor once dismissively wrote at the foot of an assignment paper: 'Many topics pursued, none overtaken'.

The whole progressive debate in Britain was eventually overtaken by economic decline, precipitated in part by the oil crisis of 1973–74. Liberal attitudes towards education are closely linked to the 'feel-good factor' generated by good economic performance. When the succession of quaintly named 'boomlets' came to an end in the 'never had it so good' Macmillan era, serious interest in educational reform gave way to educational retrenchment. As dozens of the colleges of education were either closed or amalgamated in the 1970s, Britain's weakness, economically and politically, became all too visible (Hencke 1978: 27–33). Macmillan had signalled the retreat from Empire in his 'winds of change' speech. The reality of his words came home to roost in the 1970s, when both the old and the new Commonwealth countries became assertive, rather than deferential, in their dealings with Britain. In the field of teacher training, many of the old Commonwealth countries were irritated by the colonial legacy and were determined to set up their own policies (McLaren 1974: 49–65). Conferment of nationhood on new Commonwealth countries was invariably the signal to get rid of the old ways, which had a habit of creeping back (Lauwerys and Tayar 1973: 5). British dominance of the educational disciplines during the 1970s was 'the last hurrah', the final opportunity for Australian and New Zealand academics to use their secondments to visit the golden triangle of Oxford, Cambridge and London. When the disciplines diminished in importance during the 1980s, the academic attention and interests of both old and new Commonwealth countries tended to switch to America.

Primary initial teacher training: contemporary debates

The United States of America currently sets the agenda for a global debate on education and teacher training. It is a very ill-tempered debate, couched in terms of what has been described as a 'discourse of derision'. The tone of this debate was set by Bloom's book, *The Closing of the American Mind*, significantly sub-titled, *How higher education has failed democracy and impoverished the souls of today's students* (Bloom 1987: 19–23). Bloom's hypothesis, that what currently passes for higher education is worthless because it promotes knowledge rather than understanding, is applied by Shor (1986) to the field of education. Shor argues that American conservatism, as expressed through the Republican policies of Nixon and Reagan, has eradicated educational liberalism and replaced it by 'the new vocationalism'. Shor identifies periods and issues which, while referring to America, have far wider applications for European and Pacific-rim countries (1986: 1):

- the 1960s – the culture of protest fuelled by progressivism;
- 1971–75 – the counter-offensive, career education and the focus on work;
- 1975–82 – the counter-reformation: the literacy crisis and back to basics;
- 1982–[86] – the war for educational excellence against mediocrity, however described and wherever found.

Warren (1978), Hirsch (1987) and Jacoby (1987) all provide further applications of how Shor's analysis worked in the USA. For most countries, the significant point was that 'when America sneezes, the world catches a cold'. The collective force of the American educational jeremiads was a global loss of confidence in the power of education, and a return to notions of 'less education, but better education'.

The problem is that the word 'education' is so slippery. For 'new right' politicians everywhere this in itself is irritating, because simplicity and order have to be found in a world grown complicated. It has been said that 'to every complex problem, there is always a simple answer – and it is always wrong'. This has signally failed to deter politicians of the 'new right' from giving simple answers to complex issues. In the field of initial teacher training, the 'new right' agenda abandons teacher education as being 'transformational' and, instead, returns to the need for teachers to acquire skills and competencies.

The consequence of competencies

Although Chapter 7 has shown how competencies can be used to promote reflection, that may not be their chief attraction. Teacher competencies are alluring because they are safe. They suggest that teaching is
basically a skills-oriented activity, and once the appropriate skills have
been identified, they can be learned. 'Learning by doing' has a long history within primary schooling, and therefore 'skill cycles' are ripe for
application in primary initial training. The work of Kolb (1984), Dreyfus
and Dreyfus (1986) and Schon (1987) all provide powerful reasons for
teacher trainers to become acquainted with methods of skill acquisition.
The Dreyfus and Dreyfus model (1986: 227) identifies *five* stages of skill
acquisition:

1 novice;
2 advanced beginner;
3 competent;
4 proficient;
5 expert.

Argyrsis and Schon argue that you make progress through this continuum by reflection-on-action and reflection-in-action (Argyrsis and Schon
1978). Therefore, real-life professional competencies for doctors and
teachers are best acquired by constant reviews of action (mini thought
experiments) within the ongoing flow of professional activity (Schon
1987: 57–9). Taken in conjunction with Kolb's theory of experimental
learning, there is an apparently overwhelming case for putting primary
trainees into classrooms and entrusting their training to mentors (Kolb
1984: 89; Tomlinson 1995: 20–21).

The critical issue is that, however sophisticated the competencies are,
and however neatly the skills are dovetailed and packaged, we are back
to teacher *training*. Training agendas are now commanding international
attention because the peculiarly British distrust of teaching and teachers
appears to be breaking out in the form of a contagious, global rash. As
the teacher's role is diminished a new technocracy replaces reasons and
values by 'outcomes' and 'outputs'. 'If it can be measured it must be
there, and because it's there it must be worthwhile; tick a box and capture a learning experience!' This kind of reductionism provides a rationale which has powered the introduction of national curricula, core
competencies and associated assessment processes, profiles and targets.
Shenstone (1993: 7) offers an overview of what recent New Zealand governments have been attempting along these lines. Allowing for different
emphasis, many countries have been attempting to achieve a good deal
of this 'reform agenda':

1 the creation of self governing schools;

2 the reduction of bureaucracy;
3 the introduction of objective and visible formula funding;
4 the exposure of services to competition;
5 the raising of standards through competition between schools and among pupils;
6 the development of 'national curricula' with clearly defined and monitored assessment processes and targets.

Without doing violence to Shenstone's agenda, I think it is possible to tuck within its framework a more specific 'action list' of what can be observed in initial teacher training:

• a switch to school-based training, because schools are where the action is;
• a switch to skills-based training, often reflected in students achieving mastery of teaching competencies and skill clusters;
• all of the above being predominantly achieved through mentored school experience and school practice;
• a re-definition of what constitutes a beginner teacher, with renewed emphasis on teaching techniques as compared with contextual knowledge.

Summary

The philosopher Hegel once said, 'The only thing one learns from history is that nobody ever learns anything from history'. The sad truth of Hegel's remark is evident in the present mis-application of what are claimed to be training reforms. While it is logically possible to analyse why these measures are being put in place, it is equally possible to assert that they will not, and cannot, work. Let me substantiate the accusation. We are currently faced with the bizarre spectacle of America, Britain and large parts of the old Commonwealth attempting to 'go back to the future'. This yearning for the past to answer for the present is revealed in a desire to recreate nineteenth-century trading conditions, and specifically weak labour unions and deregulated markets (Keeghan 1995: 22). In addition, associated with free market economics there is an almost unbridled belief in competition. As Shenstone identifies (1993: 7), there are potent convictions that schools and pupils can only succeed through internal and external competition. Therefore the worldwide rush to create educational markets is explained as a manifestation and further evidence of the apparent triumph of capitalism as being 'the one best system' (Harries 1992: 2).

Our Victorian predecessors found it to be a very imperfect system, especially in the field of primary education. From 1862, elementary schools in Britain were exposed to the full force of market philosophy.

This came about by the imposition of the Revised Code, a system often referred to as 'payment by results'. Satisfactory attainment by pupils in reading, writing, arithmetic, linked to attendance, earned financial grants. These grants were only paid after an increasingly severe system of inspection, verification and performance testing had been applied. Robert Lowe, who devised the scheme, was brutally frank in explaining his rationale. 'Enlist the hope of reward and the fear of penalty,' he declared, 'then see how difficulties are overcome' (Sutherland 1973).

From a provider's point of view, difficulties *were* overcome. Gladstone, as Chancellor of the Exchequer, rejoiced at discovering a system which enabled him to peg spending on schooling, and then reduce it. In any case, he could claim success. For thirty years the primary curriculum was reduced to three subjects. It was hardly surprising that attainments apparently improved (Hurt 1971: 176).

A high price was paid for chimerical success. Those who had to implement the code were not consulted: their only duty was to deliver it. Teachers became instructors, whose function was to drill, cram and grind children through what Matthew Arnold referred to as 'games of mechanical contrivance' (Arnold 1910: 12).

The limitations of such a threadbare curriculum were exposed when it became apparent that

- children could pass tests for reading when they could not read;
- the amount of money spent on testing schools was greater than the amount invested in them.

The code was abandoned in 1895.

How does all of this impact on contemporary debates concerning the provision of initial training for primary teachers? In essence, those who ignore history are condemned to relive it. We currently witness a worldwide lurch back to static models, where teacher *training* replaces teacher *education* (GTC 1993: 14–15). This seems perverse and retrograde in a world which has become more complicated and more culturally plural. The influence of teachers and teacher training is marginalised, as competencies and national curricula are more tightly specific and the role of the teacher becomes that of the technician. Further, the role of higher education in such a process is highly problematic. In Britain and Australia, there are clear signs of a desire by governments to withdraw universities and academics from teacher training (Dawkins 1988b: 290–9). If this occurs, the status of teachers will be open to re-interpretation. In particular, the perception of teaching as a trade (albeit a skilled one), and not a profession, will be restated.

For any teacher reading this, let me persuade you not to write your letter of resignation just yet! The above agenda may run for a while, but it cannot succeed. The present triumphal progress of capitalism, with all its associated trappings of markets and competitions, does not answer the question of what education is for in the twenty-first century. Kung is one of the many now arguing passionately for a 'new role ethic', where schooling and education have a major role to play in filling the moral vacuum created by our present reliance upon technocracy (Kung 1990: 6–10). Anyone working with small children knows that teaching them is far more than an information exchange, just as preparing students for teaching is something more than providing them with a bundle of skills. This intuitive knowledge is important, as Zeldin argues in his book, 'An Intimate History of Humanity' (Zeldin 1994: 1–6). Dismissing the 'system building' of the nineteenth century as a dreary game pursued by those who sacrificed normal living in pursuit of ephemeral power, Zeldin mounts a powerful case for humanity to break out of bureaucracy. In particular he declares that:

> To have a new vision of the future, it is necessary to have a new vision of the past. . . . What ordinary people can do for themselves is to increase their mutual respect, without repeating the mistakes of the past.
>
> (Zeldin 1994: 145)

For teachers, Zeldin's message and philosophy is a powerful confirmation that humanity is to be cherished and encouraged amid a world currently obsessed with meaningless inputs, outputs and competencies. Arguing that the primary purpose of education is to develop a knowledge not of facts, but of values, Zeldin attacks our tendency to polish time's distant mirror and find it more attractive than it really was. This is salutary, at a point when 'revised codes' are being re-invented across the world. While the rear-view mirror currently appears very attractive, it is, in fact, fatally cracked.

REFERENCES

Argris, C. and Schon, D. A. (1978) *Organisation Learning: a Theory of Action Perspective*, New York: Addison-Wesley.

Armytage, W. H. G. (1969) *The German Influence on English Education*, London: Routledge and Kegan Paul.

Arnold, M. (1869) *Culture and Anarchy*

—— (1888) *Evidence Given to the Cross Commission*, Royal Commission on the Elementary Acts, England and Wales, vol. XXXV, p. 127. London: House of Commons.

—— (1910) *Reports on Elementary Schools (1852–1882)*, London: HMSO.

Ball, S. J. (1994) *Education Reform: A Critical and Post-Structural Approach*, Buckingham: Open University Press.

Barnard, H. C. (1929) *The French Tradition in Education*, Cambridge: Cambridge University Press.

Bloom, A. (1987), *The Closing of the American Mind*, London: Penguin Books.

British and Foreign School Society (1977) 'General Committee Minutes, 7th May 1814', in H. C. Dent *The Training of Teachers in England and Wales 1800–1975*, London: Hodder and Stoughton; p. 7.

Central Council for Education (1967) *Children and Their Primary Schools*, vol.1 of a Report of the Central Advisory Council for Education (England), London: HMSO.

Cobban, A. (1965) *A History of Modern France*, vol. 3, Aylesbury: Penguin Books.

Dawkins, J. S. (1987) *Higher Education: A Policy Discussion Paper*, Canberra: Australian Government Publishing Service, D.E.E.T.

—— (1988a) *Report of the Commission on Higher Education Funding: Overview and Recommendations*, Canberra: Australian Government Publishing Service, D.E.E.T.

—— (1988b) *Strengthening Australia's Schools: A Consideration of the Focus and Content of Schooling*, Canberra: Parliament House, D.E.E.T.

Dent, H. C. (1977) *The Training of Teachers in England and Wales 1800–1975*, London: Hodder and Stoughton.

Dickens, C. ([1865] 1938) *Our Mutual Friend*, London: The Folio Society.

Dreyfus, H. L. and Dreyfus, S. E. (1986) *Mind Over Machine: The Power of Human Intuition and Expertise in the Era of the Computer*, New York: Macmillan.

Durkheim, E. (1938) *L'Evolution Pedagogique en France*, Paris: Presses Universitaires de France.

Eaglesham, E. J. R. (1967) *The Foundations of Twentieth Century Education in England*, London: Routledge and Kegan Paul.

GTC (1993) *The Initial Training and Education of Teachers*, London: GTC (England and Wales) Trust.

Hargreaves, A. (1994) *Changing Teachers, Changing Times: Teachers' Work and Culture in the Post-Modern Age*, London: Cassell.

Harries, R. (1992) *Is There a Gospel for the Rich?*, London: Mowbray.

Harrison, J. F. C. (1979) *Early Victorian Britain 1832–1851*, Glasgow: Fontana.

Hencke, D. (1978) *Colleges in Crisis: The Reorganisation of Teacher Training 1971–77*, London: Penguin Books.

Hirsch, E. D. (1987) *Cultural Literacy*, Boston, MA: Houghton Mifflin.

Horn, P. (1978) *Education In Rural England, 1800–1914*, London: Gillan Macmillan.

Howsary, L. (1991) *Cheap Bibles: Nineteenth-Century Publishing and the British and Foreign Bible Society*, Cambridge Studies in Publishing and Printing History, Cambridge: Cambridge University Press.

Hurt, J. (1971) *Education in Evolution: Church, State, Society and Popular Education 1800–1870*, London: Rupert Hart-Davis.

Jacoby, R. (1987) *The Last Intellectuals: American Culture in the Age of Academe*, New York: Basic Books.

Jones, L. G. E. (1924) *The Training of Teachers in England and Wales: A Critical Survey*, London: Oxford University Press.

Keeghan, W. (1995) 'A Triumph Founded on Broken Promises', *The Observer*, 6 August: p. 22.

Kolb, D. A. (1984) *Experimental Learning: Experience as the Source of Learning and Development*, Englewood Cliffs, NJ: Prentice-Hall.

Kuhn, T. S. (1962) *The Structure of Scientific Revolutions*, Chicago, IL: Chicago University Press.

Kung, H. (1990) *Global Responsibility; In Search of a New World Ethic*, Munich: SCM Press.

Lauwerys, J. and Tayar, G. (1973) *Education at Home and Abroad*, London: Routledge and Kegan Paul.

Lawson, J. (1967) *Medieval Education and the Reformation*, London: Routledge and Kegan Paul.

Lofthouse, M. T. (1992), *The Church Colleges 1918–1939: The Struggle for Survival*, Rearsby, Leics.: Billings and Company.

—— (1994) *Performance Measurement in a Comparative Context*, The 1994 Henry Fielding Lecture, Manchester: University of Manchester; pp. 1–12.

Lyly, J. ([1597] 1929) *Anatomy of Wit*, in H. Barnard *English Pedagogy*, vol. 1, 'Fuller: The Good Schoolmaster', p. 403. London: University of London Press.

McLaren, I. A. (1974) *Education in a Small Democracy: New Zealand*, London: Routledge and Kegan Paul.

Martin, J. (1989) *The Development of Teacher Training in Jamaica and the West Indies*, MA thesis, Leicester: University of Leicester.

Morris, J. (1992) *Pax Britannica*, three vols, Bath: Folio.

Muller, D. K., Ringer, F. and Simon, B. (1989) *The Rise of the Modern Educational System: Structural Change and Social Reproduction 1870–1920*, Cambridge: Cambridge University Press.

Reid, I., Constable, H. and Griffiths, R. (1994) *Teacher Education Reform*, London: Paul Chapman.

Schon, D. A. (1983) *The Reflective Practitioner: How Professionals Think in Action*, New York: Basic Books.

—— (1987) *Educating the Reflective Practitioner: Towards a New Design for Teaching and Learning in the Professions*, San Francisco, CA: Jossey-Bass.

Shenstone, M. (1993) 'The Mirror Of Reform', *Education*, 25 June.

Shor, I. (1986) *Culture Wars: School and Society in the Conservative Restoration 1969–1984*, Boston, MA: Routledge and Kegan Paul.

Simon, B. (1989) *Education and the Social Order, 1940–1990*, London: Lawrence and Wishart.

Simon, B. and Taylor, W. (1981) *Education in the Eighties: The Central Issues*, London: Batsford.

Singapore Review Committee Report (1995) *Improving Primary School Education*, Singapore: Ministry of Education.

Smith, P. and Summerfield, G. (1969) *Matthew Arnold and the Education of the New Order*, Cambridge: Cambridge University Press.

Sturt, M. (1967) *The Education of the People*, London: Routledge and Kegan Paul.

Sutherland, G. (1973) *Policy-Making in Elementary Education, 1879–1895*, Oxford: Oxford University Press.

Tibble, J. W. (ed.) (1966) *The Study of Education*, London: Routledge and Kegan Paul.

Tomlinson, P. (1995) *Understanding Mentoring: Reflective Strategies for School-Based Teacher Preparation*, Buckingham: Open University Press.

Warren, D. R. (1978) *History Educational Public Policy* Berkeley, CA: McCruthan Publishing Corporation.

Whitbred, N. (1972) *The Evolution of the Nursery-Infant School: A History of Infant and Nursery Education in Britain, 1800–1970*, London: Routledge and Kegan Paul.

Zeldin, T. (1994) *An Intimate History of Humanity*, London: Sinclair-Stevenson.

Index